Life Upon the Wicked Stage

a Memoir

To Michal Eros – So good to hear your name again

Life Upon the Wicked Stage

a Memoir

Read Ch. 19

Grace Cavalieri

Grace

NAP NEW ACADEMIA PUBLISHING | SCARITH

WASHINGTON, D.C.

LIFE UPON THE WICKED STAGE

Edited by Cindy Comitz Cavalieri
Cover photo by Paul Feinberg
Book design by Janice Olson

LCCN: 2015938623
ISBN: 978-0-9864353-4-8 paperback (alk. paper)

SCARITH an imprint of New Academia Publishing

NEW ACADEMIA PUBLISHING
PO Box 27420, Washington, DC 20038-7420
info@newacademia.com – www.newacademia.com

To my Grandchildren:
Rachel, Elizabeth, Sean, Joe.

To Grace Pryor; Dick Sage; Claire Cavalieri and
Grace Anne Cavalieri.

Grateful acknowledgement for the support of my family—
my children: Cindy, Colleen, Shelley, Angel; and their
husbands: Dan, Dennis, Walt.

And thanks to friends who saw me through this year:
Ann Bracken; Bryan Christopher; Anne Caston; Avideh
Shashaani; Becky Anderson; Bob Ertman; Brian DeShazor;
Candace Katz; Cindy Maxted; Chris DeMay; Dai Sil Kim
Gibson; Dan Murano; Geoffrey Himes; Ginny Murphy;
Irene Panayi; Jim Murphy; Jimmy Patterson; Joyce Varney
Thompson; Joye Shepperd; Karren Alenier; James H.
Beall; Katherine Wood; Kelly Doub; Laura Cleveland;
Laura Orem; Lilah Al Masri; Maria van Beuren; Merrill
Leffler; Michael Glaser; Michael Turpin; Myra Sklarew;
Nancy Coleman; Nicole Roberts; Peter Dan Levin; Phyllis
Culham; Rose Solari; Remington Potvin; Sabine Pascarelli;
Sonja James; Sue Silver.

≈

CONTENTS

≈

ELLIE SINGS:

Life upon the wicked stage
Ain't ever what a girl supposes;
Stage door Johnnies aren't rag-
Ing over you with gems and roses
…
Wild old men who give you jewels and sables
Only live in Aesop's Fables.
Life upon the wicked stage
Ain't nothin' for a girl.

—*Showboat:*
MUSIC: Oscar Hammerstein;
LYRICS: Jerome Kern

1 ~

Prelude

I LOVE REVIEWING OTHER PEOPLE'S BOOKS. I love interviewing others on the radio about their work. I love transforming words into poetry. Yet this personal writing seems hard. For some reason when Ken said this book *had to be written,* it became a favor to him. Since his death, he has come through psychics to tell me *to finish this book about living as an artist.* I'm trying to find the heart in it; and I think because Ken has only been dead a year, perhaps *that* is the difficulty—reliving my life with him since he's in every line of every chapter but in no room of the house.

I knew Ken when I was 13 years of age and, now, this is the first time he's not in my life, center stage, visibly, or through letters and messages across the miles. Now, at this time in my life, I must be 12 years old trying to write a memoir. I'll write two pages a day and make the space for what there is to say. I believe that it's easier for me to love other people's lives than my own, to value what they say; to appreciate others' writings.

I've started asking Ken questions in my mind and getting answers. One could say these answers come from my "higher" self. We could say they are spirit guides. We could say they're my imagination. But the answers are essentially true—to make a catalogue of what I've done, where I've been in my career so our daughters, Cindy, Colleen, Shelley and Angel, will have a chronology. It's as simple as that—an index of when and where—not to attempt soul-searching. This feels good to me. Easy. I write this catalogue for them.

~

This isn't a book about the house and family. That will be another. This is the book Ken wanted me to write, documenting my poetry and plays, although small efforts in the world, they are mine.

My niece was speaking to a psychic last year after Ken died and the woman said, "Did your father have four children and fly airplanes?" Karen Bordon answered, "No that was my Uncle." *He said to tell her to finish the book...tell her to finish that book.*

Many are put off by the word "psychics." In these pages I mention some experiences, all positive and enlightening. My theory is that we continue to evolve as human beings, now long after monkey tails and maybe a sixth toe, and the physical will not change but the spiritual and mental will continue to expand into other dimensions. Reading the great French philosopher and Jesuit priest Pierre Teilhard de Chardin was my introduction to this idea of spiritual evolution. My thought is that some individuals (psychics) have advanced abilities (I'll call it an extra neuron) which everyone will own in the future.

And as for the following pages—I guess it's a good thing to list what I spent my time on and, as my daughters jokingly say, *now we'll know where you were.* These four beautiful women are, and always have been, the pillars of my life on which I'm stable, and where I feel comfort and secure. And if four legs of a chair hold steady, these four girls have done that for me. Cindy, Colleen, Shelley, Angel. They've done everything for me in love and watched my efforts in the world of writing, producing, and broadcasting, giving me free reign without guilt. That, I might have given to myself; but never ever was I made to feel that I should have done one thing rather than the other; and I can't remember a complaint. Ken was my hydraulic in life and in death. The girls still are. So I write what happened for them. Just a listing. The heart and soul of my work is not *about* them, but it is *for* them.

Memory is not chronological and so neither are the chapters in this memoir. I wish each chapter would be read like a discrete essay, for chronology is not the book's purpose. I cross back and forth across time to capture the past as it comes to me.

2 ~

Meeting Bryan Christopher

My Boss at PBS, 1978, said a psychic was com-
ing to town. I blew her off because all I knew of psychics was
that Hitler had one. I was Assistant Director for Children's Programming and Education for corporate PBS. I was in charge of
the daytime schedule for the nation and I adored this job.

I had a secretary, expense account, designer suits, high heels
and trips to New York. Who needed a psychic? I did. My marriage
was off the tracks and Ken was going in one direction and I was
going in another and the kids were acting as if everything was fine.
Apparently one goes to a psychic only when she's at a crossroads
and when therapy seems to lack answers. Bryan Christopher had
never been to Washington, DC before and lived in California. He
couldn't possibly know me or my family so what did I have to
lose? I made a Saturday appointment in nearby Virginia.

Ushered into a studio room in a middle class neighborhood,
no smoke, no mirrors; I saw two men and wondered which one
was "the Seer." Bryan and his partner stood in the doorway. Then
Bryan sat me opposite his chair. The first thing he said is, "You
will never leave your husband. He's your commitment in this
lifetime. For five years you've put your marriage on a shelf. It's
time to take it down and brush it off." Then he said, "WAIT. Your
mother is here." My mother had been dead 30 years and I had
worshipped her but before I could adjust to the idea, he said "No.
It's your grandmother. Your mother is much too timid."

OH MY this was true. This man was true. My grandmother was a monumental strength, had raised seven children while starting the first Italian restaurant in Trenton, NJ, and my mother could never show up this way. My mother was as pale and gentle as the summer wheat in Sicily. My tears started rushing because I was so grateful for this man's gifts. The generosity of the gift of sight. The veil was lifted. The magic we wished for in childhood and always secretly believed in… It was here. Magic was real. Bryan told me things I'd never said out loud. No one else could possibly know the facts about my life and my children's lives that he recounted.

I rushed home to Ken who was raking leaves in the front yard, and I said, "Stop everything and go immediately to see this man. He's only in town a couple of days." Ken put down the rake and that next hour he was sitting in the borrowed studio facing a man who would change his life forever and would remove the speed bump in the road that had slowed our lives together.

Ken later said the experience was so powerful that he couldn't catch his breath. Bryan told him to take up swimming again—Ken had just returned to the Masters Swimming Program, having been a college athlete. Bryan told him to sit in the car for 20 minutes before returning home. Ken said his heart was pounding so hard that it took all that time in the car to return to normal.

Of course I made appointments for the four children the next day. And I said, "If anything ever happens to me, go to this man. He'll guide you. He's someone you can trust forever."

I sat outside that studio room when my eldest daughter Cindy had her session. She was holding her two-year-old, Rachel, and Rachel was squealing. I rushed in with a paperweight that sprinkled snow when held upside down. Bryan smiled and said of me, "Her grandmother will always do this for her."

This incident was forgotten in the past 30 years; but this Christmas (2014) our first Christmas without Ken, Cindy gave Rachel a beautiful Christmas globe filled with snow. Neither of them held its memory. I just watched Rachel open the gift. And—even without Ken—I felt safe.

3 ~

In the End
Is the Beginning

TODAY I OPENED A BROWN ENVELOPE HOLDING A PER-
MANENT PASS TO ARLINGTON NATIONAL CEMETERY WHERE I CAN VISIT
KEN'S COLUMBARIUM. Although I know he's not in that steel and
cement encasement, still the plastic announcement hurt, and left
me dizzied.

It took nine months after Ken's death for Arlington to honor his
burial with a full ceremony. In the meantime, Commander Chris
DeMay, married to my good friend Lilah Al-Masri, had a ceremony at sea, three days after Ken's death, on January 18, 2013, flying the American flag aboard "USS John C. Stennis CVN-74," in
Memoriam. The folded American flag was then sent to me. Chris
did this for us.

There's no way I can encapsulate almost 60 years of marriage
with a Naval aviator, race car driver, metal sculptor, legal adjudica-
tor, real estate broker, artist, athlete; yet I've spent one year since
his death trying to in a book of poems, *The Man Who Got Away.* So
I'll just tell about meeting him as a crossing guard at Junior High
School No. 3, where he later would say he joined the Navy because
of the way I liked him in uniform. He was voted "the best dressed"
in the 9th grade. I was in the 7th. It would be after his family went
to Sweden and back again—his father was vice president of General Motors, overseas—when he would take me on our first date. I
was 14. We went to the Strand Theater, not far from my house on
Hermitage Avenue, across from the library I loved so much. I wore

a suit with a peplum jacket. I think it was green. The movie was "IVY" with Joan Fontaine.

I was so afraid of the body, and afraid its uncertainties would represent me, that I dared not swallow for two hours. This is not a metaphor. I did not swallow the saliva in my mouth for two hours, and the agony of it, the terror. What did all that anxiety portend? That there would be something about me unacceptable? That I was basically an animal with fluids in her mouth? A flat-chested person with spit in her mouth wearing a green peplum? Not the goddess that he thought I was when he took my hand? When the lights went on and we stood up, and the chairs squeaked, I swallowed. We didn't know then how to invent ourselves. Remember, at that time we didn't own TV sets which could tell us how to act, what we should look like, how to achieve fake safety in the artificial world.

For my 15th birthday Ken bought me a dozen red carnations with matching Revlon lipstick and nail polish. Oh he was smooth. And so we would go steady. It would be three months later that he would kiss me. I had to ask him to. Obviously our love would be most comfortable among our higher selves. But our love was here to stay.

Then he'd leave again in my senior year of high school to go to Australia with his parents. Then he would leave again to go to Lehigh University. Then he'd leave again to go into the Naval Cadet flying program. Then he would leave to be on nine carriers. And today I have a pass where I can visit him anytime I want. He always came home to me.

$$\approx$$

1952

There you sit in the open cockpit
I never saw such a smile
Goggles pushed up on your head
Shoulders harnessed with a parachute
To keep you safe
This would be before you were on nine carriers
Before exile to Viet Nam
Before your children surrounded you like stars
Waiting for your kiss
Before the Autumns of our lives
Before there would be no Autumns
Before I said don't fly away
Before you would become someone else
Then back again
Before there would be so much sun outside without you
Before the winds were light and variable
Before you'd sit on the front step every time
I went to the store waiting for my return
There you are sitting in a cockpit of an SNJ
Smiling at me for all eternity
In a moment that could not last
Cleared for flight
Everything in the whole blue world
Ahead of you.

The Man Who Got Away,
New Academia/Scarith Press, 2014

4 ~
Angelo and Nettie

Write down everything you can think about your father in a list off the top of your head (funny, generous, angry, etc.), fill the page—and in another column, describe your mother (gentle, uncertain, social). Now throw away that paper. This is a writing exercise I give my college students.

And realize this. We choose our parents to complete our life journey. Maybe our soul's journey.

And whatever walls parents put up are just to sharpen desire. Every NO has a YES inside you. Every wall just makes us know more than ever what we want on the other side. Walls are valuable.

We choose our parents. I would say to my writing students, "Humor me. Just pretend that you were 'up there' before you were born and you looked down and saw what you needed to do in physical form so you chose these two people. Call it a parlor game if it makes you feel better. But think about this. Why did you choose your parents?"

By thinking this new way, we see what qualities we own, and we can stop being victims and start taking accountability for our lives. My college students think this is a game but some are sobered by the outcome.

Angelo was authoritarian and structured. He'd come to this country from Italy, the oldest of seven with a scholar for a father who could never survive America on its terms. Nettie was pure spirit, without flaw. She flickered happiness like a candle; she was light and humor and beauty.

What did these two people allow me to be?

My life's work is in broadcasting poetry. This month, February 2014, I celebrate 37 years on air and maybe 3000 poets have come through me into the ether. And it's not over yet.

Structure and spirit. Broadcasting and poetry. My father's precision, intelligence, tidy thinking, expertise. My mother's love. I was able, with all the hardships I encountered growing up, to take an art form that depended on minutes and seconds to encapsulate and then deliver pure spirit. Broadcasting the voice. Poetry. The breath of God. Breath. My mother's breath. My father's house.

Did I mind that he preferred my sister? Did I mind that my mother could not speak for me? The pain of rejection, of disappointment, of wanting to be noticed. All that, notwithstanding. I chose the walls of my father to teach me how much I needed freedom. And the vapor of my mother so that I knew I needed form. Nettie and Angelo. Angelo and Nettie.

≈

AN EXCERPT FROM THE POEM

Nettie

…

The dead are just as
    involved as anyone else if you listen closely.

They are here to work it out with the living.

…

—*Heart on A Leash,* Red Dragon Press, 1998

5 ~

Rafael Cavalieri

MY FATHER'S FATHER IS A MYTHICAL FIGURE TO ME. He spoke Italian when we visited him in New York so I never got to really know the man who pinched my cheek.

When I found out who he was—well, they say everyone writes for just one person—now I write for him.

Rafael was a PhD in agronomy, graduated from the University of Pisa, late 19th century.

In 1990, my husband and I made a trip to Italy to follow his footsteps, and stand where he stood, to breathe the same air, to see the same land, starting from Venice where he lived, to Padua where he studied, and finally the University of Pisa.

On a warm October morning with sun just shafting through clouds, Ken and I went to Pisa—in search of the student apartment where Rafael lived (probably in the 1890s). We had no address but the area around the Square and the University was small enough to travel on foot. And we stopped suddenly on one narrow cobbled street as light appeared frozen in the form of a shimmering hologram. If Ken hadn't seen it, I'd feel it was an hallucination or a trick of the eye. There, before us, occupying the entire center of a narrow street was a brilliant, multicolored, translucent rectangle, prismatic with colors I had never seen before, with a gigantic X in the center made of light. We both gasped. And then it disappeared like a soap bubble in the sun. "I think this is where he lived," Ken said quietly.

Rafael invented the first alternating two-cylinder gasoline engine that would work the hilly terrain of Italy's vineyards. Our family still has the drawings. There are variations on his story, even to his beginnings in Trieste where the Jewish family Cavalieri owned timber. We know he lost his mother and was raised by an uncle. We know his best friend courted the beautiful Giudita and that upon his friend's death, after mourning, she chose Rafael, dutifully, and probably passionless. She was a woman raised in luxury who would never be vindicated in her cold exile to America.

Rafael was a bon-vivant and spent money gambling. He also married a Catholic so his family said Kaddish for their son's loss. This must be why he accepted an offer to come to America, called to the newly burgeoning hills of California where grapes were being turned to wine.

In 1910, he visited America with only my father, Angelo, then age 12, to view what his destiny would offer. I think Rafael was a dreamer, intellectual, and allowed assumptions, not facts, to guide his uncertain path. Based on too little communication, he next brought his other children and the reluctant Giudita to New York City (children would finally total seven) only to find this country wanted nothing from him, an old Italian who couldn't even use his hands. Communication with California proved faulty and inaccurate, and finally collapsed to nothing, along with his promised opportunity in that new world of the west.

Here he was in New York City, an ocean away from velvet frockcoats, speaking Italian as pure as its roots, barely able to understand the dialect of the other Italians who were building railways in the streets. Something he was not designed to do.

It is told that once the family was allowed to borrow a friend's home outside of the city if they'd watch the farm, and tend the chickens. My father, Angelo, remembered letting chickens run out to freeze so they could eat that night. Otherwise, in the city Rafael moved in circles of Italian intellectuals, opera singers and writers, and earned a living as an after dinner speaker at soirees of artists and glitterati.

But the family suffered at home. Rafael took his eldest, Angelo, with him wherever he went. On the East side of New York

City, in a lavish apartment, my father remembers a splendid dinner offered and Rafael kicking his son under the table so that he would not eat, so that he would not show his hunger, so that pride would be kept intact. My father still recalled 80 years later the steaming platters of pasta just out of reach.

Rafael began a newspaper in New York City—and is my literary heritage.

≈

HERE'S AN EXCERPT FROM THE POEM.

In Search of My Grandfather

...

Florence was where you stayed and had your bride
    during days
numbered in their joy—Firenze—sweet capital of this
country before it moved to Rome. Floods still spill
these shores every hundred years. One can see
grief behind an old city inside old walls you
walked, a cemetery of hopes buried in your language.

...

—*The Mandate of Heaven,*
Bordighera Press, 2014

6 ~
Having Angel

AFTER 24 WEEKS OF GRIEF COUNSELING ABOUT KEN'S DEATH, PROGRESS WAS MADE. I'd gone to the counselor, Bill York, to find the tears that were locked inside. Poet May Miller once wrote, "Who dare measure grief by tears…"

The first thing York said, with his enormous kindness was, *Aren't you the tough Navy wife, though.* I didn't know what he meant although he over and again said *WHY are you still stuck in the Navy? Your husband has been retired for years?*

I had never cried. When Ken left me over and again, I never cried. When I was pregnant with Angel, and the twins were three years old, Cindy needed a tonsillectomy and I was afraid to drive over Deception Pass Bridge, I never cried. When I left Cindy at the hospital alone, with her watching me leave, because the twins needed me, I never cried. Leaving her in Bremerton's hospital alone, I headed home.

I never cried when the stalker called at midnight in Sanford, Florida during another cruise when Ken was gone, He said *I know you are alone and I am watching you.* I did not break.

When all the wives left the neighborhood because of the Cuban missile crisis and Ken was in the Mediterranean, and I was alone in Florida, I may have gotten colitis, but I did not put mattresses up in the hallway walls and bring a two-week supply of canned food there, as we were told to do—in case of a missile attack. American tanks rolled down our street in Coleman Circle but my girls and

I put on dress-ups and went outside to play. I did not break down when I vacuumed Cindy's special gold necklace, and I was too pregnant to lean over and open the vacuum cleaner to locate it.

All those years I swallowed fear but it took me 24 weeks of grief counseling to talk about having my fourth child, Angel.

In 1964, the cruise was to be nine months, and I'd gotten pregnant the night before Ken went away. Against all odds. It wasn't planned because, being RH negative, the third pregnancy, in those days, could have been life threatening. I'd had two pregnancies already with three children. Ken did not know he'd be in Laos witnessing the first airstrike in what would become the Viet Nam Conflict. I did not know how I'd keep three small children happy in the Whidbey Island rain for nine months.

When the time came for the cruise to return, and Ken called me from Japan, my water broke while I was on the phone, but it would be two weeks before Angel would come, refusing my pleas, she insisted on waiting until her father returned. The Navy doc said he'd seen this happen before.

Our social media in 1964 was to post index cards on the PX bulletin board. And so I did; I posted a notice that I needed a baby-sitter for three children so I could go to the hospital and have a baby. And I needed a ride. It was finally July. The carrier KITTY HAWK was due home, but Angel was two weeks overdue.

The Squadron Executive Officer's wife drove me to the hospital but she had her own family to care for, so I was left alone; and, because the water had broken they couldn't induce labor, and I had no prep for natural childbearing. I lay in horrible pain alone for 12 hours. Here's where the story pivots, and I could not tell it except for the fact that it just surfaced yesterday, in a safe room with a benevolent counselor.

During that labor, I was abused by a sadistic nurse (let us call her Nurse Ratchet) that, for her own reasons, and left to her own devices, treated me harshly, with disdain and even rough care, slapping the sheet on me. Checking in only every hour to see if the baby had come. It was like a concentration camp, or like being in prison at the mercy of a torturer.

When I questioned the doctor later he said, *Oh she's just old and is about to retire.* I accepted it. This was what you did. Find a babysitter, get a ride to the hospital, and have a baby without anesthetic or care—and of course Ken's arrival home wiped away the stain of that memory…until yesterday…with Bill York, my grief counselor… where I went to get in touch with that young Navy wife who never cried. And I, all along, thought I was having trouble with tears *about the death of my husband.*

Angel arrived at 6:15 in the evening. And Ken arrived from Laos at 9 am the following day.

The Whidbey Island newspaper had a photo of my three little girls, and Doris, the babysitter (a young sailor's wife). Ken was putting Hawaiian leis around their necks. The headline ran NAVY PILOT ARRIVES HOME AFTER 9 MONTHS. HIS WIFE IN THE HOSPITAL HAVING THEIR 4th DAUGHTER.

The nurse's cruelty. Could she have thought I'd been unfaithful? Because the cruise was nine months long, and Angel was two weeks late? Why had she added to my physical pain, shoving me and scolding me? And why did I not believe I deserved better?

Bill York said (in times past), "If the Navy had wanted you to have a wife, it would have issued you one in your Sea Pack."

Bill York said we believe who we are by the way we're treated. Who did I think I was?

Bill York, always kind, said, "There's more space outside for these feelings than there is inside."

≈

NAVY WIFE

If we give up loss, what will we have left

1964

Among things lost was a golden rose hanging on a chain

given by a teacher before

my 5 year old daughter had her tonsils out.

I vacuumed it up on the rug. I didn't know

how, then, to open the machine. The twins were 3 years
   old

drinking bottles, standing on the couch. I was

too pregnant to lean over, to find the chain.

I said we'd try to find another one. I promise,

but I'd have to leave her at the hospital, alone, overnight.

1970

My youngest daughter loved that new sweater, the one
   with angora animals.

She got it for Christmas, it was thrown in the wash

by accident, a gift from her Nana, tiny fuzzy creatures,
   shrunk beyond wearing.

So much was hurried. We tried to find one like it.

1944

My sweater was cut off my arm when I broke the bone.

Roosters knit on the wool, a figured sweater, the first of its
   kind,

such a generous grandmother to give such a present. I
   walked it in front

of a car. I was told to tell the insurance company

it was not my fault. The only sweater we found to replace
     it was

blue with white stars and that was 4 years later.

1950

The gold Bulova watch I wanted so much, waited for so
     long, I finally

got for high school graduation. What made me go running
     into the ocean,

the next day, swimming, without taking it off.

1964

My husband lost his friends. He says He cannot count
     them,

he cannot see their faces. He cannot say their names.

He felt their presence, flying on his wing, protecting him.
     He cared so much.

1962

The crystal earring brought back from a war cruise

was thrown out with the purse.

The present bought on shore duty, a single day off the
     carrier,

a jewel still warm in my hand. The only one left.

                    —*Navy Wife,* Casa Menendez, 2010

7 ~
Life Upon the Wicked Stage: Part 1

IT STARTED BY TALKING IN FRONT OF MY MIRROR, AS A SMALL CHILD, THIS WISH TO EXPRESS. And seeing three movies a day when my mother was helping out in her mother's restaurant. My grandmother would take a handful of bills from the cash drawer at the Venice Restaurant and press them into our hands. My sister Judy, I, and cousin Little Grace, would make the rounds of the movies all day between State and Broad and Warren Streets in downtown Trenton. And I would come home dizzied with drama, a combination of Betty Hutton, June Allyson, Claudette Colbert, acting out what I saw in a bedroom with my fake white French Provincial furniture.

All through high school and college I scored every part that moved on stage, roles of Emily in "Our Town" and The Mother in "Life With Father." I always had to have the lead and was never happier than when disguised in someone else's fiction. And then, there was summer stock in Morrisville, Pennsylvania in "Charlie's Aunt" (ok, once I was just the maid but I was the youngest member of the crew). Wherever there was a stage and a light, I stood in it.

This is why my husband always said, "You will write plays." I said *Oh Please.* He said. "You will. Just wait and see. It's just acting on paper."

In 1966 Ken received orders to be stationed at the Bureau of Naval Personnel, Washington, DC. It was shore duty and that was always lovely for me.

We arrived in Annandale, Virginia, from Whidbey Island, Washington, having traveled across country in a small 26-foot trailer with me in a cast (broken ankle) (tennis), a two-year-old Angel (in the midst of toilet training), Shelley and Colleen (seven years) and Cindy (age ten).

We lived in the camper outside of town for a month because we couldn't afford Washington, DC prices and finally settled in, renting a townhouse in Annandale, on an all-American street, 4409 Forest Glen Court, while the rest of the world was breaking old forms and creating new ones.

The Beatles had landed. Everything was pink and orange. The Cultural Revolution had moved the earth.

I was writing poems, daily, and I was always waiting by the mailbox for any interest.

Ken said, "Selling poems is just like selling used cars. One in eight."

One in Eight?

"Right, a salesman will make one sale out of eight."

I sent out eight poems a day, this was before computers, and when poems came back, I retyped them and sent them out again, like gifts to the world, and damn, by a year's end I had 13 poems accepted in 13 very good poetry journals. But think of the numbers. Exponentially. How many had been typed? Sent out?

At that time, 1968, we saw an ad in the Baltimore paper announcing a playwriting contest in a new theater, THE CORNER THEATER CAFÉ. This was the revolution at my doorstep and no one apparently knew or cared that I was a suburban Navy housewife.

Sonny and Cher were singing, the colors were psychedelic, and new theater was cropping up in storefronts and warehouse lofts. In Baltimore, Ellen Stewart, the great impresario of New York, was opening up a satellite theater with her imprimatur, and then it was to be left to its own devices, under the care of Artistic Director Les Irons, to discover new playwrights.

Every day after the children were in school, and the meat was defrosting for dinner, I sat down to write in the kitchen. And so I wrote "What Shall We Do Yesterday" which was one of the pieces that launched the Corner Theater. It won the contest. And there's nothing like winning to keep on writing. It was directed by Michal Makarovich. It was a one-act, but later I added an act making it full-length for future productions.

The play was about a housewife who loved words and waited for her husband to come home every day where they would ritualize their marriage in dance. It was about a folie á deux where two people occupy the same psychosis. The play received a marvelous review in the Baltimore newspaper about the American stage "needing this new voice."

In the ten years following, at the Corner Theater on Paul Street in Baltimore, above a dental lab, ten plays premiered and subsequently saw productions other places throughout the country, (mostly one-act plays which were the vogue in the 1960s when people perhaps had cinematic attention spans) directed by Les Irons, creator of the Corner Theater. Paul Hjelmervik and Michal Makarovich directed my work as well. These plays are all in my papers, Special Collections, George Washington University Gelman Library. In retrospect, they reveal that women playwrights were taunted to say what could not be said before.

Ken and I would go to Baltimore, I riding on the back of his BMW motorcycle. I learned not to wear layers of gold chains (the style at the time) or at night I'd come home with a frozen chest.

"Best of Friends" opened in Notre Dame College Theater in Baltimore in 1972, directed by Alice Houstle. And this wonderful occasion introduced me to the composer Vivian Adelberg Rudow, who did the score (soundtrack) and Vickie, herself a mother of three boys, and I, a mother of four girls, would become life-long partners and friends. We wrote song cycles and operas together for 40 years.

But first, the phone call from Notre Dame College about performing "Best of Friends."

Notre Dame was an "all-girls" college in Baltimore and was known nationally for its Theater and Media Department. This was an era when nuns actually wore habits (which drove my sculptor husband crazy because the art teacher would teach welding with the flame right next to her sleeve). The Mother Superior called me one day about the College's decision to do my play. It was a world-shaking phone call. I see just where I stood in the kitchen holding the wall-phone when I heard that well-modulated voice—Sister asked for "Miss Cavalieri" and with great dignity and appropriate nun-like pauses, Sister said, "The Board has met about your play and after careful decision, and much debate, we have decided to allow the use of Fuck and Shit in the script."

Thank you, Sister, I said respectfully. Nothing was said about the attack on Catholicism's obsessional practices, which was the play's premise.

It was a wonderful production because director Alice Houstle cast two young adults who played children in the roles. She had a divided stage (which was done in every production, thereafter, as the play had parallel scenes throughout). "Best of Friends" was written as part of my MA for Goddard College, along with a book (unpublished and long forgotten) on teaching Creative Writing. It was my first full-length play and I still love it. The language is shocking to me now and I realize how much we women of the 60s were trying to push back the boundaries to say We are equal to any man writing. Were we bullied to write boldly, or were we enjoying the opportunity?

There was another play in existence, apparently published, named "Best of Friends" and so I changed my title to "The Sticker Tree" at the request of director Shela Xoregos, who premiered that play in New York City in 1987 at the Quaigh Noontime Theater. It got a great review, saying something like "a solid meal where the rest on the bill are soufflés..." and it was featured on the cover of *Theater Weekly.*

In NYC's "The Sticker Tree" Shela Xoregos used actual young children and unfortunately opening night one forgot her lines and I sat frozen with fear. Ken and I had taken the slow four-hour train up to see the show and I wore my vintage soft sculpture rainbow

coat. And I sat in horror for what seemed hours while the child re-
gained her composure. It was a bumpy opening. After the play Ken
and I went to the Museum of Modern Art (MOMA) where a Frank
Stella show was hanging and I remember standing in the middle
of the room letting the colors heal me. Art heals. I can prove it. I
stood there letting the glow of great art fill my diminished energies
before we got the slow train back, in one day of varied colors.

And the play was mounted many times after that on different
stages. Here was the original:

THE STICKER TREE
by **Grace Cavalieri**

produced by the
QUAIGH THEATER
Will Lieberson, Artistic Director

Directed by: **Shela Xoregos**
Original songs by **Nicholas Levin**

with:
MARY TAHMIN
ALEX PAUL
KIA GRAVES
DAWN KELLY

Hartley House 413 West 46th Street, NYC
for ten performances November 30-December 11, 1987

8 ~
Life Upon the Wicked Stage: Part 2

"Best of Friends" won a national award given by La Pensee' Theater in Seattle and Ken and I loved that trip west. I also saw the play at Baltimore's Theater Project, directed by the great visionary Philip Arnoult, after the play had its run at my beloved Corner Theater, directed by Les Irons. It almost got mounted in Chicago, directed by Maggie Rice, but when I arrived, the cast had difficulty, and there was a gigantic fracas. Someone was on cocaine, the final rehearsals disintegrated in front of my eyes. I wound up sleeping on a mattress on the floor of Maggie's house only to return to Oxon Hill, Maryland a little disoriented, a playwright without a play.

But before all this, another reality check: In 1972 I was to have the thrill of my life—or so I thought—the WPA Theater in New York accepted a play called "Getting Ready" about an alcoholic couple. WPA is still thriving as one of the premier cutting edge theaters in NYC. Now that I look back on my play I realize that, like what a critic once said of an ee cummings play, "…watching it is like every once in a while stepping on something nasty in the dark…" I see that many of my one-acts were an attempt to break down boundaries where women were told they could speak on stage only what was spoken in the living room and not the bedroom.

In the privacy of a writing room, it's effortless to express our conduct but when you see it coming back at you on stage, every expletive is ten times bigger and louder than on paper. I didn't know this yet and we went off to NYC after having grandparents move in for the children. I remember I had black stockings and an armful of bracelets and looked every bit the part of a playwright.

Mary Ellen Long, my great collaborator in visual art, had created gorgeous silk screens. I bought two huge pieces for the two characters in the play; and the glorious images had been framed, ready for my red-carpet explosion onto the scene in New York, amidst the adoring crowds. The play was good and the audience liked it. The play was tough and these were cynical times that suited it. After the show, after the audience filed out, I went to the box office to say: *I'm the playwright. May I meet the actors? I have gifts.*

"Oh, they're gone," said the guy.

I told them I was coming.

"Yeah they left after the show. They always do."

I handed over these works of art, by now collectors' items, and said *please give them these gifts from me as thanks for their work.*

"Will do," he said.

And the next day we headed home.

But an even worse experience was in Missouri. A prize I won and the esteem I lost. In the next chapter I'll feel the sunshine on my shoulders of the productions I adored and live on in my heart but first I have to get rid of this one. The play was a one-act titled "We Regret to Inform you that the Destiny of Future Generations is Uncertain Because of a General Inability on the Part of All Night Watchmen."

The play was performed several places, and beautifully done in DC at 18th Street's Theater Lobby, the home of director Davy Marlin-Jones. The play was wacky and fashionably deconstructed, except for the last scene which was tender and sweet.

And it won a national contest given by the Theater Department of the University of Missouri.

Ken had to stay home with the girls, and I wasn't in touch with reality about the Middle Western part of our country. I was buying my clothes at the French Boot Shop in NYC through the mail because I hated going in stores and FBS clothes were cutting edge. SO what would be better than to wear my SEE-THROUGH BLOUSE (it did have pockets rightfully placed) and what could be better than looking like a "playwright."

My play shared the bill with another writer from the east coast and both one-acts were breaking ground. Remember I had never said a four-letter word in my life until I started plays and had to train my fingers to type them, and here they were going to be heard in square-cut Americana. The director who chose us thought he was being hip and exploding the uptight moralities of this campus. And we writers were feeling no pain and thinking we were on top of the world as national winners.

While in rehearsal there, the Dean showed up and the Provost, and maybe a few more heavies; and the courage drained out of our host. By the time the performances went on he was hospitalized with a cardiac-like stress attack, and the audience was hijacked by a major basketball game that night. The see-through blouse did not help any.

I wish to amend that statement that "We Regret To Inform You..." was the most unsettling experience. NO. I can't believe what I'm about to recount. There was one worse shock.

"Pinecrest Rest Haven" was to receive its premiere reading in NYC in 2000. "Pinecrest Rest Haven" was written from my book of poems that had received good readership about an old folks' home where Mr. and Mrs. P were married and shared the same memories but did not remember each other; and so, fell in love and hate, every day, again and again. I converted it to a play and, at the suggestion of New York playwright Jim McCartin, sent it to Common Basis Theater in NYC.

Ken and I set out to drive up to NYC from West Virginia where he had relocated his sculpture studios, and where we had moved full time in 1988. We stopped enroute for coffee and got a call from my oldest daughter, Cindy, saying, "Mom, turn around. You *cannot* go to New York today. The Twin Towers are in flames."

Thinking it a fire that would be controlled and extinguished, I said we'd have to stay in New Jersey then, and delay going into the city for a day. Then we saw a TV set in the restaurant, and we turned around and came home.

"Pinecrest Rest Haven" did get produced and opened in a loft theater and featured a great actress as Mrs. P (Marcia Haufrecht, who also directed) and Nick Stallone (Sylvester's cousin) played Mr. P. Nick and I became great friends. Nick died of AIDS the following year and I spoke to him in the hospital and surrounded him with all the gratitude and love in the world. The cast had some great actors, I became close to them and it was a good outcome to a calamitous beginning.

Once I asked my husband if he'd read the part of Mr. P for an upcoming library reading and he gracefully declined. Every actor who'd read Mr. P in every production died soon after, he reminded me. And in West Virginia in 1998 (the play directed by JW Rone) our 80-year "Mr. P" actually did have dementia, and lowered his pants on stage in a direction not given. He did wonderfully otherwise, as a seasoned actor, but we had to keep him seated most of the time in an armchair so he wouldn't wander off stage. Everyone played around him.

I cannot emphasize enough how few women playwrights were contributing to the stage in the 1960s. How we tried to stand shoulder to shoulder, and how we looked unseemly to the world, women playwrights were "a pain in the arts." We were pushy, strident, and, like all voices that had not been heard, sometimes tending toward excess.

Writing about relationships was my forte because I was in one, and that was my commitment and I saw the world that way. And also because relationships were changing from the Cultural Revolution and male/female roles were reversed and genders were crossing and some of my one-acts dealt with this.

A play I had in Bethesda under the aegis of the Writing Center and a neighboring theater company was "Old Favorites." I wrote it in the early 1970s for the Corner Theater, when everything was up for grabs and O CALCUTTA! even had a nude cast on Broadway. "Old Favorites" seemed OK at the time it first appeared (no nudity); but, 20 years later, sitting by a respected ballet dancer who had come because I was known to her as "a poet," it was an uncomfortable debut. A work, fitting for the 60s, appeared tasteless to me in the 1990s.

All my plays were made worse and better by directors but were never exactly what I wrote, and in the next chapter I'll talk about my plays that I love.

Director Shela Xoregos and I became partners for 28 years and still work together at this writing. She's a joy to work with because she's a literary director and words matter—every syllable, every nuance. Just what a writer dreams of. Some directors are environmental, but Shela is a text person, a gift to the playwright.

There's one play I wrote which was produced at the Corner Theater in the 1960s that had characters in drag. It was hilarious but I can't even remember the title or what became of it. I don't have the script anymore. I just know it was so funny that I sat laughing in the front row until the man behind me said, "That lady sure does like this play."

9 ~

Plays/Productions I Loved

"The right director—one who understands your work and has the skills to bring it to life in three dimensions—is a blessing. The wrong one can be disastrous. The key to creating and nurturing the perfect writer-director relationship, of course, is first recognizing what's most important to you in the way you want to work and the way you want your work to work ..."

Dramatists Guild Magazine, 2013

"BEST OF FRIENDS" (AKA "THE STICKER TREE") HAS MY HEART SEWN INSIDE. It's autobiographical.

When I was very young, my cousin Little Grace came to live with us. Her mother had died when she was a toddler and Little Grace had been in Villa Victoria, a nearby convent, for a safe stay while her father maintained his job and restored his equilibrium. When she refused to go back after vacation, we all realized that it was not a merciful place, because her personal benefactor, Sister Lillian, had gone away.

She came to our house. I was thrilled. She was my own little sister delivered to me to have forever, and she was three years younger. Perfect. My older sister Judy was never a playmate and preferred to be alone, or quiet, or reading, or playing the piano—solitary sports—and so here was someone given to me from out of the blue.

We had an enchanted childhood where every day was a carousel and an adventure. All my creativity was focused on this new little sister that I adored and who obeyed my every command. She was mine. I wrote out what we would do every day and in detail, Little Grace responded happily. We even got up at three am every night to feed our dolls. She was the perfect companion.

Then Grace's father remarried and she was taken away. I think I have amnesia about that but I felt somehow it was my fault. It must be. Wasn't she my property? I must have been a terrible person or I would not have lost the thing I loved best. Being "Catholic "figures in here, for Little Grace and I—with overextended imaginations—attributed all happenings to divine sources.

The play "Best of Friends" is about control. Big Mary uses religion to keep Little Mary under her spell. On a parallel stage there are two circus workers where Cassandra keeps Rocky in control, using sex and booze. (We lived not far from a railroad track where sometimes in the distance itinerants camped and then moved on, fueling my childhood fantasies.)

In the play, Little Mary and Big Mary visit the circus performer, Rocky Sprague, camping nearby and he is kind and loving to them. Little Mary is especially enamored. Big Mary is furious that someone has stolen Little's affection, that she feels is rightfully hers. Little Mary is HERS! She concocts a story about Rocky molesting Little Mary and the townspeople lynch him (this being set in the south in the early 1930s). Then Big Mary is alone. Just as I was, when Little Grace was taken away from me.

Little Grace saw the premier of our story in the form of a play at Notre Dame in 1972. It's a powerful play because the "felt life" in it is my own life.

≈

"QUILTING THE SUN"

In 1990, Bill Gilcher of the University of Maryland's "Visual Press" approached me with the idea of writing the Harriet Powers story. He was in collaboration with Andrew Ferguson, Head of Media, The Smithsonian Institution. I'd worked with Bill at the

National Endowment for the Humanities for five years (1983-88), and I had broadcast Andrew's children's TV series "Footprints," while I was doing Children's programming for PBS in 1978-1982.

We had goodwill connections.

Harriet Powers' quilt hung in the Smithsonian and another in the Boston Museum of Fine Arts. She was an ex-slave quilt maker and it would make a fabulous story. All I could think of was finding genius in unknown places and I was high on the idea. There were only three things known about Harriet Powers: 1) She was a leader of her community in Sandy Springs, GA; 2) She was married to Armstrong, and had children; 3) She sold her precious quilt (now in the Smithsonian) to Jennie Smith, an art teacher in Athens, GA, for $5.00, half the asking price.

It was my job to imagine why a woman who had always been poor suddenly sold a quilt which apparently she'd dedicated much of her life to making. The only thing I could imagine was that she'd have sold it to save a sick child's life. After all, this was a fictional story based on actual life facts, and I was to create a world and populate it with characters as truly and vividly as I could.

I would sit between Bill and Andrew at meetings while they shot ideas across me and Andrew would say, "Got that?" Bill, a fellow artist, was sensitive to all I did, but we were three people with three points of view.

Bill and I and our scholarly adviser, Gladys Fry, renowned scholar on quilting and the discoverer of Harriet Powers, spent a weekend in Athens, Georgia, poking through yellowed papers in damp boxes deep in the basement of the Athens Courthouse. We also set out to find where Harriet's house had been in the Sandy Springs woods. It was a marvelous adventure except for the fact that Gladys and I shared a motel room and she could only sleep with a TV on all night, and I can only sleep in absolute unmitigated silence. Nevertheless, our spirits were high on adventure.

At the George Washington University Special Collections (Grace Cavalieri papers) there's a coffin of drafts for "Quilting the Sun." I would say thousands of pages. Different versions. Additionally, Bill Gilcher wrote his own film documentary at one point and also his own screenplay after the project was to take two separate routes. None has been produced. Andrew Ferguson died before seeing any of these projects realized.

Playwriting is easier when young, because writing for theater is about conflict and ideas. And the younger the writer, the more fire. How else could I have written ten one-acts in one year? But this was 25 years later. To get energy to write daily I would remember my cautions to students: You can't have more going out than is coming in. It's all about energy and I would have to gin some up every morning by physical movement, lighting candles, steeping in hot baths, listening to music, holding crystals, reading slave narratives, before imagining the black culture of the 19th century in Georgia.

After many iterations, funding never could be unearthed for the television screenplay I wrote, and when the copyright reverted to me in 2000, I turned "Quilting the Sun" into a stage play.

From a screenplay written for a large cast with aerial overhead shots, etc. I changed the play for the stage using few characters, changing it from a horizontal work to a vertical piece, compressed for psychological rather than physical action.

After staged readings directed by Shela Xoregos (2001 and 2002 in NYC libraries) the play was invited to the Smithsonian for a splashy reading (2003). All dignitaries were invited and Harriet Powers' quilt was to be displayed. The Smithsonian gave $5000 to bring the NYC cast down to DC for 24 hours.

I never did anything to harm anyone, so I don't know why destiny chose me to play its tricks when my plays opened, but on the very night of this grand event, a crazy farmer drove his tractor full of explosives up from some beleaguered southern farm to protest a congressional farm bill, and he parked it in the Lincoln Memorial Reflecting Pool. Constitution Avenue was cordoned off and the buses from black churches cancelled, and my daughter Shelley coming in from Virginia couldn't even make the event. The auditorium was filled somehow but many others were unable to attend; we went on with the reading.

The Smithsonian reading was history-making. With the quilt

on display under glass in the lobby and Gladys Fry, our scholar, giving an animated introduction, it was an unforgettable event.

But what of a white person writing black theater? Do you think this went unnoticed? During an earlier reading in New York, the actress portraying Harriet once stopped the action and said to me, "Why did you write this play?" This was a heartbreaking question for her to ask and for me to answer.

I said, "Because I know about loss." I took it to the universal because I believed what I said. I can't say there weren't tensions, I believe unjustified, because I would—and have—championed a black writer writing white theater, and I always cheered this. Our inveterate director Shela Xoregos never saw race, gender or age except how it suited a character, yet she did fire actors who resisted her direction or questioned her integrity.

I'm proud of one thing. I did not use stylized dialect. I wrote dialogue in cadence and phraseology which allowed the culture without caricature.

In 2007, "Quilting the Sun" premiered in a full production in Centre Stage, Greenville, South Carolina. An actress who'd read in another play of mine in New York previously had moved there to live, and passed the script along. Let me say this premiere was my one week of celebrity with a capital C. The themes of race had never been on stage there with such a powerful message, with such a great historical precedent, Harriet Powers. And thanks to the person who would play "Big Mama," who was on the City Council, all the spirits in the Heavens came to her calling. She organized the entire state of quilters (as she was one) to convene in Greenville the week of my play to announce its arrival and create quilting events all over the city. The Mayor presented me with a key to the city, marking one of the happiest times in my life.

Ken and I were given a loft in a beautiful house by one of the theater supporters. As someone said to me in Greenville, "We may act slow but we like our money." Also it was epochal that Ken and I ate frozen dinners there some nights. We are both gourmands, and never had explored these phenomena before together. It was a great adventure for us in every way. Frozen dinners aren't bad when accompanied with Martinis for two. Cindy and her husband flew down and made my high even higher.

In the main hotel in town there was a luncheon where, for the first time in history, 300 blacks and whites—the largest "mixed" assembly at the hotel, to date—arrived under the umbrella of the historical society and museum. A black choir punctuated the event and then I spoke of how I wrote the play and why.

There were antagonists in the audience, but Harriet was there by my side. My intentions had been only to bring Harriet Powers to life and have her live long after I died, so I couldn't have her light quelled by small dissents.

Day after day, we attended events of mostly black quilters, all paying homage to Harriet. The apex of the week was a visit to an all-black church in a rural outer part of the city. Ken and I stood singing with the crowd with tears streaming down our cheeks, blessed, accepted, tears of love, of being loved. I was called to the stage for an ovation. I am crying as I write this.

And as for the production? A director from the Theater Department of Clemson University had to do this at her busiest academic part of the year and, among other mistakes, used a doll to represent the baby Harriet would try to save—the very reason for selling the quilt. The prop was not used well and was sometimes left lying in the middle of the stage. There were other flaws. And still every actor surpassed my dreams of how the characters could be realized. However, there was only one critic, one single theater reviewer in Greenville, in the only newspaper in town, an avowed atheist, who rankled at the massive religiosity of the play. She wrote a poor review. It is a God-centered play. She said it was a quilt that had not been sewn together. The whole celebrating community collapsed by her pin in the festive balloon.

This was unfair because the actors were so brilliant and impassioned and the lines are truly channeled through Harriet. There was much to admire that was left unsung by a single ungenerous person who could never in all her years write a play. She never mentioned the excellent acting.

~

43

But fortunately, because Spirit never abandons our dreams, JW Rone and Jenny, his wife, had driven over to the opening from Beaufort, South Carolina. JW had directed "Pinecrest Rest Haven" at the Ice House Theater in Berkeley Springs, West Virginia, in 1998. JW had moved to SC to create an art center in an arid land. He adored the play and saw what was needed, and he made plans to recreate the work for me the way I'd envisioned it.

"Quilting the Sun" opened in Beaufort in 2011 and I believe this was one of the times I've seen a play imagined by direction the way it was imagined by writing. The stage manager had left abruptly and JW had hammered the set together himself, making a series of pieces that, together, made a flat backdrop of wood; and where single segments turned open to contrast black life interiors against the whites' elegance of the period. This was a week to remember. Ken and I stayed at the Beaufort Marine Base, and relished a time with my 90-year old Uncle Freddie, who lived nearby, and his 100-year-old girlfriend, Hazel.

My daughter Shelley and her husband attended, and added the love and sparkle needed. The actors were professional, one having just arrived, relocating from NYC, was fantastic as "Uncle Jerry," The JuJu Man. How can we talk about luck when we mean divine guidance?

Ken and I drove home, satisfied and fulfilled. And knowing that the only reason I wrote—and he supported and surrounded this—was because it gave us the playground together we wanted. Psychic Bryan Christopher said, "You two will go through life picking flowers together." And we did. We did.

≈

For a Bibliography of Grace Cavalieri's plays
see the APPENDIX TO CHAPTER NINE, *page 247.*

44

10 ~

"Hyena In Petticoats"

TIME: 18TH CENTURY (BEGINS 1776, ENDS 1797)

PLACE: ENGLAND (BEGINS IN EPPING, ENDS IN LONDON)

CHARACTERS:

Mary Wollstonecraft—(age 17, ages up to 30s during play) The mother of modern feminism, who wrote the first serious book in English. Strong, manipulative, aggressive, argumentative, moves to vulnerable.

Everina—(Mary's younger sister) Stoic, dry, sensible, angry, moves to compassion.

Liza—(Mary's youngest sister) Elflike, vacant, capricious, nervous, silly, moves to strength and resolve.

Clergyman Clare—(middle-aged) Clare taught young Mary to read and write, or so he thought.

Gilbert Imlay—(American, 30ish) Imlay was an American author, a lover, who fathered Mary's first child, Fanny Imlay.

Joseph Johnson—(middle-aged) The great publisher who introduced Mary to the world, but betrayed her in private life.

William Godwin—(30ish) English philosopher who wrote against conventions of England, married Mary W. and fathered her baby Little Mary. (Mary Wollstonecraft died in childbirth.)

Punch—(played by Man) Classic character. The circus came to London in the 18th century, Mary's time.

Judy—(played by Woman) Classic character.

Lady Kingsborough—(voice over) Mary's first employer who opposed Mary's ambitions and beliefs, and who fired Nanny Mary.

~

≈

I HAD DISCOVERED MARY WOLLSTONECRAFT in graduate school, studying English, at the University of Maryland, College Park, in 1974. I couldn't believe this. While researching 18th-century literature I came upon the first woman to write a serious book in English, and who knew of her? There were only a handful of books about her. I remember Eleanor Flexner's book was the best. At that time, Mary Wollstonecraft Shelley got all the press because she wrote *Frankenstein* and married the poet Shelley, yet her mother, Mary, was unknown to the general public.

Mary Wollstonecraft (1759-1797) haunted me for 25 years. She'd written *The Vindication of The Rights of Women*. She was burned in effigy for seeking educational rights for women while other woman authors at the time were writing fluff and formulaic romanticism under pseudonyms. And as I'd later say through narrators Punch and Judy, "Mary wanted to stand shoulder to shoulder to men / while lying underneath of them." What a fascinating character she was.

Twenty five years later she was still incubating in me, and wanted out. I went back to research (by this time, there were many books about her) and I was impassioned to write a book of poems in her voice: *What I Would Do for Love* is the book that resulted.

Jean and Bill Emerson's Jacaranda Press in San Jose, California, published the book of poems in 2004. As of today, January 24, 2014, it's going into a 3rd printing. Although now Bill has died and Jean alone sanctioned the latest reprint. At this writing *What I Would Do for Love* has been translated into Italian by Sabine Pascarelli and published as *Cosa farei per amore*.

When I decided to write the play about Mary, I was visiting the Library of Congress one day and talking to Prosser Gifford, then head of Scholarly Programs. While talking up my Mary, I was telling him how the conservative philosopher, Edmund Burke, had called her a hyena in petticoats—and suddenly that title came to me as perfect for the work—in the play I have Mary say "I am not a hyena. Hyenas run in packs and I am very much alone."

Oh I loved this Mary; I talked to her night and day. She whispered in my ear. I spoke in her voice. If I spoke black southern language for "Quilting the Sun," now my mind spoke in 18th-century English for "Hyena in Petticoats." If Harriet lived with me for three years, now Mary Wollstonecraft was my constant companion. Ken said he never knew who would be coming for breakfast.

Faithful and good Shela Xoregos presented an incredible staged reading of "Hyena" in 2006 at the New York City Public Library in Manhattan, after development in New York library readings during two previous years.

March 2006. This was a moment of other-worldly intervention because—the night of the opening at the New York Public Library—across the street, in the other Library building was *A FULL EXHIBIT OF MARY WOLLSTONECRAFT*, her clothes, her handwriting under glass, her (only) portrait, memorabilia. Before the play would be read, Ken and I walked, stunned among the exhibits, tearful and grateful and thankful. Then we went across the street to see Mary brought to life.

The place was filled. So many people crammed into the main space, they had to call in more seating, then bring in still more chairs. Yet more people stood.

Composer and music historian, Gene Abrams, coordinated a mix of original and 18th century music which he played on an electronic piano. Perfect. My oldest and youngest daughters came with us and, surprisingly, many of my high school friends showed up. It was bliss. I was in Heaven. Mary was vindicated and so was I.

Among other readings of this play, a marvelous moment was in Durango, Colorado with the Ft. Lewis College Theater Department. A staged reading in costume at an outdoor amphitheater under the stars.

There was another art event to follow the play. I had been invited to Durango by my friend of 50 years, the great installation artist Mary Ellen Long. Colleen, my second daughter, came with us and she enjoyed assisting Mary Ellen as they mounted a retrospective of Mary Ellen's work in the Durango Art Center.

I'd written a long poem for Mary Ellen about our lifelong collaboration called MAP, (see appendix) and professional dancers enacted the poem, as it was broadcast on amplifier. And somehow Mary Ellen and I had a "movement" part at the end of the piece which terrified me. I am not now a dancer and by now we were 70-plus years old. I had to borrow a long yellow muumuu from Mary Ellen and somehow I got my feet together in our five-minute bit on what seemed an unsteady floor. The words were not heard well because of the mixed media, but the intent was beautiful and much beauty clamored. And being with Colleen and Ken was the real fun. All the rest was rehearsal as far as I was concerned.

≈

Postscript on "Hyena in Petticoats:"

Some of my sweetest moments with Mary Wollstonecraft were readings on stages for local audiences. Learning the history about an 18th century dynamo was a plus, many said. Ken and I often read scenes to writers' groups, the most interesting, in the living room of Katherine J. Williams, psychologist/poet, to a room of psychiatrists and mental health workers who studied the creative process. That meeting would be the last time Ken would appear as my leading man, reading scenes from the play.

I used to open any event by saying to a group, "I wrote the poems and, after that, the characters were just hanging around the house so there was nothing to do but put them in a play." Ken surprised me one night when we were presenting in Takoma Park's Art Center by coming on stage saying, "I was just one of the characters hanging around the house." Everyone loved him.

Here was that intimate event:

Friday May 14, 8 pm Takoma Park Community Center
7500 Maple Avenue
Takoma Park MD 20912

HYENA IN PETTICOATS
(READING: Selected Scenes)
one hour 8-9 pm

Scenes chosen are of her relationships with the men in her life.

Mary Wollstonecraft: read by Rose Solari
award-winning poet, author of *Orpheus In The Park*

Clergyman Clare/Joseph Johnson: read by Kenneth Flynn
renowned metal sculptor/ former Naval Aviator

Gilbert Imlay/William Godwin: read by James J. Patterson
musician/writer/author of *Bamboo Shorts*

≈

For more on Mary Wollstonecraft see the
Appendix to Chapter Ten, page 251.

11 ~
"Anna Nicole: Blonde Glory"

AFTER MARY WOLLSTONECRAFT AND HARRIET POW-
ERS ENTERED ME, WHERE WAS THERE TO GO BUT TO ANNA NICOLE SMITH?
Anna Nicole was the perfect example of celebrity tragedy. She'd
been a model and *Playboy* centerfold. She had less emotional support in the world than Marilyn Monroe, Judy Garland, Jayne Mansfield, and their tragedies all put together; she was considered a train
wreck. Her family, a destructive father and mother, a rape, physical
and emotional abuse had destroyed her. Her handlers filled her with
drugs and propped her up. The exploiters concocted a TV reality
show and made her a clown. Anna married a 90-year-old billionaire
who died and left her a fortune, contested in court for seven years.

Here is where I got hooked. Anna had one teenage son weaving
in and out of these escapades and when he was a 20-year-old, Anna
had a baby girl. When I saw the photo shoots on TV of her in the
hospital holding her new baby, I saw a different Anna Nicole. No
make-up, hair pulled back in a pony-tail, and her true beauty showed
through. Those beautiful cheekbones, the tired mother after birth.
Here was a real person and no one recognized this. What if I could
write a play about someone who saw her true beauty, all that vulnerability; someone who saw that she could have offered something
genuine to the world. For a second I saw Anna's authenticity.

After birthing her baby girl, Anna's son died in her hospital
room! Of a drug overdose! Anna died similarly not long after. The

baby's father was up for grabs: several men claimed paternity. After much flashing of cameras and scandal, Larry Birkhead claimed the child via DNA, and he now raises her alone. Dannielynn is already modeling at seven years old. The inheritance from her mother's marriage to the billionaire awarded her ten million dollars.

After readings at the Muhlenberg Library in New York City, and in Washington at Bethesa Writers' Center, director Shela Xoregos arranged a staged reading at Arias Theater in New York, March 2011.

The perfect Anna was found in a glorious reading with a packed house. In NYC there's no lack of big blondes but Shela found the perfect one. Mary Riley. A clone to Anna in looks and a brilliant replica. She captured every nuance of Anna's breakable nerves. It was a high moment in my life. Friends showed up, as well as poets and family. and I was so grateful for a superb reading.

The idea for the play started two years previously, as most of my full-lengths do, with a book: *Anna Nicole: Poems*, begun in Toad Hall, New Hampshire, where Maria van Beuren runs a writers' retreat. Maria is a brilliant book indexer by trade and a doyenne of an estate by choice, Toad Hall. Ken and I went the first week of every August for several years; Ken, worked on sculpting; I, on writing. With peace and solitude and not worrying about the stove timer going off (meals provided), I got the lion's share of Anna onto the page. It was not her voice I captured but her life in a painful dark comedic set of poems which were published by Didi Menendez's press, Casa Menendez, and it was a finalist for the national Paterson Poetry Prize. (It won Paterson's Literary Excellence Award, 2008.)

I had all the stage characters already there in the book of poems: I had the crass manager, the would-be lover, those tugging on her celebrity without true commitment. So there was nothing to do but stand them up on stage and let them slug it out in front of us. I added one crucial element because theater needs conflict, where poetry does not. I imagined Anna having a twin sister (Anima) who died at birth but who followed Anna through life, cursing her good luck for surviving and causing the addictions and failures that Anna endured.

In a previous chapter I mentioned the World Trade Center explosions when "Pinecrest Rest Haven" was to open in NYC, and the threatened explosives in Washington, DC the night the Smithsonian premiered "Quilting the Sun." And so the great council of jokesters in the heavens who test our will, saw fit to produce one of the worst hurricanes of the decade, flooding New York City during my "Anna Nicole: Blonde Glory" opening week early in August, 2011. I had seen opening night at the Dream Up Festival, Theatre for the New City, but the director admitted that it was a rushed production; and I longed to see the next night's show. It promised to be even more spectacular in visuals and acting.

Although the first night is usually not the best for a play's rhythm, I still loved it. And adored Mary Riley, and fell in love with Anna Nicole and her bruised heart all over again. Shela had done a fabulous job getting designers and in one scene Anna wore a dress made entirely of flowers.

The next few days were a wipe out. The subways were flooded, Broadway was dark, and us along with it. All tickets were refunded. And I sat stunned and numb at the curious turn of events. It was to be a two-week showcase run (hoping to entice producers) and the actors, after that, had other jobs to go to and, of course, the show was ended. I did not say doomed because it is never doomed. Not as long as I brought a person to life from paper who will live longer than I will, and may see light again someday.

The play has been circulated since that time but seems to want for something—a person who believes as I do in Anna Nicole Smith's story. An opera was mounted in London, after my book came out, and the English piece was brought to America at BAMA; a TV series trashed her, but I believe my play is the only vehicle showing her as the goddess she could have been: "Anna Nicole: Blonde Glory." The title speaks of that.

Once I had a dream that Anna held me against her and the energy and electricity was beyond earthly understanding. I know that her spirit, ridiculed on earth, is seen for much more beauty in that land where the dead now live.

*Cavalieri's play is a universal story of women
through the ages who are valued as mere sex symbols.
The play demonstrates truth with wit, candor, tragedy,
drama, and humor. It is gratifying and edifying to experience Grace's skill as a poetic dramatist.*

— Daniela Gioseffi, American Book Award winner/
former Equity actress and drama critic

*Grace Cavalieri's new play is a case of poetic justice.
With heartbreaking sensitivity, the quintessential dumb
blonde is transformed into a truly tragic figure.*

— Maria Enrico, translator/professor, Spanish/Italian

*It was brilliantly directed, probably one of the best
I'd seen. And I was impressed with the writing... Grace
really did find a heart in that material.*

— Guy Shahar, actor/director/writer (WGA)

*The psychological subtext of Grace Cavalieri's play
is clear and accurate. Cavalieri proves herself to be a
dramatist capable of biting wit and empathetic psychological understanding about the primary needs of the
human psyche.*

—Allan B. Rubin, M.D. psychiatrist
Psychiatry Residency, Mount Sinai Hospital, NY, former
Chief of Neuropsychiatry, US Army General Hospital

Tragic and misunderstood were the words I was thinking during the whole play today. Grace and the Director really brought Anna's story to light and made me think about her in a much different light. We LOVED the whole experience.

— Nadia Al-Masri, Speech therapist, Boston, MA

The Anna Nicole reading was truly a triumph. I never really connected the word "profound" with anything about Anna Nicole, but it was profound! The play was full of humor, and is a true representation of tragic comedy, and the struggle to find "oneself." Hope it will have a full production soon.

— Dai Sil Kim-Gibson, filmmaker, author

The play was a unique glimpse inside the heart of this person whom I previously would not have taken seriously or noticed, just dismissed as an opportunistic bimbo. She came alive and showed her pain. It will change how she is viewed forever.

— Tim Frasca, author/journalist

≈

ANNA'S ESTATE

At the ½ star hotel
the lower lip is painted bigger, to match
her dreams of being a star.
She blessed the lumpy beds, bought her own silk sheets.
This was before the moral issues, the legal issues,
the spirit of the law, the letter of the law,
the causes of death, junkies, drug addicts,
probable criminal cause, bodies exhumed,
frozen sperm, mystery sons,
living in sorrow, wrongful death,
undue influences.
Before the opalescent oceans
where she could never find the truth in things,
where she wanted a photo album so bad,
so she wouldn't die without memories—
one day, standing at the free continental breakfast
dragging her sleeve in the jelly,
someone walked by, touching her waist like a prayer,
like an enfranchisement,
and she was on her way,
in a dress made for someone much smaller,
trusting a stranger because he said,
The Good Lord can't see what happens in Hollywood.

Anna Nicole: Poems, Casa Menendez, 2008

≈

For more on Anna Nicole Smith see the
APPENDIX TO CHAPTER ELEVEN, page 253.

12 ~
Married to a Sculptor

KENNETH C. FLYNN
(JANUARY 20, 1930 - JANUARY 15, 2013)

My husband, Ken Flynn, was a metal sculptor and he's taught me a lot about writing. He always loved metal, playing with it, and working with it. Heavy metal: Racing sports cars, working assembly lines, making his own airplane, flying very big ones as a Naval Aviator. And he was at the same time always a visual artist. When he came back from the unfathomable experience of Laos—he had promised himself that if he ever came home he'd never put off his love of welding—the first thing he did was to buy leathers, torch, and all the fixings. This was 1964.

He had a howl in the belly and wanted to turn that over to the powers of invention. Ken had watched his friend, Chuck Klusmann, get shot down and captured as the first Naval Aviator POW in Laos. He tried to rescue him, and was nearly lost in trying. This memory resulted in a bronze rendition of Chuck that was juried into an all California art exhibit. Ken was too reticent to submit his first work, so a neighbor artist did this without his knowing. Ken's works are beautiful, organic shapes of bronze on steel, smooth to the touch, but with sharp and dangerous nails within. This, we could call memory.

His process is now patented and comes from carving wood shapes, covering them with molten metal, and burning the original form so nothing is left but metal laced with light and space. The Lost Wood Process. Here is where I learned my lessons in discard. Writers would be so much better off if they believed the waste basket were not sacrosanct. Ken could spend nine months on a wood carving and, after the dripping and the welding, he'd purposely destroy the wood inside the metal. I can honestly say I've worked nine months on something, but that's different from starting with the intention of destroying it. Even revision, even plundering our own work, is not quite the same. This is because Ken's wood carving is in itself a work of art before he sacrifices it for a greater good.

I learned something from Ken every day about our arts. I'm lucky because I could carry a pen or laptop wherever we'd go, anytime, anywhere. His procedure is so complicated, the equipment so heavy, materials so expensive, no convenience—none at all. Also, writers can stuff their work into drawers and discs. Ken's is always visible, once occupying five acres in West Virginia, now crowding a smaller place in our Maryland home.

I know three things about sculptors: They like solitude, they hate marketing, and they'll do anything to make what they want.

I watched Ken stand outside in the bitter cold with a heating pad on his feet to carve a piece in wood, one that would be a contribution to God. Then I saw him spend three months burning the wood out, standing outside with a fan directed to the fire and bits of charcoal coming out. Once I saw him place a small bronze "lost wood" piece in the fireplace to finish the burning.

He was a modest man and didn't even want a website for his work. His pieces are owned by galleries and collectors all over the world. And in my living room, he shines through copper and steel every day, saying I WAS HERE. "For this I came."

≈

OBITUARY

Navy Capt. (ret.) Kenneth C. Flynn died peacefully in Annapolis, Maryland, on January 15, 2013, days before his 83rd birthday, from complications of pneumonia.

During his Naval carrier, Kenneth Flynn was an aviator assigned to several carriers as a Landing Signal Officer. The most significant tour of duty was on the USS Kitty Hawk. On June 6, 1964, LCDR Flynn performed an aerial mission to rescue the first POW shot down in the vicinity of Laos. Flynn was recommended for a Naval Air Medal, however, because of classified activities, it was 30 years before the honor was presented from President Clinton via Senator Benjamin Cardin's office.

Kenneth Flynn was active in US Masters Swimming from 1977 to 2008, often a gold medalist. At age 69, he achieved the honor of US Masters All American, setting a national record.

After retiring from the Navy in 1975, Flynn's profession was metal sculpture and fine art. His first recognized sculpture was "SEASIA," the subject for whom the Air Medal was awarded. Flynn's "lost-wood" bronze sculpting process was patented in 1994. He taught sculpting at Glen Echo Park during the mid-1970s and was instrumental in converting the amusement park to an arts center. He was also a founding member of the group that formed the Torpedo Factory.

From 1999, Flynn spent three years designing and hand-building a small aircraft, which he flew successfully.

He is survived by his wife of 60 years, poet/playwright Grace Cavalieri; his four daughters, Cynthia Cavalieri, Colleen Flynn, Shelley Flynn, and Angela Phelan; a brother, Richard Sage; and four grandchildren, Rachel Price, Elizabeth Comitz, Sean Phelan and Joseph Phelan. He resided in Annapolis, MD.

A service is planned with full military honors at Arlington National Cemetery.

≈

THE ART OF DISCARD

Said the Sculptor to the Writer:

"Somebody wants what you're writing but nobody cares if I sit hour after hour dripping molten bronze on hot steel. I don't care. It's the watching I want, the way I hold my hand so still, if I wait too long the metal will melt. If I move too quickly the bronze will harden. I live for this. The watching. The moment to touch bronze to steel, the second to pull it back. If I move too quickly the bronze will harden. If I wait, the steel metal will melt. All you need is a pencil. I have leather, masks, rods, machines, sanders, polishers, fire. You can hide your rejects in a drawer. Mine stand in front of me, larger than I am, gleaming and incomplete. What do you have faith in, he asked me. I have faith in failure, he said, then making it beautiful, something that will last."

The Man Who Got Away, New Academia/Scarith Press, 2014

For Ken's essay on Southeast Asia about the experience that awarded him the single air medal see the APPENDIX TO CHAPTER TWELVE, *page 256.*

13 ~
Antioch College

IN 1970, PHIL ARNOULT HEADED THE THEATER DE-PARTMENT AT ANTIOCH COLLEGE. He was the cutting edge of the cutting edge, had visiting guests like the Avant Theater's great Jerzy Grotowski with groups from Poland. Phil introduced the newest body of theater to America, pieces so far out that I joked they fell just short of being legally actionable. This was great art and Phil thrives today building bridges for international theater. Phil had seen my plays in Baltimore and he came for lunch in Oxon Hill, Maryland one day—we moved there in 1970—and offered me the job as Playwright in Residence at Antioch College.

Antioch's Mother Lode was in Ohio and it was the most progressive harbinger of education in the country. Three campuses were set up in the late 1960s, in Baltimore, Washington, DC, and Columbia, Maryland where a central building housed the arts, a red brick mansion, circa 1800s.

Phil ran the Theater Project, downtown Baltimore, which was the scene of new visions of the Cultural Revolution and beyond. It still thrives, though now serving as a stage for professional entertainment, music, etc.

When I left to teach at Antioch, I had technically been in the house for ten years, raising my ducklings, and writing the last few of those years. I didn't know how to do this, how to get to Baltimore and back before the 3 pm school bus, how to contribute by teaching courses other than Playwriting, and whether the $1000 yearly salary would pay for the car's fuel. Ken, on a Navy Commander's salary, had bought a new Porsche and I thought that would be just the thing—but where would I park?

The College had little money, just getting started, and needed everyone to put a shoulder to the wheel.

When I arrived I saw that Phil had a plaster of Paris mold of his penis mounted on the wall behind his desk. For years I thought it was an abstract art sculpture. So the Navy artist housewife was being thrown to surf the 100-foot wave of the Arts.

My interview: I walked into the main building, Columbia, Maryland, having gotten lost along the way and asked directions; I was more than flustered and nervous when introduced to the most benevolent and extraordinary Welsh novelist, Joyce Varney. She laughed her head off the moment we met when I told her about the student who I picked up hitch hiking along the way. And I was in love with my new Boss. The Welsh are full bodied, full throated, fulsome, fulfilling, and lyrical. I was where I belonged. She was setting up writing programs. I had degrees in English and Education but finally, I was in the sandbox I had always dreamed of—being with young people who were to be artists.

Most students were geniuses or burn-outs. The school van driver had nose bleeds from cocaine, and I made sure I never drank the punch at college functions. The school had a mighty Social Science Program and had beckoned many ghetto kids from Baltimore, giving scholarships and aid to bring forth a new generation of graduates. Many would never have received degrees otherwise. I was energized by everyone who crossed my path.

I could teach what I wanted and it turned out to be more poetry than playwriting. During 1970-1975, several hundreds of students came through Joyce for prose, and me for poetry, and we felt like keepers at a zoo. And much good came of it.

I got a raise to $1800 the second year but I don't think my annual salary was ever more than $2400. Never mind, I was happy. I, who hated to drive, jumped out of bed, eager to go; and when Angel was not in school she packed her Barbie dolls and lunch box and went along to watch the magic.

I would not allow marijuana smoking and I think I was the most Victorian of the faculty members. This was really homeschooling. Joyce and I were housemothers, nurses, confidants. We heard complaints about bad LSD trips, herpes, and many times I brought students home to recover in bed, serving them my soup on a tray. There were midnight suicide calls. And my family adjusted to strange visitors. All part of the job description.

It was the Revolution. And the voices that had been oppressed forever were now rising to the surface. Blacks, Women, Gays. Like all things under strata, compression makes diamonds. The poetry that was written was extraordinary. Gay icon Rita Mae Brown visited. I had legendary theater director/critic Davy Marlin-Jones lecture, and all the top poets I knew visited my classes. Everyone came to the party.

An aside: Joyce held a special theater seminar in her home for Marlin-Jones. Ken and I picked him up in Washington (as he had but three hours free) so I packed a picnic basket with linens, champagne and gourmet sandwiches so he could dine in the back seat on the way to Columbia and be back to his stage, Theater Lobby, in DC by 3 pm. This was high maintenance education.

Some magnificent students: Geoffrey Himes wrote a major exegesis on the Beatles' song lyrics. What other college would have been so flexible? He is, today, a top music critic in America, author of the Bruce Springsteen biography and a Country Music Hall of Fame historian. Mark Dunau, brilliant playwright; Paz Cohen breathtaking prose/poetry writer/translator; Marty Brown, terrific; Paul Bartlett, sweet poet—they are among the top creative people today contributing to our canon of letters. I still hear from many students from 40 plus years ago. I just got a Christmas card from Theresa Kendall, speaking of her Antioch poetry times with me in 1972.

And there were extremes: The school was run as a work/study program so "community work" earned students college credits. I had a fair share of ghetto students who worked industriously to move to a better world. I had one young woman who wanted work credits because she delivered drugs to the dealer and when

I asked her why she thought this would qualify (she kept track of all the hours) she said she "had learned so much from the experience." We were supposed to be supportive in all cases, but I was nonplussed and sent her to the Registrar, Ann Rice. Ann was nurturing and I knew would give her a gentle hearing before she was denied.

The place was racially charged. This was the early 70s, remember. And there was one teacher more radical than one could ever dream. Racism against blacks existed. It was a fact and a disease. Problems resist solution if people have a psychological/personal problem and use racism as the sword, then there's little one can do to heal it.

I used to cook dinner at 6 am in the morning before I left for Baltimore so it would be ready to heat up when I got home. Angel would say, "I'm not eating this. The food tastes tense." She would then punctuate her disapproval by eating only French bread pizzas and baloney sandwiches during my Antioch tour.

One particular African-American professor had been chilled by the ice water of racism. We ate cookies together every day when I went in her office. But one day she snapped. She was a honcho in the Social Sciences Department, and when the Baltimore campus moved to the old Belvedere Hotel, she locked us in the Ballroom. It was supposed to be a faculty meeting and she said no one was getting out until we admitted we were all racists plotting against her. I knew it was nearly 3 pm and my kids were coming home from school. There was much intellectual debate and repartee from the activists, and I kept looking at my watch and worrying until 5 pm. I was the first to say, "I'm a racist. Let me out." And I went home. Fortunately, there were many more rational encounters than this and much good came from them.

The most tumultuous moment I had was when I was to teach a Black Literature poetry class. I was blocked by the all-black group in the DC Antioch Center. I got into the classroom and proved that I knew black poetry and was armed with proof. I was completely sympathetic to the feelings of my students in a disruptive political climate. Sometimes I wish I could've worn a placard around my neck that said, I HELPED MOVE THE FIRST BLACK FAMILY INTO LEVITTOWN, PENNSYLVANIA, INTEGRATING THE CITY, IN 1956; I KNOW THE DEAL. But my credentials didn't count. Only the process of time would help us. That's what it was like back then.

I talked of all the literary ancestors and read from their works. The rest of the term was good. We studied Ed Bullins and LeRoi Jones' (Amiri Baraka) plays; and poetry from Paul Lawrence Dunbar to Gwendolyn Brooks. It was an honest knowledge of a body of work I valued.

Black literature was a field I knew and a course I was proud of, unlike my Baltimore screenplay class—I had never written a screenplay—and had to study each night to use the right words in front of advanced filmmakers. Antioch had a substantial film department taught by esteemed moviemaker, Tom Johnson. These filmmakers were pretty wild. I did hear about film students licking whipped cream off a naked female student one night but I tried not to think about it.

Some of the most attractive educational features in Antioch were the spin-offs. There was a Humanistic Institute for Education which I embraced wholeheartedly. The central idea was to allow the student to know the leader (teacher) was made of the same emotional stuff that they were. For example, we could start a lesson by saying, "I'm very nervous about meeting you and I had a very disorienting dream which I'll tell you before we begin…." Private thoughts like that. There were also team Legos, where we would observe students to see who jumped in aggressively, who sat back, those who would not play at all; and then who among them was the observer who recorded the process. I forget what was done with the information but it was railing against the totalitarianism in classrooms elsewhere. We thought we were changing society to the good; and were probably just changing ourselves to a higher degree of self-righteousness. I certainly thought all other education was spawned by the KGB—and this would get me into trouble back in my own neighborhood at a later time.

Angel was always trooping along side of me when she had days off from Apple Grove Elementary. Once I produced a radio play, "Cuffed Frays," and the only studio space was on the top floor of a school for autistic children. The child factory was a primitive attempt at herding the hurt creatures and the bad energy was devastating. When we walked through the entrance, we saw one child with arms strapped down and another trying to peel his skin off; we hastened up the stairs and Angel turned pure white. I had no idea of the environment when I agreed to the space, and I couldn't get home fast enough. That was the last time she'd accompany me to any event that was not prepped and staged first.

Angel did develop a love for theater through these meanderings, when Antioch star student, Maggie Rice, started Commonwealth Theater off-campus and Angel got her first taste. This would next take Maggie to study with Robert Alexander and Rebecca Rice at Arena Stage in DC for eight years and to create the richness for 'a life within' and a new way to see the world.

Antioch was like no other place on earth. One schizophrenic student was living on the street and described to me what it was like to be on heroin. "You feel like that file cabinet over there," he said, "Like nothing." But he was there by guess and by god and learning something about poetry, the last great thought before he would OD, I'm sure. The geniuses were there also and the books that were written since, and the plays by those writers make me happy with the thought of them.

One student wanted to lay his head on my lap while I taught. I demurred.

I wrote an unproduced play about Antioch called "Smarts." Since then, I've plundered and disassembled the piece to use parts in other plays. Basically it was about two conventional Jewish ladies who visit their sons at Antioch and what they encounter—high jinx, including a clock that always had the same time and a revolution on campus. It was pretty silly but I wish I had the energy to rewrite it.

What drove me to Baltimore and Columbia and DC everyday? Desire. The great impulse. The force. What makes us want what we want? Whatever it is, row, run, swim toward it. Desire keeps us alive and it made me the most alive I've ever been during those five years. I burned out my thyroid in the process and I had colitis when I had to leave home for three days at a time, running poetry retreats at the Ilchester, Maryland, convent, but I had the clothes for it. The neighbors must have gossiped as I left for work in converted hippie nightgowns, ankle-length cottons, made into dresses with belts.

My daughters were wonderful, entertaining the brilliant, weird and disenchanted who shared our supper table. I pray those students didn't get more than their share of my children's time. But I fear some days they did.

≈

EXCERPT FROM A POEM ABOUT LEAVING ANTIOCH.

Working for the Government

...

Tell them about me, that I was no easy lady
More like an old dog, chasing a bird in a
Moment of sun who leaves now for good saying
Isn't it a beautiful Autumn.
If these are my tears, I can do what I want
                                    with them.

—*Bliss*, Hillmunn Roberts Publishing Company, 1986

14 ~

Devy Bendit and More on Antioch

I CAN'T MENTION THOSE ANTIOCH YEARS WITHOUT TALKING OF DEVY BENDIT. She was a lawyer teaching at Antioch who wanted to immerse herself in poetry and she did—by immersing herself in me. The first day I met Devy, she came into my office and said she wanted to be a poet. 1970. She said she had a headache, and 'did I have an Advil?' I took a bottle of emergency pills out, which had one of everything one might need when away from home, a tiny medicine chest. She grabbed it and to my horror swallowed them all. Fortunately they were not toxic and mostly benign. Fourteen years later she suicided, 1984.

Devy bonded to me the moment I entered Antioch. Devy was gorgeous and smart and looked like Audrey Hepburn. However, she was afflicted with anorexia, a terrible disease which I was not skilled enough to cure. We spent hours together; and for fourteen years she visited, called or wrote me every single day.

I think I was relieved in a way when she finally went to rest. It was an impossible situation. She came to our house for every Thanksgiving and Easter, all holidays, and she always threw her Cornish hen or steak in the garbage, and then would eat an entire cake. It was horrifying. She even made more than one pass at my husband and we'd find her swimming naked in our swimming pool when we were gone from the house. She lived an hour away in Baltimore, thankfully, but why did we put up with it? She was so adorable and what rescuer can possibly turn away from that great seductress—need.

Devy was due for our family's Christmas dinner, 1984, and would not answer her phone for days. People who saw her the day before said she was very animated. I hear that's the way suicides behave when they know there's finally a solution, relief in sight. She had a vendetta against her mother who was, I thought, lovely, and this fantasy led Devy to a final torment—to leave everything she owned to me—written to me on a post card by her bed. She took a stash of Seconal pills and drank half a bottle of white wine, and covered her sweet head in a blanket.

Devy, who was a lawyer, knew that her mother was legally next in line to inherit her possessions. But she wanted to see if her mother would honor what she wanted by making her last request on a postcard—willing her possessions to me. It could easily be disqualified. Once again Devy tested her mother, even taunted her. We were humiliated and told the family to please ignore this and take everything but they were ethical and had a highly developed Jewish sense of rightfulness. They did take her father's violin and the family treasures.

I still wear Devy's earrings and her coats. We donated all her law books to the Antioch Law School in DC. My daughter, Cindy, and I had a small poetry publishing house, The Bunny and the Crocodile Press, and we published two of Devy's books, *Selling Parsley* and *Solid Gold*, in the mid 1970s. Devy'd been married, she'd had lovers, she'd tried LSD and wound up in the hospital. She was funny, surprising, and smart; but her body showed the signs of malnourishment—she was 70 pounds when she died. She was in her early 40s.

I think we all disappointed her. Everyone she ever knew. The most painful gesture was a book of blank pages, left by her bed, which was inscribed. "To Grace. May these images match her love." It was empty.

≈

At Antioch I was antiseptic, virtuous, a mentor, but in Oxon Hill, Maryland, I was considered a renegade, a mother who never went to PTA, a hippie in long skirts.

During my five years at the East Coast Antioch College the new administration was seeking accreditation. The day the accreditation team came, our writing department had its ducks in a row, including our poetry publication *SAMIZDAT* (named after a famous Russian underground magazine). I was so proud to see it lined up on the show-off table. I felt I'd been part of something big.

I asked Joyce Varney (now Joyce Thompson) to write a remembrance of her time there, for another project, and here's the letter I got. It's filled with approbation but that's what the distance of 44 years does for you.

Hi Darling:

So much of the best part of Antioch will be censored. But that is what I most remember, and treasure. But coming there in the late 60s after two years at Harvard was like getting a blast of hot fudge on ice-cream.

How I ended up at Antioch in 1960 something, after spending two exciting years as a Fellow at Radcliffe with a Harvard appointment, is still a live mystery. It could only happen in America. It was what you might call a freak of nature. I had no education to speak of. I did not pay enough attention in the Welsh School where all miners' children went. However, I was always an avid reader if a lousy speller. At nineteen years, I arrived as a GI bride from South Wales to America, with nothing more burdensome than taking care of my baby, husband, and becoming the best damn cook, and wife. After Wartime England I came to make chocolate chip cookies, brownies, Thanksgiving turkey, and Pumpkin pie. The last thing on my mind was becoming a writer.

I left school at fourteen in South Wales with no wish to return to that school for coal miners'children. Where the desks were nailed to the floor from 9-to-4, along with the children. I guess I was what you might call an inspired illiterate. And quite happy with that. But my husband went to Dartmouth, and his Mom wanted his wife to get some education.

So America had other plans for me. My lapse into Literature came about when I went to a Writer's Conference at the local University of New Hampshire to keep a friend company. Charles Angoff, a famous journalist, was there at the conference and gave all of us an assignment. A Chinese quote. "When Grandparents Enter the Room Discipline Flies Out the Window" and told us to develop it. I wrote about my Welsh grandparents who raised and spoilt me and I came away with a prize for the short story. I remember feeling as though the professor had said—"I now crown you Miss America."

This encouragement led me to take special courses at UNH, and after many Es and Ds I finally learned how to frame a paragraph, but never became a good speller.

This was at least 20 years away from Antioch or Harvard. But I kept writing and taking courses and eventually published A WELSH STORY, which launched my career. On the strength of one award-winning book, I became a Radcliffe Fellow, and later a director of the writing program at Antioch College in the USA and abroad, and by then I became the author of several books for adults and children. And also published plays, short stories and poetry.

I choose Antioch because I met Judson Jerome at Breadloaf Writer's Conference. Jud was a full professor at Antioch, a poet, a cheerful little elf of a man, with his pants on fire to change American education. His name was all over Time Magazine insisting that "A culture was dying, and a culture was dying to be born." Educators must get rid of the bricks and academic hall of ivy and open up schools of learning in store fronts. Educate the illiterate. He was preaching this at Breadloaf Writer's Conference to skeptical editors and professors. But this was the 1960s and anything was possible. We were going to change the world. Anyway, Jud persuaded me to come to Antioch and earn an MA in Arts and Teaching even though I didn't even have a high school degree. And because I was a writer I earned one.

Now I come to the best part—meeting Grace Cavalieri. Had I chosen Tufts instead of Antioch I might never have met Grace. And what a loss that would be. I will never forget my first introductions. I had been at Antioch about a month, and well over my head with work when Phil Arnoult suggested I get in touch with Grace who was looking for a job. I will never forget her walking into that Manor House Antioch had rented. She walked in the room, followed by an enormous Lad, and her first words were: "I gave this man a ride to Antioch because he promised not to rape me. I have four children." She smiled with those melting brown eyes, and her voice was such that however low she spoke you could hear every word. My instinct was to laugh. Instead I stared into those eyes and said simply, "You're hired."

And that's how it all began. Although we worked like slaves, Grace certainly did, we never stopped laughing. Grace with her one-liners kept it that way.

Grace Cavalieri, with her down-to-earth common
sense, sense of humor, as well as being well educated,
was an inspired teacher. She helped students to keep
at least one toenail on the ground in those bedazzled
years. In a few short weeks her classes were packed with
spellbound kids. She was the Pied Piper and she had
drop-outs from the best Ivy League schools, gobbling up
all she could to teach them. She could make the saddest
student laugh out loud, as she did with everyone she
met. Students would line up outside her door just to steal
more time. I remember one earnest lad, pleading 'when
could she see him,' she had tutorials lined up every hour
of the day. He'd been up late writing a poem just for
her. Grace gave him a dazzling smile and said sweetly,
"Hopefully before my menopause."

I could go on and on, but you would be up late read-
ing.

Most Sincerely,

Joyce V. Thompson.

~

Joyce invited me to teach at Oxford University one summer
where she hosted Antioch College Abroad. I could only squeeze one
week away from home, but she was always my leader with a magic
wand dinging everyone human, and I followed in her stardust.

≈

As I was writing this chapter (February 10, 2014) I received a letter from an Antioch 1973 graduate, Marty Brown. He wrote the following remarks I made while teaching. He didn't know I was writing these reminiscences today. I hadn't heard from him since the 1970s.

Marty wrote:

"I remember you saying to me, "you write using the trombone style of writing"

(about my lines being of greatly uneven length).

i remember you quoting frank o'hara, "you go on your nerve..."

i remember you being curious about how fond several writing students

at Antioch, myself included, were for the poetry of Gregory Orr."

15 ~
A Heartfelt Apology to Mrs. B'shira

A BAND OF TEACHERS FROM APPLE GROVE ELEMEN-TARY SCHOOL, ALONG WITH ME AND MY HUSBAND—IN JARGON—"TOOK DOWN" THE SCHOOL PRINCIPAL, MRS. B'SHIRA. In other words, we had her fired.

I regret this terrible action on my part, all because I thought her educational ideology was dangerous. It was ultra-rigid and I never realized my anger was because of my own opposing ideology. All fixed notions are dangerous. The teachers who headed the action had other agendas, but I can only regret my own lack of insight.

At the time, 1970, three of my children were attending this school in the suburban tree-lined Maryland neighborhood, Shelley and Colleen in grade five, and Angel in kindergarten. Cindy was in junior high at the time.

The 1960s and 70s were a great time for change—the Beatles had descended. Poetry was benefited by song lyrics that broke up phrases and made new forms. Old forms were broken so new ones could be made. The world had been waiting for a sunrise and Jesus Christ Super Star let it happen on stage.

Education was polarized as distinctly as today where the Republican Tea Party opposes President Obama. Mrs. B'shira was the epitome of old school. She was probably not a bad person, but she was vindictive about those who did not adhere. The young teachers became friends of ours and socialized with us, complaining of the restrictions, and lack of creativity. Mrs. B'shira was threatened by anything creative or new. The young teachers were the products of this new age of liberal humanized learning. They coalesced and somehow maneuvered, charmed, seduced us to listen to their complaints. We were sympathetic but some new events turned the corner to radicalize our collective discontent.

I taught at Antioch three days a week and would substitute occasionally in public schools other days. Apple Grove called me to come in as a kindergarten substitute. I wore a beautiful red floor length calico dress (much like a folk singer might have in that day). It was the kind of thing I wore to Antioch and was respectable, if not puritanical, by Antioch tastes. That night I got a call that I had upset all the children (not true) and my dress was inappropriate and I was fired from any future substitute jobs in that school.

It was not ego that hurt but it was clearly the rejection of what I represented. Something outside the norm. I then saw the dilemma of the teachers who were banding against Mrs. B'shira. Angel's kindergarten teacher, Miss Kelly, an enlightened educator, was to be dismissed because she wore pantsuits to school. There was no dress code announced or all of us would have conformed, but random punishments occurred without notice. Colleen and Shelley were sent home for wearing knee-length culottes to school. The clothing issues were symptoms of irrational and spontaneous reactions from a principal who punished where no policy was in place. And we were determined to save Miss Kelly's job. She was an outstanding teacher by all standards.

My husband was outraged and I think we were inflamed more by the teachers' grumblings than our own small arguments. Our children were getting a good education and thriving so perhaps we should have looked the other way.

Ken was caught in his own war of worlds. He was a Navy Commander who was by now a fully developed and committed artist. He went to work at the Bureau of Naval Personnel on a BMW motorbike every day (the classic office joke at BUPERS was: would his sword or his sandals get caught in the spokes?). He was finishing his degree at Antioch College—where he was disdained as military. Remember, Viet Nam Vets were treated like lepers when they returned, so he, neither fish nor fowl, was offended by Mrs. B'shira's lack of generosity. He sympathized with the rebelling teachers.

We should have stayed clear of it. We should never have sacrificed one person for our ideals that were based as much on prejudice as those of the offender. Ideas should be strong enough to stand without harming others.

The teachers' dispute finally reached the Board of Education where my husband represented our family and it was nasty, finally with Mr. B'shira threatening my husband. Anger all the way around. Mrs. B'shira was removed and sent to another school. Her own loyalist team of teachers was kind enough not to take it out on my children.

I've never felt that we did the right thing by escalating the situation. We'd been activists in the peace movement. We were respectable progressives. And respectable parents. But nothing was at stake here but different philosophies—no true wrongs like racism or injustice—a clash of ideologies, about what is best for children. I often wonder if that was enough to ruin a person's career.

Now that I'm part of a Buddhist sangha, compassion is the practice. So please Mrs. B'shira wherever you are, accept this 40 year old apology. Rebels with a different cause from yours. But history has proven us right! Creativity is the way to teach.

16 ~

Where Are the Children?

EVERYONE WILL SAY: *SHE GETS TO CHAPTER 16 WITH-OUT MENTIONING RAISING FOUR CHILDREN?* The great thing, the wonderful thing, the beautiful, miraculous, holy and blessed part of this is, it's OK with them.

Some subjects, like the sun, are too great to look into.

Raising small children was the most creative time and happiest time of my life. Now after 16 books and 26 plays, I know it called for more ingenuity, innovations, and imagination than all those projects together. I know one thing for real: I always saw the world from their points of view. That's all that's needed. I saw it their way.

My girls are the only way I know who I am. They don't care if I win the Pulitzer or have my name on a poster. Or whether I have one hem hanging and a shoelace untied. I am their Mom and that's who and what I am. They love me for myself and even when that is weak and failed, they love. When I am playing dress-ups with artists, they love.

I wanted to start this, not with an apology, but Lucille Clifton had five children and would bristle when asked about that. "Why can't I be a writer and still raise five children?" Nancy Pelosi swears she made cookies. I can't picture it but I think she was a good mom.

I regret some of the football games I missed when my girls were cheerleaders, but I certainly did not miss hearing the cheer-leading practices in our garage. My daughters were happily pursuing their own interests at school while I was visiting some of PBS's TV stations (1978-82), or NPR's stations for NEH (1982-88), or teaching at St. Mary's College. I regret that now. Oprah once said, "You can have everything you want. But not all at once."

It's February 2014 right now and a grey, cold day and Ken, who was the designated parent at those games, is gone. And I wish I could go see the school events I missed then.

But the children say they never felt deprived of me, and I have consulted others besides. Psychics who tell it as it is. My girls lived in my love and grew there. If I was guilty of anything it was sewing the light of poetry and, some days, leaving the children only the cloth.

However, one title of this chapter should be "Every Good Mother Feels Guilt." Because it is true, whether we're late with supper or producing a play. There's no difference in what a mother feels if her attention is anywhere but with her children.

I'd written a book of poems, *Migrations,* with all my pain and loss about children. Psychic Bryan Christopher said we abandon them the moment we birth them. And I have multiple poems about this, because the only road for children is away from us. In fact much of my art is about this loss.

The book *Migrations* is illuminated by Mary Ellen Long's magnificent photos. She, my artist collaborator since 1964, has photos of broken dolls, and antique dolls, accompanying the poems. It is shattering. All the heartbreak of bringing children into the world just to have to say goodbye to them. Hello to my loves. Goodbye goodbye. I love you. Please don't cry.

Edna Kirksey, a spiritual leader I knew in Florida, started a publishing house (Vision Library) and *Migrations* was one of her first publications. The book is a visual work of art and yet hardly found a market. Certainly not a Hallmark card, and who wants to give a Mother's Day gift book about guilt, inadequacy and loss, however eternal its truth.

Vivian Adelberg Rudow was my composer from the years 1974 to date and in 1995 she set the poems to music. She kept saying, "Grace this is too sad! We must find light in loss."

Ken went into the hospital for an emergency triple heart by-pass at this time. He'd been competing in Masters Swimming since 1982 and at a race in Ft. Lauderdale (1993), Shelley and I saw him stop a race and climb out. A routine check-up followed at Bethesda Naval Hospital. While he had an angiogram, just to pass the time, I went to the Navy Exchange to buy towels. When I returned the docs said he was in the emergency operating room. I, to this day will never buy towels again. It was a rough nine days as he was hemorrhaging and they had to "go in again," as they put it, three times. I slept in the waiting room most of the time. My girls were always there. And since home was too far, in West Virginia, I finally rested in a local motel.

Here's a point about children and art—or art about children. After Ken was recuperating comfortably, I stood in the hall outside his room on a payphone (no cell phones yet) and worked on the "opera" with Vickie. We set the poems to the music from the hall-way of Bethesda US Naval Center Cardiology ward. The result of Vickie's music is incredibly beautiful. She combines the lyricism of love, the hip hop of vitality, the sweet moan of loss.

When Ken's skies were clear, we had a multimedia event at the Franz Bader Gallery in Washington, DC. A fine place. There was a brick wall separating spaces so we had audiences on both sides. My cousin, Jane Sharnoff, was in the Seda Galenian's dance troupe and they danced to the poems, with Vickie's music, while the TV monitor showed Mary Ellen's photos from the book. We had iden-tical dancers on each side of the wall—a mirrored simultaneous event. But the TV monitor didn't display the visuals properly in the middle of the audiences. Mary Ellen and husband Wendell Long came from California expressly for the event. So I was a wreck.

What felt like one of the worst moments on earth was at the end of the show, when Vickie and I stood, hands held together high for the applause, and I failed/flustered/forgot to ask Mary Ellen to stand up and be acknowledged. She forgave me after a while.

And here is where I forgive myself again. I begin writing about children and I end up writing about writing about children. They don't care. They know who they are. They know who I am. Although children come through us, they are not of us. They are our offspring that we nurture through their tears, but if you are an artist, you do this while riding a wild dark horse.

Angel came for dinner tonight and I told her about this chapter I was writing. She said, "You proved to us that a person could be authentic. That we had to find our imprint and be true to that." I always wondered why they supported my writing with heart and soul. Perhaps it was the path to their own truth. What a concept.

And as I always say jokingly to them, "Thank you, the Management." So the Management wishes to acknowledge, among lifelong support, recent events below:

Thank you, Angel, for weekly meditation sessions with me. Thank you, Shelley and Colleen, for coming to Seattle's Associated Writing Program Conference with me. Thank you, Cindy, for coming to the Poets & Artists Opening in Chicago with me, and for driving to New Jersey so I could receive an award. And thank you all for the hundreds of times in between these events.

Dr. Evans, longtime psychiatrist/friend, said children should be children, not be assistants. Oh no. Dr. Evans, mine are much more than all of that. They are my muses, although they do assist.

Cindy teaches me how to be generous, to keep an open heart, to embrace everything without judgment. Colleen shows me all about loyalty, dignity and elegance. Shelley gives me the gift of imagination, laughter, playfulness. Angel gives me integrity and a spiritual life without end. And the miracle is, each daughter has ALL of the attributes of the others.

Bryan Christopher said, "You have been blessed by the universe in ways you do not know."

17 ~

The German
Embassy, 1980

I LOVED MY JOB AT PUBLIC BROADCASTING SERVICE,
WHERE I WAS THE ASSOCIATE DIRECTOR OF EDUCATION AND CHIL-
DREN'S PROGRAMMING FROM 1978 TO 1982. In charge of the daytime schedule, I had the super nova program "Sesame Street"
lighting up the sky, taken by 100 percent of the PBS stations.
Many other countries were also taking the series, some illegally,
but there was no way to police this. However, an invitation came
to our department for a cocktail party at the German Embassy.

Ken loved embassies, having been raised abroad in Sweden,
Australia and England, and I loved putting on high heels. And we
both adored vodka straight up and out of the freezer. This was to
be a splendid night; I was sure the dignitaries wanted to talk about
Sesame Street and, if not, who cared. Ken and I loved a date, pref-
erably one with hors d'oeuvres.

It was a magnificent large building, and we had stimulating, if
superficial, conversational moments with guests about television
and children. Everyone was interested in PBS and its reach and
significance. It was fun.

Ken, an artist, wandered from room to room admiring the gorgeous hangings and sculpture and said much too loudly, I'm afraid,
"How in the world did you people ever manage to smuggle all
these things out of East Germany without getting slaughtered?"

He went on, I cringe to say, with some more jokes on the
subject. But no one was laughing. In fact, the room fell dead—I

mean dead—silent. Ken and I looked at each other. We never analyzed the invitation: GDR? The German Democratic Republic? How could we have confused it with the FRG: the Federal Republic of Germany? So many consonants in the abbreviation. So few vowels.

We were in the East German Embassy. And our popularity dissolved like frozen vodka in Hell.

Once the cocktail party chatter resumed, we got our coats and quietly, very quietly, stole away.

18 ~
Small Presses for Poetry

THE BUNNY AND THE CROCODILE PRESS WAS START-
ED IN 1976, BY GRACE CAVALIERI AND DAUGHTER CINDY. Then, that
same year, I joined our friend, John McNally, in establishing the
Washington Writers' Publishing House.

The name "Bunny and Crocodile" came from a *New Yorker*
cartoon that poet David Bristol sent me with a huge crocodile
mouth, and two bunnies inside the open jaws, hugging, unaware
of any danger. This surely was poetry in the world. People always
attributed the press's name to Ken and me but truly it was just an
imprint we thought perfect.

The small press movement is time-honored in America. In the
1960s and 70s, the movement gained momentum, taking on the
mission of publishing good poets whom big houses ignored. Big
publishers were owned by AT&T and Westinghouse, corporate
America. But small presses didn't have a bottom line, or even a
line, and all kinds of books were produced—even mimeographs
were published in poets' basements.

The Bunny/Crocodile depended on an established poet finding
his/her own grant to sustain publication. Most of our poets were in
academia and, at that time, colleges supported and subsidized publications. Of course, my household had to provide more funding than
anticipated because of incidentals that we—an illusioned entity—
could never foresee. When it came to finances, "The Bunny" was
always outside chewing grass while "The Crocodile" slept in the sun.

Also, we did not want to focus on bookkeeping so the authors received 100 percent of their books and sales money. What did we have? We had the great pleasure of making a book, making something that did not exist before—call it collaboration with God, but there was something wonderful about packaging a poet's words and sending them out into the world like a letter of love.

The reason our press was not a vanity press (i.e., writers pay to be printed) is because of one word: selection. We received many manuscripts, and we chose carefully among those poets who were excellent, who had tried traditional houses first, were deserving in the community and—admittedly—sometimes were also our friends.

Cindy was an accomplished artist who designed our books and covers. She was in college when we began. We found a printer in southern Maryland who made books that were reasonably priced with good textbook paper. The largest portion of our publishing lives was helped along by George Klear's Printing Press in Leonardtown, Maryland. After George died, his son Kerry worked for us.

George Klear, an angel in the rough, was amazed at the idea that anyone would print poetry instead of VFW news or fishing calendars. He always gave a great price and once, when covers for the WPFW anthology were injured, George reprinted 500 books for free—without us even asking ("That's what giving is," my husband always said).

From 1976 to 2014 we did books sporadically, one or two a year. We had other interests, and publishing was on the margin of our lives. During the last ten active years of publishing we accepted novels. Finally we decided to close the press in 2013. Thirty-six years of work with no revenue was a drain. The energy we received from shining light on other writers called for more batteries than we had left.

But a new submission came from Joyce Varney Thompson who, in 2013, had a manuscript just as we were about to lock the doors. And so we would publish this one last book. We had, the year before, published Joyce's son, Robert Varney. He wrote a cunning mystery novel, *Do Unto Others*. "Robin" was a distinguished judge in New Hampshire and his courtroom drama saw immediate success. But it was Joyce who was the whipped cream and cherry on top. What an exit publication.

Every time Joyce had shared an anecdote from her youth with me I'd leap and say she must write fiction based on all that she encountered, a scared young Welsh girl who would rise to celebrity. She'd been collecting notes for years and had bits and pieces tucked away, and a good semblance of a novel on a rocky computer that kept crashing. She sent the manuscript to me and I knew there was a world of readers who'd care—but more importantly, Joyce knew she must write it, no matter who read it.

I was able to comb through and restructure, and massage the chapters. The heft was all there. The writing power of Joyce Varney had gone nowhere at all. The book sparkled with her wit and music. In less than a year's time, we sent the manuscript to Libby Howland for copyediting and super indexer Maria van Beuren to proof perfect.

British GI Brides in America: Among Alien Corn, our final production, was a beautiful tribute to a lifelong project.

Our hands-on production person designed a beautiful book for Joyce and obtained rights for the cover image—a ship full of GI Brides waving on arrival to America—just like Joyce remembered. (It was $350 for the rights to print the photo.)

Our press moved from offset printing to Lightning Source's Print-on-Demand, which relieved everyone of boxes of unsold books in authors' closets—a great improvement from the time when we would order 500 or 1000 books at a time and the author would have to house them, then carry books from store to store. Poetry is hardly Capitalism; ours was the world of the small press. We published poetry because we loved making writing permanent.

I'd met Joyce Varney in 1970 when she'd been setting up writing programs at Antioch and I was in love. I still heard from Joyce and never lost sight of her, looking over my shoulder through the years, even after we left Antioch and she moved to Maine to write full time. In the 1990s, Joyce Varney married Tommy Thompson, a New England physician who'd been in love with her for 30 years. Time took its toll, they moved to Florida and she lost her husband.

The silver thread between us was never broken and when I lost my own husband, Joyce's letters truly got me through my misery. She knew the human heart more than anyone I ever knew. She was 90 years old when her book came out from our press.

I loved all our book children, as Howard Nemerov used to say of his poems, "even the squat and ugly." But none of ours were that.

The most sweeping success of any of our books was *The WPFW Anthology* where the Bunny and Crocodile published the first 300 poets to appear on my radio series "The Poet and the Poem from WPFW-FM." Some poets had never been in print. Others were Poets Laureate, some had never been on radio before, and every one gave us the beauty of a poem. We were able—I cannot believe the hundreds of grants I've written—to distribute the anthology to every library and every public school in the District of Columbia.

These were the books George Klear replaced because someone in his shop moved the covers before the varnish was dry. So I still have a box of extras in my closet, and I am saving them for the most special of all occasions, although I can't imagine what that will be.

In 1986, Robert Sargent, my constant friend and companion and Bunny Board member, had just retired from his career at the Pentagon, working under Robert McNamara. He put his clerical skills to work by helping me apply for nonprofit status, incorporated in the District of Columbia. Now we could do more work. An entity can be incorporated in every state so when I moved to West Virginia in 1988, I added Forest Woods Media as a moniker as we were doing more poetry distribution in media than in print.

At the time of the Bunny's inception, I met John McNally. He was a wonderful, energetic person, who worked with my husband at the Bureau of Naval Personnel. Ken, his "superior officer," was a Commander and John was a Lieutenant so when Ken brought him home, John was naturally called Ken's "inferior" officer. John had seen horrible action in Viet Nam in a river boat with dead bodies falling on him. But he never spoke of it. He was sweet, handsome, on his way to law school, and he loved poetry; he was an excellent poet.

It was John's idea to start a publishing house that was not quite as jejune as "The Bunny and Crocodile" and he had a grand vision. This was the time of cooperatives and collectives. John thought we should start a collective and he knew a great graphic artist in DC who would design elegant small chapbooks. The idea was to start with three poets, then those published poets would become workers for the press, selecting three more, then we'd have six. It was an inverted pyramid which would become a small press empire.

The first three books were slender, about 26 pages: Deirdra Baldwin, Harrison Fisher, and my own. Nice glossy covers and good paper. Not like paper in other books at the time. E Ethelbert Miller was among our next three, Terence Winch followed, and John McNally's idea flourished.

The Washington Writers' Publishing House is still thriving today, with hundreds of titles to its credit. John moved on to study law. I was President of the Washington Writers' Publishing House the first two years, then Robert Sargent for several years. Poor Robert, I left cardboard boxes filled with unfiled papers for him to sort out. Jean Nordhaus shouldered the press for many years after that. She'd been Poetry Coordinator for the Folger Shakespeare Library Poetry Series. We were all poets publishing poets. Elisavietta Ritchie is the responsible one now in 2014 and there are bounties of books on shelves with the WWPH imprimatur.

But the best part was our book distribution.

Robert Sargent, my buddy, helped me with poetry distribution for The Bunny books and WWPH books. I was somewhat of a poetry guerrilla in those days, employing underground tactics to get poetry out into the world. I would run into a bookstore and place books on the shelves and dash out. Robert would be double parked and we would speed away like Bonnie and Clyde. We got no money from those sales but poetry books were sold and our distribution system worked just fine. Give everything and ask for nothing and you'll have success. Those are the economics of the arts.

≈

An aside about Robert Sargent:

Robert drove me everywhere to do Bunny business and later WPFW business. Also, he took me to my poetry gigs during the day at various colleges. He died at age 94 and was my best friend for 40 years. The Bunny published five of his collections. When I had full-time jobs in DC at Public Broadcasting Service, and later at the National Endowment for the Humanities, we met every single Wednesday for lunch. I would come outside my building to find him sitting on a bench in the sun reading a book. He always carried a yellow memo pad, from his Pentagon days, with an agenda of what we'd talk about. As we gossiped or shared poetry acceptances and rejections, telling our secrets, he would cross off the topic with pencil.

We always shared a single dish of French fries. And neither of us worried about who got the last fry. After his second wife Chris died, he asked me to marry him. I had never thought of Robert in romantic terms and I was shocked. I said, "Thank you Robert, but I'm already married." We never spoke of it after that.

Born in Mississippi, Robert was courtly, a southern gentleman and had a deep drawl but he was a devil. He kept a fake journal for his wife to read and, although he adored her, he wanted his other women kept to himself. He sometimes wrote innocent dalliances in his fake journal so she'd believe them true.

Robert and I had our arguments and they were fierce. He is the only person who could rouse my fury. Politically, we were opposite, and this was a point of contention. But he was my poetry valet. And a loyal partner in poetry crime.

≈

EQUIPOISE

(for Robert Sargent at 94)

Today I tripped and dropped the cake
        outside your window
spreading the grass with whipped cream for sparrows to eat.

My hands were emptied of pleasure, but
        I went inside. You were
dressed for company, a bright blue shirt to match your eyes.

"She's here" the helper shouts and your blind eyes see,
        just as, almost deaf,
you can always hear me.

Today I tell you to go on with your writing.
        although 94 and knocked back by stroke,
I ask your "process." *Poetry*, you say. "But how can you write?"

You say you hold a pencil, do a line, then have it read back to
        you.
        You think you can manage.
"Family secrets" I whisper. A good idea for a poem.

I lean in as we did every week over lunch.
        I repeat the story you told me 30 years ago.
You lowered your voice then to tell me how your mother was
        found

sleeping with your uncle. Today I make you enter
        the house of memory,
"And who found her?" I ask. *Winifred, my little sister.*

I wanted to know who else was told, what your mother said,
        why your mother's other sister helped her out,
loaned a room in the house. Adultery. We talk about adultery,

how you put false information in your journal for your wife to
    find.
        Your eyes are cloudy
yet you look straight in my face. It says we've been through
    a lot,

stories told each other over the years, our friendship a fragile
    line,
        we walked and never fell off.
Once I said you did not express enough appreciation.

Today I say "I Love You" and you say *Thank you Thank you.*
        You say it 5 times in one hour.
The line sweeps back, holds us in, correcting its curve.

There is nothing we do not know. I avoid painful subjects.
        I close the door,
stepping over the sweet confection melting in the sun.

— *Sounds Like Something I Would Say*, Casa Menendez, 2012

For a list of Bunny books see the APPENDIX TO
CHAPTER EIGHTEEN, *page 263.*

19 ~

Poets Laureate I Have Known

PART 1

I learned that Maxine Kumin died yesterday.

When she came to DC she was on my radio show, "The Poet and the Poem" on WPFW. 1981. She had just come to town to take office as Consultant in Poetry at the Library of Congress. I remember standing on the corner of 7th and H in Chinatown, where WPFW-FM was then housed. Victor, her husband, was with her this night and she put her head on his shoulder, I didn't need to know more about their relationship. Later she told me that she'd prepared dozens of dinners and frozen them for Victor as she set up residence in DC for her tenure.

She was chosen Poetry Consultant, a term that would be legislated by Congress in 1987 to become "Poet Laureate of the US." Maxine entertained noontime brown bag lunches with women poets in her poetry office in the Library's Jefferson Building. She was a feminist, and a populist. I was very busy at PBS and couldn't make the scenes during the day but I never missed her readings. She brought a humane, homespun, no-nonsense presence to the nation's capital.

She and Anne Sexton were the only models we women had in the 1950s. Sylvia Plath had fled to England and didn't seem to represent America. But Maxine did. And still does.

Poets who were Laureates have all been on my radio show creating many adventures for me. Mostly within myself.

~

I would spend the summer before each October inauguration rereading everything the incoming Laureate had written. This was the only way I'd be able to face the poet across the table on microphone with a sense of confidence. The words had to be part of my DNA.

This worked out very well for all events with significant poets. Once, prior to being a Poet Laureate, W.S. Merwin was reading as a guest of the Library. He arrived for a one-hour session on microphone with me without a single book in his hand. What did he think we were to talk about? Fortunately I had ten of his vintage books—some from my library and some Devy Bendit left me from her death, rare ones which he was excited, surprised and pleased to see. We had a good show as I handed him book after book across the table. He gave me history, anecdotes, publishing gossip and poetry. It was terrific. That episode proved to me that preparation prevents disaster.

One other time that I was blindsided in the same way. A.R. Ammons was at the Library to win the Bollingen Award for *Garbage*. Luckily my fear of failure served me well, when he arrived empty-handed, I had his works underarm, plus the winning book.

A.R. Ammons was very important to me because he is the poet I can point to who "gave me permission" to start writing seriously, in 1968. He had just written *Tape for the Turn of the Year*, an entire book written on a cash register size "tape" and the poems went from margin to margin. And in it he said those magical words: "If you are nothing/ you can say and du anything."

I thought "I have the credentials!" He even spelled 'do' wrong to let us know we could *du* anything.

I was so sad when, not too long after our interview, A.R. Ammons died. He had given me the energy early on to jump-start a career, which would fuel me a lifetime.

CHRONICLING THE LAUREATES:

The first poet actually designated "Poet Laureate" was **Robert Penn Warren (1986-87)** and he was not well at that time. He would not meet for a private interview, but I was one of a press core that thronged to a small room to hear his words. I did record them and sent them to Pacifica Archives on reel-to reel tape, but after that I had the great joy and honor of sitting face to face with each and every Laureate except one other. Because of illness, Mona Van Duyn went home from her DC post early and had to cancel our session.

Let me begin with Richard Wilbur. He was the Clark Gable of poets, so sweet, so handsome. The Public Relations office wanted me to do a video interview with him, and I was obsessed. I practiced my questions night and day. The PR office said I should wear something neutral (times have changed, if I look at TV these days) but luckily I had a beige cashmere dress. I love that video. Somehow I looked as if I knew what I was doing on camera. My major question was, "What do you want from poetry?" Wilbur, god of formalism and dignity, was caught for a second and then said, "To keep on writing." He was smooth as almond milk and gin.

Later at a luncheon, I said to Wilbur's wife, "I'm Grace Cavalieri. I made your husband famous." She iced me without a blink, and said, "He was already famous." It was her pit-bull devotion of love for him that spoke, not really a reaction to me. But I wish I had just quietly eaten my sherbet.

Howard Nemerov (1988-90) was a love. He had served as Consultant before, 1963 to 64. We strolled arm in arm though the Library and I remembered that once he sent a poem to the *New Yorker* (or the *New York Times*), and he was not offered enough money and withdrew the poem. This man knew who he was. The anecdote is amazing to those of us who would pay those publications to feature us.

Nemerov's sister was the renowned photographer, Diane Arbus; they came from a monied family and were, each, vastly different from the other. Diane was a renegade risk taker, famous photographer of oddities, who ultimately killed herself. I just saw a movie based on her life, *Fur*, featuring Nicole Kidman as Diane. Nemerov was a university professor with a midwest house, a family and cats. He told me he only wrote six or eight poems a year. My great satisfaction was discussing the plays he'd written that were so little known and which I treasured. We had a fine discussion about those, on air, and also about his war poems. I remembered something he forgot, for naturally I had boned up, and he said, "That was a long time ago." And the sweet sadness in his eyes touched me. I realized and learned that we do not have to know the answer to every question. Life will forgive us, especially if it was "a long time ago."

Howard Nemerov died in 1991. When I called his wife Peggy to ask permission to use a poem, she was sobbing during our talk. That was one year after he died.

If we know the poet's work there is nothing to fear, so when Greek God **Mark Strand (1990-1991)** arrived, it was not too daunting although his work had awed and stunned me. Little known pieces like *Monument* are among the literary icons of our civilization. I believe that piece will be studied in philosophy classes someday. I certainly used it in teaching. Strand's work is well stained by his origins in Nova Scotia—the greys and blues of tone. He'd been a painter before becoming a poet, and it was evident in his visual cast on words

Years before his Library residency, I remember Mark Strand reading at the Folger Shakespeare Library. He was wearing a peach jacket. I would not have forgotten such a thing. Later on air, I commented on that and he said, "I have never owned a peach jacket in my life." Dead silence. I felt like arguing but left that without editing. Just goes to show, memory is a trickster—his or mine.

Mark Strand died this week. December 2014. I'm glad our recording exists and the transcription is published.

Rita Dove (1993-95) was a dream. She was the youngest Poet Laureate, and the first black poet since Gwendolyn Brooks had been Consultant in 1985-86. Dove was the youngest black to win a Pulitzer Prize. It seems wrong to categorize by color as "first" but this is historical and precedent setting. Our interview was fun but she had to scoot off for breakfast with the Clintons in the White House. I told her, "I'm glad I wasn't invited because once they have you over, you have to have them back and it goes on and on."

That night at Dove's inaugural reading, standing between magnificent white marble pillars, Rita read the one poem I could not believe she'd read, *Mickey in the Night Kitchen*. It is about vaginas, talking with her young daughter and teaching her about their bodies. Now, that's all good. Motherly. But this was the Library of Congress, and the Library might not like body parts on Inaugural Night. What I saw and learned is that Rita Dove was going to be the same person inside the shiny building as she was outside. She was Rita Dove whether in the writing studio or classroom and I felt all the windows and doors in the world suddenly open letting in fresh air. She used her time as Poet Laureate to bring poetry and jazz on stage.

Robert Hass (1995-97) broadened the frame for poetry and ecology and, a west coaster, he brought in the century's leading thinkers. On our show he talked of imagination as being a community. I remember spending too much time talking about little red flowers that grew in California and near me at that time in West Virginia while on-air. What was I thinking? But it was a good show with good information and is a contribution to the canon made by a progressive poet activist.

Robert Pinsky (1997-2000) had three terms in office because he launched an ambitious "Favorite Poets" project. He traveled the country and collected favorite poems that had influenced the lives of ordinary folks—Jane and John Q. Public—the butcher, the baker, the soldier, etc. And these poems were collected and published. There were readings of the book nationwide and spin-offs of the project. Robert Pinsky had a regular feature on the PBS News Hour, placing poetry center stage in America's living rooms.

Pinksy was to host a star-studded panel at the Library during the Bicentennial and he appeared sick with laryngitis and no voice whatsoever. Sometimes it's good for the crowds to see that a famous poet is still someone who is in a very human body.

I love Pinsky. I had interviewed him before he was Laureate about his translation of Dante and he said he always wanted to do the difficult and had started the translation as a game with other poets because he liked the exercise of organizing the metrics, like a mathematical challenge. The other poets fell away and he decided to finish the book. It is in terza rima, and I think the only translation of its kind.

And nervous breakdown time for me. Four hour-long programs back-to-back in one day. It was the bicentennial of the Library of Congress. I'd been commissioned, by contract, by the Library, to interview the four "guest Laureates" for the bicentennial: Louise Glück, W.S. Merwin, Robert Pinsky (then sitting Poet Laureate) and Rita Dove. There was to be a big celebration to herald the anniversary year. All four poets were arriving the day of the event and I lived at that time in West Virginia. I scheduled the studio for four hours and I squared my shoulders. I needed to know each one's recent work, and have the stamina to enter each poet's reality on microphone, and there was no time for more than one "take" per person.

I got through Dove, always cooperative, and Merwin who brought no books to read (as I already discussed) and then, enter Louise Glück. I cannot express how I value her poetry. And her clothes are as good as her poems. She was truly important to me. And suddenly I am told she did not do radio interviews. Oh really?

Nobly, Glück entered and reluctantly she sat; I was happy until halfway through the interview when she stopped and said, "I'm tired now. I think I'll stop." So did my heart. "Oh this is an hour show, Louise. Public radio expects the series to be an hour." *And so does the Library,* I thought. *I cannot lose this opportunity.* I started talking to her about her work, deeply and intimately, her work, her work, and that is something a poet responds to—someone knowing their work.

We eased ourselves into a hot tub of discussion and finally reached the top of the hour. Make no mistake; this could not happen if I were not truly a fan. There is no substitute for genuine appreciation. I may have the only recording of a radio interview with Louise Glück. This is archived along with the only radio interview of the great Sterling Brown, star of the Harlem Renaissance, Washington, DC's first Poet Laureate. These programs are important.

This day of the bicentennial recording marathon, I had three poets recorded and one to go. The celebration was to begin in revelry upstairs in but hours, when I received a call from Robert Pinsky. He was cool, saying, "I'm still at the airport in Boston. I'll be there as soon as I can." I waited without falling apart, and he arrived, putting on his tie, to go directly to the party where he was to host. And it was a sweet interview. He is a complete gentleman.

I saw Robert Pinsky's play, an adaption of Wallenstein, in 2013, at The Shakespeare Theatre in DC. I attended with my friend Karren Alenier, and we saw Pinsky rush out at intermission with his wife. We went searching for him and found him secreted in an enclave of the upstairs lobby. He said he got some of his production ideas from Bertolt Brecht and some from comedian Adam Sandler. He was humble about this masterwork. And nervous. Sometimes our works are bolder than we could ever imagine once they are on stage. He has recently written an opera libretto that is cutting edge with robots, working in collaboration with the MIT media lab. I consider him the smartest boy in the senior class who loves the difficult, and he does it with great imagination and intelligence.

An aside about Pinsky. Once I was teaching at the International Poetry Society, not a popular place with The Academy. It was a commercial enterprise which added us teacher/poets to include an educational and idealistic poetry component, and we worked very hard on this. The conferences attracted thousands and continued annually for several years. I had a great time teaching 500 at a time. Pinsky was invited to speak and I knew he did not approve of what appeared as "commerce" exploiting poetry. By contract, he would only give 15 minutes at the podium. He happened to be in California visiting his grandchild so he agreed to come say a few words. He spent a third of his time praising my radio contributions to poetry. *He* spoke of *me*. I'm sure the conference entrepreneurs felt they didn't get their 15 minutes worth.

My first introduction to **Stanley Kunitz (2001-03)** was on his inauguration day as Poet Laureate. His taping was flawless and, at the luncheon after, he kissed my hand. Stanley loved the ladies, and when my husband was at times more than charming to a woman, I remember Stanley and the great good energy he gave women.

Billy Collins (2001-03) was wry, funny, and read on-air like liquid gold. His wife Diane was not impressed, she told me, by the fanfare. She was a strong, beautiful woman, a furniture designer, and I felt so bad later when they divorced, remembering a gorgeous poem Collins read about cherished horse sculptures she had given him. They were both lovely.

Collins is about the most popular poet in America because he is among the few whose excellence is serious humor. He told me that tragedy and comedy exist on the head of a pin and it was his obsession to make them work together. I was interested in the fact that he had a Jesuit education for 16 years of schooling even through graduate days. This accounted for his love of chant, and the lyricism he first heard in Latin, at Mass. There is nobility about this. I just read that he sold his papers to the University of Houston for a large sum. Worth every penny, I thought.

Louise Glück (2003-04) was our Laureate and, as I said, never have I seen such stylish clothes. On the opening reading, she wore a black chiffon dress with uneven hems. Everything about her was elegance. No wrinkle in the line, or the frock. She wrote to the bone and may still be my favorite woman poet in America.

Ted Kooser came in at Poet Laureate in 2004 and was our first Laureate from the Plains states. The LOC seemed to choose so many Laureates from the eastern corridor, and Kooser did Nebraska proud. He had a no-nonsense loving presence. I did more than one show with him, because after he left office he returned with a new book, *The Poet's Toolbox*, which I wanted to feature on-air. Ted had recovered from a brain tumor and was at the end of his life when a sudden resurgence brought him to perfect health. He traveled the country with great energy as an ambassador of poetry. I'm a terrible traveler and asked him where he got his stamina. He said he never drank alcohol, yet I think a renewed life force had a lot to do with it. In our first interview we had a careful discussion on the nature of flat bugs. I asked him what university owned his paper and he said his corn crib, where he kept his writing desk.

Ted's wife was a newspaper editor in Garland, Nebraska where he lived, and she helped him implement the "American Life in Poetry" series which publishes poems in newspapers and online across the country. So nice to read with morning tea. He printed this one of mine which was also read by Garrison Keillor in his daily verse on NPR.

TOMATO PIES, 25 Cents

Tomato pies are what we called them, those days,
before Pizza came in,
at my Grandmother's restaurant,
in Trenton New Jersey.
My grandfather is rolling meatballs
in the back. He studied to be a priest in Sicily but
saved his sister Maggie from marrying a bad guy
by coming to America.
Uncle Joey is rolling dough and spooning sauce.
Uncle Joey, is always scrubbed clean,
sobered up, in a white starched shirt, after
cops delivered him home just hours before.
The waitresses are helping
themselves to handfuls of cash out of the drawer,
playing the numbers with Moon Mullin
and Shad, sent in from Broad Street. 1942,
tomato pies with cheese, 25 cents.
With anchovies, large, 50 cents.
A whole dinner is 60 cents (before 6 pm).
How the soldiers, bussed in from Fort Dix,
would stand outside all the way down Warren Street,
waiting for this new taste treat,
young guys in uniform,
lined up and laughing, learning Italian,
before being shipped out to fight the last great war.

— *Sounds Like Something I Would Say*, Casa Menendez, 2012

≈

*For a review of Pinsky's play "Wallenstein" see
the* APPENDIX TO CHAPTER NINETEEN, *page 265.*

20 ~
Coming to Poetry in Washington, DC

To repeat past history: In 1966 we had just moved to Annandale, Virginia, a cross-country trip in a small camper with four children under nine years of age. I had my leg in a cast, broken on the west coast, from playing tennis, the day before the movers came. Angel was two years old and being toilet trained on a high toilet with a specially built big box under her so her feet would touch something. By the way, she had it down just fine by the time we hit Utah.

We'd bought the camper to go skiing one weekend on Stevens Pass in the beautiful Olympic Mountain chain, Washington State, and—*surprise!*—the US Navy suddenly had orders for Ken to go to Washington, DC to the Bureau of Naval Personnel for shore duty. At least it was not a ship, and we now had a mode of transportation. The camper was pulled by a van which lost its brakes while going down a mountain but it turned out well. As interesting as a near death experience is, it's not what I set out to write about.

When we arrived in Virginia, we could not believe the cost of houses in the Washington, DC area. So we found a realtor, a Navy Captain's ex-wife who escorted us daily to the forbidden places and we sat around our evening dinner pondering our fate. The girls were enrolled in school nearby, brought there each day from a campground outside the metropolitan area. Ken was duty father as I couldn't drive with a broken leg in a cast, and Angel and I hung out in our small space and had lots of play time together.

There is one anecdote I cannot miss. This memoir is not to be about the cute things kids say but—traveling across country when we were using public restrooms in restaurants, I always washed the little girls after toilet trips with Scope to assure no germs. I figured if you could gargle this, it can't hurt. When we finally got to our east coast destination, Shelley was watching a TV commercial and ran out to tell me with horror. *Mommy, you should see what some people use Scope for!* I realize this is not an appropriate story for a chapter on meeting my first poet laureate. But truth trumps everything.

Finally we decided to rent a home. It took a while for the housing reality to set in but we found a great townhouse with three levels, lots of bedrooms and baths, and even space for Ken to pursue his art. As I said, from here I started my first plays and began sending out my poems with regularity.

Now we get to my first encounter with a poet laureate. In 1967 I took notice of a magazine out of American University named *Kauri,* created by Will Inman, the university poet in residence. I sent in some poems and plays and all subsequent issues accepted them; and published along with me was the Washington poet Elisavietta Ritchey. We were printed together, 1967 through 1969 issues. Lisa and I made contact with one another and we decided to put on a poetry reading in Washington, DC. At that time DC had no readings other than colleges and the Library of Congress, amazing as it seems, because now there are at least three simultaneous events in various locations, any given night.

I was able to secure the Polemic Theater on Kennedy Street as I'd just had a play performed there, and I knew the owner. The theater was vacant during the day so we got together some family and friends, a sound system, and Lisa and I read together. William Jay Smith was Library of Congress "Poetry Consultant" 1968-70 (a role later termed Poet Laureate) and he attended the reading. What a generous gesture. We certainly felt we'd arrived on a poetry scene that was emerging, and that Washington, DC was certain to become a locus for literature. By the year 1990, I proclaimed DC as the third poetry capital in the nation, after New York and San Francisco.

In 1977, my first public reading was at the Folger Shakespeare Library, at the invitation of poetry director Leni Spenser. I can remember the happy moment. The velvet seats.

≈

A NOTE ON *KAURI'S* WILL INMAN.

He became a fast friend of my family until 1970 when we moved to Maryland. He was a card-carrying communist and these were the days when this was against the laws of our country. He spent much time at dinners in our townhouse in Annandale, Virginia, bringing poets and artists and political activists with him. He had been active with Phillip and Daniel Berrigan, and Mary Corita who spilled blood on the papers at the Pentagon in protest of the Viet Nam war. At some point our phone was tapped, and we felt the pressure, while marching in peace demonstrations. But our intentions were honorable; our actions were principled by our beliefs and fueled by Ken's horrific experience in the Viet Nam era. Ken was a very loyal and effective Navy Commander and from this point on, we fell between two worlds.

Will was homosexual, an activist advancing the cause in the 1960s. He married a student whom he loved very much. I guess this means he was bisexual. After a good marriage they parted and Barbara is a professor of English now in a college in New York State. Will did significant work in prisons, homeless shelters, and with AIDs victims in later years, and died living alone in a camper in Arizona in 2010. I see his poems pop up in anthologies still. What a good man.

21 ~
Laureates Jacobsen, Hayden & Meredith

IN 1977 PRESIDENT CARTER HELD AN UNPRECEDENT-
ED OCCASION TO ACKNOWLEDGE POETS. And curiously Allen Ginsberg
was not invited, or so it was rumored. It could be the White House
actually ignored the Beat poets for fear of a lack of decorum at a
State event. I remember I wore a maroon velvet suit and I remember this because Ken picked a thread off my collar before we went
through the receiving line, just as if his little girl was going to her
first day of school. The place was jammed, of course, and Washington, DC's poetry icon, May Miller, fainted in another room from
the excitement. "Blues Poet" Sterling Brown was there and all our
best and finest. The ridiculous part is that we'd parked at a meter
and had to run out before too long. What were we thinking? We are
invited to the White House and we put quarters in a meter? As if it
were a night at MacDonald's? This is how people act coming home
from work maneuvering children and rushing out. The meatloaf
and the White House got about the same percentage of planning.

Josephine Jacobsen (1971-73), a lady from times past, became
a personal friend when she was Poetry Consultant to the Library of
Congress. Her work was elegant and she astonished everyone by hiring a car and driver from Baltimore to DC to commute to her post.
I didn't visit her fine home in Baltimore but she'd been on my radio
program. But, years later when she was getting older, her friend Martha Mendenhall and I went to Cockeysville where Josephine and her
husband shared a three-bedroom garden apartment, crammed with

a few of their art treasures moved from their large house. It was an assisted living complex and she was not feeling well.

Martha was inveterate although she herself was in her 70s at the time, and insisted we make the visit. Martha was a videographer and hooked us up to a marvelous interview which aired on cable television for a long time in Virginia. Martha produced a series for the American Association of University Women called "On The Go." I would later host this series featuring women poets. I have to say here, that Martha was sort of a pink panther of a technician and I'd been with her on many jaunts where she'd forgotten the extension cord, battery, or camera. But Josephine Jacobsen was delighted to immerse herself in her poetry and got the color back into her cheeks while being filmed, reading. She then had a martini for lunch and she admitted she would get deathly ill with colitis after, but this was her daily special treat.

I'm so glad Martha dragged me there that day. It would be the last time I'd ever see Josephine again. When I think about her poems I remember best the poignancy of one where she watches her husband sleep and realizes there are some terrains we can never enter, no matter how much we love another. I must forgive myself the paraphrasing here. Another poem most memorable is about losing a piece of diamond jewelry in Granada while vacationing and supposing the hotel maid stole it, with all the self-incriminations and self-doubt such accusations inflict on us. And the poem addresses racism indirectly. She was a cultivated intelligence. A lady.

My husband loved **Bob Hayden (1976-78)**. Robert Hayden was Professor at the University of Michigan and his wife was an accomplished pianist. He was the first African-American Poetry Consultant and he brought a gentility and nobility to the post that had only been imagined before. Amazingly, he'd had limited publication, a chapbook from Broadside Press. Today he is widely published; I believe his poetry is among the most quotable in America. "Those Winter Sundays" is in every classroom in America, and teaches us more about relationships with our fathers than we ever knew before with profound simplicity and humility.

It happened that I was to interview Hayden on WPFW at the time of his arrival in town. I was doing a twelve-hour marathon program on Paul Lawrence Dunbar, and he was part of the commentary. We were also in the midst of a fund drive at the station, and he took out his checkbook and wrote a donation. A move completely unsolicited. In the cab when we were returning to the Library, he leaned over to Ken and said, "Please, call me Bob." There was something about that Ken would never forget, the intimacy allowed, when most others called him Professor Hayden or Robert. He saw that Ken was awed by his work and honored to be a companion for the time together. Hayden was so sensitive; he never missed an occasion to make someone feel better. His poem "Night Blooming Cereus" is an immortal work of art. And so is his life.

Following as Poetry Consultant to the Library of Congress was **William Meredith (1978-80).** I was working at PBS at the time and I had to set up a microphone in my office for our interview. I guess I couldn't get away. We met for lunch in the tunnel underneath L'Enfant Plaza next to our PBS offices. He called it "the long magnificent walk." Only William could make a tunnel into a poem. That night at his reading in the Library (he wore a blue velvet jacket) he had forgotten his glasses and called on anyone in the audience about his age to lend theirs. And someone handed him a pair. I marveled that one could read at the Library of Congress at all, much less be so nonchalant as to leave one's glasses at home.

William was in a monogamous relationship with the poet Richard Harteis who was 30 years his junior, and we were their constant companions during the 1980s and on. We stayed with William and Richard in Connecticut after William's stroke. I brought a lasagna and banana bread through five states in our car. I got flea bites in the Red Roof motel enroute and, allergic, my face was the size of a pumpkin. I arrived an ugly, swollen guest.

In Connecticut, we went out to a small fishery restaurant that night and there were two roughnecks pointing out William and Richard with derision. William and Richard behaved as if they didn't notice it. I guess it was customary as Uncasville was a tiny village and their relationship at that time in history was uncommon.

When they lived in Bethesda, Richard and William hosted yearly formal New Year's Eve parties. One night the caterer did not arrive and I can tell you I stood in the kitchen in my evening gown and helped two other guests cook and serve food. It seems we put chicken in something.

'While living in their Bradley Boulevard home in Bethesda, MD, William purchased a gorgeous sculpture of Ken's called ORYX, two gigantic horns from Ken's collection of lost wood sculptures. They kept it outside by the swimming pool, and when they moved to Florida, brought it to their courtyard. I worry about the patina because Ken would often service pieces he'd sold to clients to maintain their burnish. But he is gone and the sculpture remains and, like our children, when they leave we cannot refresh them but from a distance.

We stayed three nights at the Meredith/Harteis Florida condo on our way to Key West. I cooked with fervor. One night I made Cornish hens with orange glaze for supper. Richard outlived his William and has done momentous work in print and film. The full length movie *Marathon* is taken from Richard's book by that title—about their relationship. Richard wrote and, for the first time, produced that film, and it was entered in film festivals all over the country.

Richard can do anything and often does; he is somewhat of a genius and is a glorious poet. I saw him just last month here, a year after Ken died. He came with sculptor Nancy Frankel to pay respects. They were prepared to take me out for lunch but we were drinking champagne and eating caviar I'd hoarded, so I was able to make a cabbage and gnocchi dish instead of leaving the house. I told him it was a Balkan meal but actually I hadn't gone shopping and that was all I could rustle up—very appropriate since William and Richard have official titles with the Bulgarian government and a William Meredith Center for the Arts exists there.

Richard's memoir *WBM (White Brain Matter)* just arrived in the mail yesterday (December 4, 2014).

One sad moment occurred regarding William Meredith. When we were living on 16th Street in DC, William and Richard came for dinner (bouillabaisse as I recall). William had been an aviator in World War II, so Ken graciously purchased a pair of golden naval aviator wings as a gift. William had not had a good experience in the Navy, however well he performed as a pilot, and it may have been the unpleasant memories or else William derided all war at this point, but for whatever reason, he refused the gift. Richard placed his hand over William's and said, "Ken has given you a part of the life you both shared." William demurred, and murmured his thanks. He was still incapacitated from a stroke so we felt this may have altered his reactions.

William was badly handicapped by that stroke. When William and Richard spent a weekend in our country house in West Virginia, William was sitting at the dining table and fell off the chair. Let me rush to say that he was fine, fine, because what I say next will sound horrid. He broke a leg—not his own—but our Nakashima handmade chair. This chair can only be found today in the Museum of Modern Art. We'd bought Nakashima furniture from the Master, George Nakashima himself, when we were first married and lived near New Hope, Pennsylvania. George Nakashima's workshop was open for visits on Sundays, and we bought dining room chairs in 1956 for $35.00 each, now worth thousands each. As William slipped to the ground, everyone screamed WILLIAM! And I—to my shame—said OH MY GOD MY NAKASHIMA. Ken was eventually able to tool a leg that replaced the ruined one, and I think it would fool everyone but the art dealer who someday will evaluate it for my children's estate.

Anthony Hecht (1982-84) came into the Library and we had a curious beginning. He had just moved to a fine home on Nebraska Avenue near American University with his wife and a small son at the time; and, to conduct him to WPFW to be on-air, I picked him up and took him first to dinner at the Hawk & Dove on Capitol Hill. He asked if he could order steak, and I thought that was strange, asking permission. At this time I was going through a personal crisis. Unlike many who go inward with troubles, I tend to fill the air with them.

One of my daughters had a troubled husband who was locked in his apartment and would not let us enter. We were frantic and were planning a family intervention. I was inconsolable and Hecht, in his bowtie, looking more and more like a frightened rabbit, listened attentively and must have thought, "Is this what a Poet Laureate must endure, dinner with a nut job?"

The evening must have had every star out of alignment. After dinner, we had what I thought was a wonderful time on radio, with poetry that is really immortal. I was getting my balance back. Anthony Hecht (I never felt privileged to call him Tony after this evening) read his Jon Clare poems. Now, these poems about the great prodigal poet refer to gypsies. Somehow a listener walking through a room somewhere, got it out of context and found a racial equivalent to gypsies in her mind. Who could have imagined this? Or prevented it?

After the show that listener called in to talk to our featured guest. Usually callers call in with words of praise, questions about where to buy the book and wishes for a successful Laureateship. This woman blasted Hecht for being a racist and more that I could not hear. Anthony Hecht was so shaken when he got off the phone—first, dinner with an hysteric, then a humiliation, a rash of insults on his first public appearance in Washington. Let me just say, I was heartbroken. When my book *Creature Comforts* came out that year, I inscribed a copy to Anthony and years later found it abandoned in the poetry office. Who could blame him for not wanting memories of that unsettling night?

I was able to make up a little to Anthony when I helped shepherd "Voices and Visions" on air, while working at the National Endowment for the Humanities. "Voices and Visions" was the first prime-time poetry series in the history of public broadcasting. I'd been breathing life into it since its inception at PBS, where I worked just the year before I went to NEH. Anthony, his wife, and a friend visited NEH and were hosted and acknowledged by the staff for the dignitaries they were and given a private showing. Hecht's wife had just written an elegant, much touted Italian cookbook and we also were able to celebrate that. Ignoring our first meeting was like trying to forget a gunshot in church.

22 ~

Reed Whittemore

REED WHITTEMORE (POETRY CONSULTANT 1984-85) WAS MY MENTOR. I owed so much to him even before he became Consultant. He invited me to read my poetry at the University of Maryland with Ann Darr (1977). I read from *Swan Research* just published by Word Works and I was honored.

When I left teaching at Antioch in 1975 I enrolled in the graduate school of English at the University of Maryland. Well, it wasn't all that effortless. I was still getting an MA from Goddard College but was unhappy with that program; I felt self-study wasn't teaching me anything. I'd started grad school at Rollins College in Florida, in 1963, when Ken was on a cruise, studying after hours when the girls were asleep, and I'd had academic success.

With all As, I thought I could breeze into the Maryland Graduate School of Education. When rejected I was unreasonable and wrote letters about 'how dare they.' I'd been an Assistant Professor at Antioch for five years, had an active poetry press, etc., but later calmed down when I found that a state school is swamped with education enrollees more than any other department and one had to have a 4.0 average during undergrad days—which I admit—under the bowers and flowers of poetry and theater, I did not.

I complained to a friend, poet Rod Jellema who taught at Maryland, and he advised me that I did not really want more Education training; I really wanted to pursue my love and livelihood, English. I was admitted then, maybe with his assistance, I'll never know, but I gobbled up 18th century literature and found Mary Woll-stonecraft, who would change my life. My life was being guided to the good. My 18th century course professor was about to retire and I think she did actually from that time. She served green Kool-Aid and cookies on our last day of class. It felt like kindergarten but at least I wasn't afraid to drink the Kool-Aid at the University of Maryland, safer than Antioch.

Most of all I was happy because I could study with Reed Whit-temore. Reed was writing his book *Poet from Jersey*, and we students surrounded him like stars in a constellation. We like to think we contributed to his writings as we discussed William Carlos Williams. I was in early 20th century heaven with Whittemore's first-hand accounts of literature of the early and mid-1900s. We were witnesses, researchers, and participants to his process.

Whittemore was the definitive authority on the small-press movement and responsible for the current national organizations supporting literary magazines today.

Forty years after studying with Reed Whittemore, I was writing a review of another William Carlos Williams biography for the *Washington Independent Review of Books*; I was able to call upon a memory that served me. The author was explicating the meaning of the Williams' poem "Genius in My Own Household" and he had it all wrong, according to my memory with Whittemore. In writing a review I never try to trump the author who knows far more about the subject than the reviewer. In this case I explicitly remembered Reed thinking of using that title for his own book title. He was talking about how William Carlos Williams had gone to the ballet with his wife, across the river to New York, and had come home to dance naked in front of his mirror. I could picture Reed standing there in the class telling us this, and I was able to quote Whittemore about the true inception of the poem.

One thing about Reed: he was not confrontational. He had been assailed by feminism during the past five years at Maryland University and when I asked who his favorite woman poet was he banged his fist on the table and said he could not think, then blurted, "Carolyn Kizer." He then settled back satisfied he'd ended the conversation. I didn't mean to start a political discussion. I was genuinely curious about his tastes.

About Carolyn Kizer: In 1964 I sent my first manuscript to the editor of *Poetry Northwest*. I was a Navy wife, alone with small children on Whidbey Island, husband at sea, what did I have to lose. She changed my life. She said she could not take the manuscripts, but recommended I send it to *The Tamarack Review* in Canada and she would write a note. Let me say here and now that such an act of kindness fueled my life forever. I vowed that, if ever I were in a position like hers, I would further poets who came across my desk like she did for me. Years later, friends who knew the story surprised me. Alan Austin (producer of *Black Box Audio Magazine*) and other poets introduced Carolyn to me at a Folger Shakespeare Library event, saying they wanted me to meet a "Mrs. John Woodbridge," and they enjoyed my gasp when Carolyn came over to me.

Carolyn died this year (2014). It was the year they gave poets away. Maxine Kumin, Galway Kinnell, Maya Angelou, Mark Strand. All gone.

In academia: After some good courses at U/Maryland I'd hoped to get on track for PhD, but I dropped out because four children were at home—and I was teaching a poetry workshop at Glen Echo and running a small publishing house, also diminishing my returns. But I got the best of the best while there and I cherish the time of rigorous research and academics.

When Reed Whittemore became Consultant in Poetry at the Library, he followed the custom of inviting local guest poets to read. Previously the other Poetry Consultants didn't choose locals, because how could poets be prophets in their own land? However Reed invited Robert Sargent, my best friend, and me, to read in the Coolidge Auditorium. 1985. A gold star year.

To discuss the occasion, Reed took us to lunch. No one had the temerity to decide who would be the "second" reader. The last reader is always the most important. So we flipped a coin. I won. I could see Reed was disappointed because Robert was then in his late 70s and good manners should honor this. But I was glad I won and did not intend to give up my victory.

That was a highlight. I wore a white coat dress with a red silk blouse beneath because I knew I would rash up at the neck. Nancy Galbraith, head of the Poetry Office, was bemused that local poets were to be center stage, and later was dumfounded when the Coolidge Auditorium filled with over 500 people and had standing room only. DC is a poetry community and everyone we knew was there.

I invited all of NEH, of course, and WPFW staff. Candace Katz, my colleague at NEH and still my buddy, said, "Grace divided the world up from that day on—those who came, and those who did not."

When Robert concluded his reading I stood up for the standing ovation for him. But there was a rumble at the back door as a group of black friends walked out. Robert was from old Mississippi and used the word "nigger" in the context of a long poem. It was meant to be part of a narrative, not as a pejorative but, either way it was unacceptable. How could he do this? The friends who left in anger had been members of my radio audience on WPFW's "The Poet and the Poem." They had come to honor my appearance. Later they would say, "Only at the Library of Congress could a man say *nigger* and get a standing ovation." It would stain my memory forever.

Robert and I had a falling out about that when I chastised him for the selection. Later, when I was to air our reading of the program on radio, I told him I was editing the word out. He fought me using arguments of semantics and lexicon. WPFW was a black-managed radio station, but that was not the reason that I cut it out. I was furious and aired the damn thing, edited. We were at odds for a long while.

A better moment during my reading with Robert Sargent that fateful night came from poet Roland Flint. He called out a compliment from the audience. He said, "That's my favorite!" when I read my circus poems from *Body Fluids,* making me really feel at home and among friends.

Before I go on to the next chapter of Laureates, I have to remark on that white coat dress I wore to the Library of Congress reading on March 4, 1985.

Ken and I had gone up and down Wisconsin Avenue looking for just the right thing for me. I found a red silk blouse and skirt but wanted a white wool coat dress I saw in the window. It was stunning. Looked like a Chanel, said Ken, who wanted to be a fashion designer, had the best taste in women's clothes. I loved it and would wear it over the red silk. I still have that blouse and it fills my heart to move it aside in my closet. Such fun to shop with Ken who loved stores and had to drag an agoraphobic with him.

I was to wear this outfit two times in one month because my show on WPFW had won second place nationally in the Media Awards by the National Commission on Working Women. (First Place went to Linda Lavin for a popular prime-time TV series, "Alice.") Of course, I already had the best outfit, the one chosen for my Library of Congress debut.

Life is a balance. Psychic Bryan Christopher always told me that 'positive attracts negative' in life as in physics. Look at my moment at the Robert Sargent reading and I could cite other examples.

The National Media Awards were held in a DC hotel banquet room, and when I walked to the podium to receive this coveted honor (*poetry as entertainment,* thank you!), the judge and I stopped next to one another frozen in time. There we stood in our identical elegant white wool coats, both belted now to look like coat dresses. Perhaps the only two such garments on this earth were together on one stage. What are the chances of that, standing before a smiling audience, who was enjoying the show for more than one reason.

23 ~
More Laureates

GWENDOLYN BROOKS, JOSEPH BRODSKY, DONALD
HALL, CHARLES SIMIC, KAY RYAN, W.S. MERWIN,
PHILIP LEVINE, NATASHA TRETHEWEY

Gwendolyn Brooks (1985-86) didn't fly in airplanes. She commuted by train from Detroit to the Library and stayed at the Hay Adams Hotel. She wore a head kerchief at readings and brought the warmth and welcoming rich earth to her voice and to her benevolent stay. I was glad to see her again because we'd had a rocky beginning in 1976.

Before WPFW went on-air, 1976, I was recording all the notables who came through town before we were launched so I'd get the best possible poets. Gwendolyn Brooks was reading at Howard University and kindly agreed to come to our studio at 15th and L Streets, NW, above the drug store, across from the *Washington Post* building. It was a studio held together with silly putty and scotch tape but we were really getting ready to become the premiere jazz/poetry station in a region of 200,000 listeners.

Gwendolyn Brooks was a political activist at the time, or most recently had been, and she was in an emotional place that brooked no nonsense. But she was always fair. This was the mid-70s when people were confronting racial feelings. I, at one point said, "You've been a teacher for us all." Somehow it did not sit right. She said sharply, "*You* all?" She added, "I am black first, a woman second and a poet third." She made some more distinctions. I didn't improve the day with flattery. Gwendolyn wouldn't trust anyone who flattered her even if I tried. I happened to have the first national review written of her work by poet Reed Whittemore in *The New Republic* from 1950. She was glad that I knew her true self—and not her as icon; so then our friendship emerged. I had designed, with another producer, a recording of a dramatic reading of "A Street in Bronzeville." The show was appearing at Howard University as a staged reading. She was pleased with the radio edition. I was saved.

In 1985, when Brooks became Poetry Consultant I wonder if she'd recall much more than my name because I wanted to introduce her to Reed Whitmore, the poetry editor who'd discovered her early works. Ken and I arranged a luncheon for Reed, and Helen, his wife, at Jennifer Lawson's beautiful home in the historic Adams Morgan section of Washington. Jennifer was the first African American female director to head PBS' Arts Department (Prime Time Programming) and her husband, Tony Perkins, was a film critic. Tony had broken ground with the Black Film Institute in DC and would become an important leader of film in the nation.

Ken and I drove the Whittemores from College Park, Maryland, to pick up Gwendolyn at the Hay Adams Hotel, and we had a somewhat formal gathering but a warm and welcoming moment to usher the great Pulitzer Prize winner into the city.

When Gwendolyn invited me as a featured reader at the LOC, under her aegis, she chose the following poem from my book *Creature Comforts* to be written on the "broadside" program.

> ***This is***
> ***The September of our loss***
> ***The old man who was to die took a nap anyway***
> ***I admire that.***

Gwendolyn compared the poem to Anna Akhmatova, the Russian poet she liked, who often wrote encomiums. Brooks is a woman who broke the rich earth for everything to grow.

Let me now praise **Joseph Brodsky (1991-92)**, émigré from the Soviet Union after spending seven years in a labor camp for writing in the folkloric language of the people instead of the official authoritarian mandate at that time. He learned English by reading T.S. Eliot, as good a use of Eliot as all others. And with a friendly sponsor, Brodsky was able to come to America and start a new life, settling in New England and ultimately marrying a new wife and having a baby.

I'll never forget Brodsky's presence. In one lecture at the Library he spoke of poetry as 'the highest locution,' saying we have no other record of humankind from ancient Roman days. Land sales and transactions left no record of human sensibilities—poetry is how we know what was thought and felt. I have paraphrased this somewhat but that was the essence.

His Nobel Prize speech is essential reading to know his brilliant mind and great heart. On the air with me he laughingly said he stayed up all night writing the Nobel acceptance speech and so he recommends that everyone should have a Nobel speech written ahead of time just in case it's needed.

He told me he typed with just one finger. I asked which one. He said right fore finger. We can't have too much specific information about a genius. He gave a great interview but for one misbehavior. There is absolutely no smoking in the recording studios because of the sensitivity of the equipment. Although told many times by the engineers, he continued to chain smoke. Another bad habit was to start every answer to my questions with "No!" and then he'd go on to be more agreeable. Every answer began with a negative. He was in danger of sounding like a Grinch unless I could veer him, but I had no luck.

At home that night in my own studio, I cut out all the NO's on the tape and he sounded quite convivial. I wanted to string 50 *nyets* on a single reel and just play that sometime, all different tones, somewhat like a symphony of negativity. A NO as defense system; yet his following remarks always intimated "yes."

Smoking would do Brodsky damage and he died young of a heart attack in 1996. He was 55 years old.

Donald Hall (2006-07) arrived in a wheelchair pushed by a young woman companion, Linda. She'd been a teacher in an alternative high school in New Hampshire near his farm, and now, although she didn't "live in," she visited daily and eventually toured the world with the poet. Donald Hall's marriage with Jane Kenyon had been the love story of the century and the subject of each other's poems. Since Kenyon died of cancer so young, every moment had been chronicled. The world was in love with Jane Kenyon. I taught her in every classroom.

I'd met Jane Kenyon when I was at the National Endowment for the Humanities where I worked in the 1980s. She was accompanying Don on a celebratory tour for his new book release. At a party the night before at Betty Parry's house (the Pearl Mesta of DC), I invited her to be on my show.

Jane came to the Endowment and I did a program with her in a conference room with my portable equipment. I remember sharing a bunch of grapes and having a lovely time. She was bemused that she was only thought of as Don's partner, but neither of us knew how that would change and her name would someday be known in the household of every living poet.

Donald Hall was one of the most influential poets in America because early on, since the 1960s, he was writing biographies of other poets as well as producing his own poetry. He was prolific and popular, a mentor to so many. He'd had liver cancer since 1998 and he was still performing. Allen Ginsberg, who'd had liver cancer, succumbed in six weeks' time.

Flash forward to 2006. In readiness for my program with the new Laureate, I met Donald Hall and his companion, Linda, at the Public Affairs Office of the Madison Building and we went across the street through the underground tunnel to the Jefferson Building which would be his new home.

One curious moment: in preparing for his reading, I'd ordered all the books he'd ever written from my local Eastport Library in Annapolis. This was customary when I was to interview a poet. The Library would put out a call throughout the state and collect books for me. Someone took me literally when I requested all his writings. The University of Michigan Special Collections sent an original handwritten manuscript of his, on rough paper, with pasted photos of his friend's works, the sculptor Henry Moore. My husband and I held it like a newborn baby and returned it immediately, telling the Library to inform the University of Michigan to never, please, allow this out from under glass again.

Hall's opening reading brought the audience to its feet. The next day, on my show, he spoke of a children's book notion and he promised me, as his assignment, he'd go home to write it.

Charles Simic and I had two radio experiences, one bittersweet, and the first created a problem, but nothing to do with Simic directly. He was a reading guest of Roland Flint, Georgetown professor, poet and my dear friend. I seized an opportunity to secure an interview. Simic had met my friend Devy Bendit at Breadloaf Writers' Conference in Vermont, and she'd sweetened his life by her admiration and loyalty. When she committed suicide in 1984 he spoke to me on the phone and so I knew him remotely only in this way.

Simic had once commented on my book *Body Fluids* in 1976, raved about it, wrote me a postcard, and said it was fantastic and too bad he didn't write blurbs. Hmmm. Too bad indeed. But I still have the written proof.

Roland drove Simic to the studio and left him with me for the hour. The station was at that time in Chinatown at 7th and H Streets on the 5th floor. That's how I know the event had to be before 1987 when the station moved to Columbia Road. Let me say that if I knew I would write a memoir, I'd have taken notes as I went along. But looking back, my memory on dates is approximate at best.

I'd worked all day, then at the National Endowment for the Humanities, an extremely intense scholarly organization. Ken and I had moved to the city (DC) after selling our Maryland home in 1982 and Ken was working in his studio in West Virginia, coming home weekends. So I didn't always have my back-up man with me who was usually my steady force.

I remember running from work to our 16th Street condo because my daughter Colleen was home and I wanted to prepare a meal; then I got back to the station to wait for Simic. The engineer never showed up. I knew the equipment well but, with such an important poet, it was better for me to concentrate on presentation rather than voice levels. Somehow, I survived the stress of the whole day and the program sounded calm and relaxed, mostly because Simic could not be otherwise if he tried.

I'd gone to great lengths to make that day a success so I was upset when Roland published a poem about his day with Simic including a trip to the 'crazy Italian.' For some reason, I told Roland how hurt I was. If I had not efficiently done the work of three people that day I wouldn't have reacted, and I now wish I hadn't for Roland was very sensitive and close to me, and he told me he'd never read that poem again, and that I was responsible for his destroying it. It lay between us for years, as in Edna St. Vincent Millay's lines "like a troubled sword."

We repaired in time and Roland was our weekend guest in West Virginia before he died of pancreatic cancer. In fact, I cooked for days and prepared feast after feast for his three days. One dish I remember was Torte della Nonna, a grandmother's apple tart. And late at night we went to my studio/loft and he recorded his entire new book, *Easy*. That would be the final recording he made before he got ill. It was played at his Memorial celebration at the Writers' Center after his death in 2001.

After that circuitous route, my second meeting with **Charles Simic (2007-2008)** was fine. He came in as Laureate and gave a brilliant show. I'd read his autobiography and we enjoyed his life's remembrance. He made a joke about the French, but I jotted a note on that as we spoke. After we were off air and walked to the studio his wife Helen, who'd watched the monitor, said, "Charlie. You cannot say such things about the French!" I told her we were of one mind, and it would be edited out.

I've seen the Simics at occasions in DC since that time, and they were genuinely sympathetic to learn Ken had died. Everyone loved Ken. He was present as my "associate director" of every recording and was our "photo op" man, rushing into the studio after each taping to remark on what he heard and how affected he was. Always genuine, enthusiastic, supportive, loving. I would say every Poet Laureate of the United States loved Ken Flynn.

My ritual with Ken, when we were to go to Library of Congress recordings, makes me ache for him. We'd wake early and have tea and his homemade bread. He'd have a briefcase packed with stopwatch, clipboard and camera with newly charged batteries. We'd park near the Jefferson Building to greet the parking lot's attendant, Garibaldi, from San Domingo, who saved one parking spot for us. Garibaldi played opera music in his ticket booth, called his mother every day, and was saving money to go back to visit her. (He finally achieved this in 2014.)

Ken and I'd cross the street to Starbucks and have tea, coffee latte for him, and a sweet treat; then, carrying our hot cups to the Jefferson building, we'd wait for our poet to show. If the poet were a Laureate we'd meet in the Madison PR office with Library officials.

Upon arriving at the studio, Mike Turpin, my engineer since 1997, would usher the guest into the studio and seat the companions outside in front of a giant monitor. Ken would arrange his articles on his desk to time the poems and note anything for edit after the show.

I'd sit with the poet and have paper work filled out for releases and permissions, Mike would test voice levels and for 17 years we did a one-hour show, now formatted to 30 minutes because of radio tastes. The world is compressed and time and space with it.

After the show, if the guest was a Laureate, he/she would be whisked off to another meeting; otherwise, Ken and I escorted the poet(s) across the street to treat them to a Chinese lunch at a table in the corner where we could talk. We called it the "Producer's Table." Of course the restaurant owners thought it was just a table. I now attend alone, and there's a huge invisible hole torn in the side of the world.

Kay Ryan (2008-2009) was the first gay woman to be named Poet Laureate and this is a strange way to introduce her but much was made of it and she welcomed the PR. She brought in a cadre of friends from the west coast to a poetry office lunch one day and those women were such fun.

I loved Kay and she came in to my office when her partner, Carol, was dying. Carol had been the one who sent Kay's work out for publication, and Kay would not otherwise be known, or published, much less become Laureate. She was a populist poet and spent her time bolstering community colleges and small libraries, the tiny stars that would otherwise go unnoticed.

Kay's interview was a significant conversation about her poems, each one the size of a pocket comb, and packing a philosophical wallop that would take anyone else three pages to say.

She told me how to mousse my hair straight up with my hands so it could look like hers.

Carol died during Kay's term of office and the next time Kay appeared at the Library she'd lost 15 pounds, as she was running in the California hills every day.

Before Kay's farewell reading, she hugged me, and I was talking and caught her ear by mistake and bit it in the flurry. She went onstage with what I thought was my blood on her ear, but it was just lipstick. The LOC photographer caught the scene with the ear/hug/kiss/bite. I wonder how much he wants for the photo.

Kay gave me a rare, first edition, out-of-print book of her poems, *Dragon Acts and Dragon Ends.*

The grand gentleman of poetry, **W.S. Merwin (2010-2011)**, commuted from Hawaii to become Laureate, and he lighted the room with his presence. I'd had an extensive time with him in 2000 exploring ten of his books on microphone so this would be about current work. He was nicer than ever, and the show was a moonlight ride on a lake. His wife handled his written communications and was very attentive to me. They owned a conservation plantation in Hawaii and tended their trees to sustain certain species. I asked Merwin on microphone what his house looked like and he became very animated in describing how he designed it and I think I got the first information on the sliding doors. A scoop. Something no one had about Merwin before. Today, Dec 5, 2014, I learned his wife is dying.

Philip Levine (2011-2012) was the working man's poet; he came out of the factories of Detroit and was hailed universally for his hardhat poetry. He was all business that day across the table from me. I didn't know he had liver cancer. Philip had a baseball cap on, he'd just come in from Brooklyn; when he met Ken and found he was a Viet Nam veteran he welcomed us in like family. Authenticity is acting the way you feel, and this was Philip, and this was what we wanted from him.

As I proof this writing, I find Philip cancelled his trip to the Midwest Conference where he was to receive the Mark Twain Award. His friends were flying to Fresno to say goodbye; he was dying.

What a cruel year for us, but the angels must want more poetry. Especially from the grinding machines of the heart, the pulse of factories and cities. When I published the Levine interview, I took all of my words out and just left in Philip's explication of his poems and ideas about poetry. The article is very lively, in fact brilliant.

Philip Levine died on February 14th.

When **Natasha Trethewey (2012-2014)** took office and came on stage I'd never seen a woman with more presence. She was perfect. She wore a man's suit and possessed every ounce of space on that stage. Women, more than men, turn back the applause. She held the space for it and commanded all the energy to gather around her force field. We were frozen with admiration.

Her work explores the world of being biracial with all the difficulties. I knew the Pulitzer Prize work she read but I learned something about women in the world that night that I only thought I'd known: How one could control an audience by self-esteem and self-knowledge.

I thought my session on air with Natasha would be reserved and it was quite the opposite—fun, warm, intimate and filled with love.

Natasha toured the country in her PL mission, finding poetry in unknown places while PBS News Hour's Jeffrey Brown accompanied her visits to schools, old age homes, safe houses. She didn't appear "important" nor did she attempt to be special. She has a lot to teach us by this. She made a remarkable statement on camera about poetry being something for everyone to express, and that some people just use more elevated language than others.

24 ~
Two DC Laureates

DOLORES KENDRICK & STERLING BROWN

DOLORES KENDRICK WAS THE FIRST BLACK WOMAN TO TEACH AND RETIRE FROM EXETER, a private New England Academy. She became Washington's second Poet Laureate in 1999, and is our Aretha Franklin, Gwen Brooks, Versace and Prada combined. Now in her mid-80s she still wears high heels and goes to Mass every Sunday. She is decorum and ceremony. But when we're alone she's a girlfriend and great for swapping secrets: when the Chair of the NEA said something private to her, or some person stole the idea of the narrative voice in a poem, etc.

Ken and I asked where Dolores wanted to meet for breakfast one day and she said, "The Mandarin Hotel." She rented a suite there several times a year one mile from her condo, as a place of seclusion to write. She took her meals there often. When we drove to the door, the parking valet started talking about a poem she helped him with, and all the staff swarmed around her as their personal celebrity. I call her Washington's "Poet of the People" and we tried to attend all her Fiestas over the years. That breakfast, by the way, was $130.00 and we thought maybe *we'd* pick the place next time—or maybe not—such fun to be with her in the palace of her choosing.

We brought our four girls to The Mandarin the next month for a birthday lunch (they were all born in the same week, different years), to share the décor. Dolores was a pathfinder to luxury.

Dolores was on my show several times, the most momentous was when her book *Women of Plums* was issued. That is the book of the decade. The poems are in the voices of women slaves, and the narratives were also set to music and mounted on stage. It was worthy of the Pulitzer if anything ever was.

In the radio studio with Dolores, WPFW, I had a number of things to accomplish before taping, not the least of which was to find my engineer, get release forms signed, and find her voice levels, and I thrust a paper to her in a hurry to get the signing done— and she stopped cold in the chair and said, "I will do THAT after I do THIS," and then carefully and slowly took her time with each chore presented.

For the rest of our lives, when Ken or I would try to rush the other, the reply was always, "I will do THIS after I do THAT."

Dolores was a great supporter of my poetry and presented me with the coveted DC Poet Laureate Award in Poetry bestowed from her office. It hangs on my wall right now reminding me of the days with Dolores, when Ken was escort around town for two women poets. She now features my work on her Poet Laureate website in a space called "Gracing Poetry." I wish she'd call when she has a moment. I love to gossip.

STERLING BROWN WAS NAMED THE FIRST POET LAUREATE OF WASHINGTON IN 1984 and one of the most venerable figures of the Harlem Renaissance, although he was left out of the book of that title and he never recovered from that. In 1979 the city declared May 1st *Sterling Brown Day*. I had some involvement with that by way of the City Council.

Sterling Brown made history on the page turning the blues into a poetic metric and his work is as well known to black people as opera is in Italy. His life was tragic because, during his 30-plus years at Howard University, his tenure ran smack into the middle of the turbulent 60s and 70s student protests. He was once taunted, thought to be too white, and rebuked by others for not being a Black Nationalist. He listened to jazz when Chopin and Mozart were popular among the Howard faculty. He said Howard University was still in the 1950s, mainstreaming "Negro" respectability. Sterling Brown embodied and overcame every racial confusion but it left him hurt and disappointed. Brown was the first black person to go to Williams College and to Harvard. He told me he played jazz recordings at Williams and stuffed a towel under the door so no one would hear.

When WPFW went on air, I visited his home and became close to Daisy Brown, his wife. She reminded me of Nettie, my mother, so pure and almost fragile, all spirit and good love. She had her hands full with Sterling and his Wild Turkey moods and adoring followers. I was able to do a program with him on location. The sound is not great but it is his only radio interview that I know exists.

E. Ethelbert Miller was a graduate of Howard, a great poet, and a leader in the DC community. James Early was an intellectual and political activist who had worked with me at NEH and was now a Director at the Smithsonian Institution. Together we were a coalition. I wrote a resolution to establish the post of Poet Laureate of DC and presented it to Hilda Mason, a DC City Council Member, who then presented, and had the proposal passed, by the Council.

Ethelbert and James were well known in the city and I had the NEH and WPFW imprimaturs so we weren't dismissed. The day he was appointed, Ethelbert was busy at work but James and I took a cab to Sterling's house to present him a plaque, and he was joyous.

The city reveled during Brown's term. It was as if he was always their Laureate. We just needed him out front. I think of him every year and light a candle in my mind for all he endured and how he will be known beyond his time for turning a corner in American Poetry, using folk music and the blues on the page, and changing American letters forever.

25 ~

Navy Wife:
The First Years

MAYBE BECAUSE WE WERE CHILDREN OF THE DEPRES-
SION AND CAME UP IN THE 1950S, but we thought that to be a Naval
Officer was a noble profession. Later my husband and I would be
part of the Peace Movement and against the foreign policy on Viet
Nam; but we always believed that the Navy was a high calling. Now
when I hear the jeers and jokes, I see the old Navy is gone. We truly
believed there was something to serve larger than our own lives.
Maybe it was partly jingoistic, or partly that we were too naive to
know better, or maybe it was true after all.

Ken left Lehigh University and commenced upon a grueling 18
months as a Naval Cadet, more rigorous than a Marine boot camp,
and he earned his golden aviator's wings.

The Navy was a hardship for me from the beginning but I didn't
see it that way. I thought it was the way it was supposed to be. First,
when getting married while I was still in college. Ken had to earn
his wings on the last carrier before he became Ensign; and the commanding officer postponed the carrier qualifications three times. We
thought that was to be expected in the Navy. I had 300 wedding invitations sent out and then resent three times between October 18 and
October 31. By the time the wedding came, some people received
invitations to the reception and no wedding invites, some just the
wedding announcement, and some had none at all.

My ceremony was further marred because my best friend was
not invited. Bill Cook was my buddy back in college, and we had

been in high school together. He was the smartest man I ever knew and would have been Valedictorian of the Trenton High Class of 1950 if he were not black.

My wedding was in 1953 and there was racial turmoil in Trenton and picketing outside the hotel where I was to have a reception (three different postponed dates). My father was fearful and I was told I couldn't invite Bill. I should have said then I will not get married, but remember Ken had off only three days of leave before being sent to sea, and that allegiance came first. To this day Bill and I never spoke of this; and because of the multiple invitations sent out, the confusion probably saved me.

Ken and I were married on Saturday and left for New York City for the weekend. To leave for the "honeymoon," I wore a blue suit with a small blue hat and veil and a suitcase filled with high fashion clothes for a two-day vacation. I'd worked in a retail store after school all through high school, part-time in college, and spent all my earnings on clothes, with just two days to wear them.

Ken was always leaving, it seems. His stepfather, Chet Flynn, was vice president of General Motors Overseas. Ken left me for his high school years in Sweden, then during my senior year of high school, he left for Australia. I wrote three letters a day for 18 months during that tour. Now he would be headed for Texas the Tuesday after our Saturday wedding and I'd be back in class with my Senior English/ History majors at New Jersey College at Trenton with Lahna Diskin, Bill Cook, Kathy Dodwell, Tom Dolan, Lee Steelman, my buddies. No Ken. I'd be single again.

Our honeymoon: We were in room 1932, the year of my birth, at the New Yorker Hotel and Ken's mother called every hour because she insisted that she'd paid for the room and wanted to be included. Her son was only home a short time. That would foretell the nature of our relationship with Harriette for the next 50 years. Until the day she died.

Something better than that showed me what life would be like with Ken. I wanted steamed clams for dinner. And he complied for no other reason but because I wanted them. This would be a mantra for our marriage. We walked 20 blocks that Halloween weekend and found them next to a Horn and Hardart restaurant. For the rest of our lives, sometimes I'd ask for things 'just because I wanted them' and for no better reason. And Ken honored that feeling as if it were the golden grail. I believe it carried us across many thresholds; because sometimes the marriage terrain was tough; and if a person honors that 'wanting' without reason in another person, all bad feelings dissolve. It is an ultimate acceptance.

I taught school in Yardley, Pennsylvania while Ken was away, living with my parents where they'd moved to Levittown, Pennsylvania. I was so stressed and so without self-definition that I had anxiety attacks made worse by a rowdy bunch of fourth graders. Once I had to call in the alpha male teacher next door who'd been brought up with creative punishment from his Catholic education. He threatened the children with having to hold a flower pot in outstretched hands for 20 minutes. I have the gift of patience (or repressed anger) and I did love every wild heart in the class who couldn't sit still. But I'd be able to express my teaching creativity in future years; in this class it was survival.

When Ken came home for me, the mothers all gave me a gift—a black satin nightgown. My face was purple. I never thought they'd think of me that way. As I opened the gift, surrounded by fourth graders and mothers—I felt the same haze of confusion I began with. But I'd been blessed by fire and found out, from the parents, I'd been given the most incorrigible students because I was the youngest teacher. The stress was not from my lack of skill after all.

Driving south I was the happiest I'd ever been. I had never been far away from New Jersey and I cannot believe the feeling of bliss from being with Ken and finally starting an uninterrupted life with him—at least for an entire year.

≈

GOING SOUTH

I love to think of it
Traveling south that time

Thirty years ago
Stopping

A sunlit town
A weekday afternoon

A town so small
Four corners with

Its children
Coming home from school

Green lawns, sweet air
Georgia or

Some other foreign place
Never seen before

No highways then
Bypassing

Sounds
Of people walking, talking

On the street
I couldn't believe my eyes

Three o'clock far away
My shoulders, a pink halter

No one dead
My mother, father, sister still alive

Nothing much to worry me
But the road

Ahead
Flowers, soft aromas

Strange trees
And a restaurant

I see just where we sat
That corner over there

The smell and feel of honey
But most of all warm sun

Beside a road
By a car headed south

Flavors of a southern town
Years ago, my first time down.

≈

We had funky apartments that we bestowed with modern style and bold designs. We had exchanged silver and crystal wedding gifts for sleek modern pewter ware and pottery. And we cleaned and cooked as if we were the Taj Mahal. Jacksonville, Florida, 1954, living on a swamp that now is a condo. Pine needles on the ground and a penetrating smell of sulphur from paper mills. Pure Heaven. I would go back in time to that place and forego all my next lifetimes.

At some point we moved to San Juan Avenue into a townhouse. It became the home for naval aviator bachelors in the squadron; martinis every day after playing tennis. In Florida, life was amped up with young bachelors arranging their flight schedules to be done at 2 pm to come party at our house. Young ensigns and lieutenants with the whole wide world ahead of them and four gorgeous young "Pru girls" who lived next door. Prudential Insurance Company was one of the largest employers in Jacksonville in the early 1950s. One of our favorites, Betty Jean Bessent, would marry a young lawyer and, because she had no parents, we gave a small wedding with champagne and cake in our three-room house. B.J. became a glorious tennis champion, but has Alzheimer's now, and Dan is a retired Judge in Tallahassee. Most of those glamorous pilots are gone but for handsome Jerry (Nick) Tappan, who came to Ken's funeral this year from California, and Mel Everhart who traveled from North Carolina to Arlington Cemetery.

I started teaching at Jacksonville Elementary School. When we first walked up to the Board of Education, there was a hand printed poster saying TEACHERS WANTED, like waitresses. But I met the best friend of my life, another Navy wife, Helen Morgan, from Arizona, who lived a block away and it was all fun. We were out to bring fresh progressive cuttings to Florida educational conservatism.

I want to talk about teaching in Jacksonville in a room with no air conditioning and 30 students, where the cafeteria served fried fish, grits and greens on Fridays. If I were asked for the one moment in my life where everything came together for me to create learning the way I believed, it was here. Once again, because I was the youngest teacher, I was given the dregs, students in the fifth grade who couldn't read, one violent girl, a boy who'd been "left back" three times, a mess of kids. There was nothing to lose and that's a wonderful way to live, and I taught from my heart. The past dictums obviously didn't work. What inspires? Art inspires and when students create their own learning, there is no failure.

While there were academic strictures in Pennsylvania and supervisors roaming the halls, here no one cared, and so I could. Until we could get reading skills up to grade level, social studies would be difficult to teach. So every day at 3 pm we had Drama. And we acted out the events in history. I loved it more than they did. In a year's time my three-time loser became the star, my violent girl stopped wetting her bed, and these young people knew social studies better than any other fifth grade class.

To study Hawaii we sat on the floor in costumes and ate pineapple. Along with traditional methods, I provided the experiential. I remembered my childhood in Gregory School, a progressive educational experiment in Trenton, where we made our own paper in the fourth grade. These are the tools I brought with me—not my studies during college years of Education. Discipline was not a problem anymore and the students acted as if they were the gifted ones in this school, and they were.

I'm not saying the principal was enlightened by us. Oh no. Once Ken came in and helped students make sculpture out of clothes hangers and the class won the county art show. The principal at a faculty meeting ridiculed, "Those who bend wires and call it art." He could not hurt me. We were on a winning streak. Every Friday Ken would bring in ice cream Dixie cups for the class. He'd bring in his parachute and explain airplanes. We were a team.

Helen and Ted Morgan, Ken and I would have a pitcher of rum drinks on the weekend. We thought being in the Navy was the dream fulfilled. We didn't even know there was a Far East about to change our lives in 10 years. And then I became pregnant and the cafeteria's fried fish on Fridays sent me running to the teacher's lounge. But I'll never forget that class of fifth graders where we had fun together and how they learned to read, and scored higher than others in most areas. Especially in (the drama of) History. I still look at their pictures. And believe I've never been so fulfilled.

Ken sent me home by plane in June, 1956, and he was to follow. My baby was due in July. I had made all my maternity tops (two side seams, two shoulder seams, the extent of my ability) and my Aunt Alice drove my mother, Nettie, to the airport to meet me. I had one day with my mother, my beloved Nettie that I'd come home to be with. I had made Ken give up the Navy to be a civilian so I could be with my Nettie.

The next day my sister and her husband and two young boys arrived from Detroit. Judy and Frank left immediately for New York leaving us babysitting—I cannot say what I feel about their parenting or the book will go up in flames—but the next morning, I woke and the boys were running wild in the neighborhood and it was 10 am. And no sound from my mother's room. I knew this was not right. I knew something was not right.

I opened her bedroom door and saw her. The color of pale lilac. A blood clot to her beautiful brain.

Soon Cindy would be born into a house of grief.

26 ~

Back To The Navy

AFTER MY MOTHER'S DEATH, KEN AND I BOUGHT A HOUSE IN LEVITTOWN, PENNSYLVANIA. Seven Quaker Hill Road. The only declaration of an art spirit in that street of homes was our garage door. Ken did a Mondrian design with each of the squares making the structure a blaze of yellows, reds, blacks; not difficult for visiting friends to locate. It said "Here we are. We are here."

I struggled through the loss of my precious mother, a difficult birth with Cindy, my father's anguish, returning to the hospital with colitis after Cindy was born, and the onslaught of having Ken's mother, Harriette, nearby. Not the least of our problems was the fact that Harriette thought the baby was hers and raced down the steps to feed her, before I could get there, for the first two weeks of Cindy's life.

I learned assertion through this and, with a counselor's help, and with loving attention, kept Harriette from pulling out our flower beds, thinking they were weeds, and decorating my house behind my back.

In 50 years of being with Ken's mother, in spite of the gross improprieties, I knew she truly loved us—and that carried us over troubled waters. She was the Joan Crawford of her day, a femme fatale with one son only, and now enjoying her third marriage enroute to five. But she was wealthy, gorgeous, and brought glamour to our mundane lives, and she adored Cindy. That should not be a bad thing if I could only gather in my own raw needs enough to bear it. (No single feeling is without complexity. So I should mention the gown that Harriette had made me for my senior prom. Blue and white. Layers upon layers of blue upon white. How happy she made me then.) For my entire life, Harriette bestowed finery on me and the girls we could never, without her, have afforded. That this was an entanglement goes without saying.

Because my mother had just died, the many people I knew and their relatives, thought the baby and I needed visits. Thus my return to a stay in the hospital, with colitis, having to leave Cindy with Harriette. Could the gods be crueler?

We'd left the Navy because Harriette's husband owned a plastics factory in Trenton and she claimed Ken (an engineer by trade) was wanted there. This was incorrect. When Ken showed up, after giving up a Navy Commission, Ken was offered $75 a week by Harriette's husband, Godfrey Zentmayer. Godfrey never wanted Ken in his life in any way whatsoever and he made Ken's life miserable every day. Finally, his story ended when all the anger he was storing in a rocky marriage to Ken's mother and subsequent divorce caused him to later shoot himself.

Ken invented three items for that company, Martindell Molding, and never got more than his weekly stipend. Ken designed the coffee pot with an outside plastic stem that showed the amount of liquid, the same outside device on a steam iron, the pen holder for the Esterbrook's desktop pen, plus the first plastic tampon holder. This is true. The policy is when you work for a company, it owns copyright. We never knew any better. A simple bonus would have been appropriate for Ken's contributions.

I was miserable and in two years' time, although I feared leaving my father on his own after my mother's death, Ken sought reinstatement in the US Navy. He'd given up his regular commission but could return as a permanent Naval Reserve officer.

It was a hard drive south this time to Pensacola, singing "This Old Man. He Had Ten. This Old Man He Had Nine…" over and over to my two-year-old, but my nausea, I found out when we arrived, was not from the repetition of songs, but a new baby coming.

Back to where we belonged, in a rented cottage on the water outside of the base, with a dock and a row boat and a yard full of birds. I could write lovingly to my mother-in-law from there and truly feel no rancor. We'd had it out when Cindy was eight months old, Harriette's interference was intolerable, and Ken's treatment at work was abominable. But the day after the battle for my independence from my mother-in-law, I found out I had won a trip to Sweden from writing an essay against censorship in the arts.

So I digress from the Navy to burrow into this experience for a moment. CBS had a new daytime show, the Today Show with Arlene Francis and Hugh Downs, trying for an intellectual daytime component. The show inaugurated a writing contest on issues of the day. I, of course, entered every one and the day after I cut off ties with my mother-in-law I found we needed a babysitter.

It was providential because Ken had been in boarding school in Sweden during for high school and Harriette and Chet dragged their son abroad in the second American ship to travel there after World War II. Ken had always wanted to show me Sweden, and as we knew, it was not possible on $75 a week with a house mortgage, but now we could go. A "nervous stomach" was my weakness under crisis but I was determined not to collapse.

We didn't know what would be given us but that we were to be accompanied by a Swedish embassy host. Ken knew Swedish. It was all perfect, almost. We took $50 with us and that was all we had. My Aunt Alice came to our house as intermediary to carry the baby to Harriette for care, which I had no doubt would be total and adoring; I was not speaking to Harriette, and could not face her. And off to New York we went to be on the Today Show.

I wore a black dress from the French Boot Shop where I would order clothes for the next 20 years, as I hated shopping. Probably from years of working retail after school. The dress was simple and elegant. The skirt was straight to the knees, long tight sleeves and a round neck. I was so excited and Arlene Francis said, "Keep that. Don't let the bubble break," in sardonic advice. Another mantra we would carry through the years, bringing us to our knees with laughter.

Before we went on camera, an assistant rushed in and said FLYNN? You won the trip to Japan also with an essay against tranquilizers. (These drugs were just coming out in the 50s and I wrote a scathing essay against the use of such medication while actually I wouldn't mind having some.) The gopher went on to say I still had a choice of countries. And prizes. I stayed with my choice for Sweden as Japan sounded too far away to leave Cindy with Harriette.

The trip to Sweden was sent from my mother in Heaven as our belated gift. How else could we ever manage to see Ken's boyhood country? We visited Ken's school in Sigtuna. In the month of May the snow was two feet deep, although I wore high heel strappy shoes of course, and a black velvet coat from the French Boot Shop. Everyone there had boots and fur hoods.

As I said, we had but $50 to take with us and never knew what was to be expected of us or what check would be presented at a restaurant; yet all went as promised by CBS and all we spent was $30 of our cash on a purse for Harriette for caring for Cindy—a purse that would be handed over by a third party, Aunt Alice.

The most momentous Swedish event was a plane ride to Orrefors in the midst of a forest where artists and craftsmen lived in isolation in a commune, making glass. We were hosted by the first person to invent a process to engrave figures onto glass, Edvard Hald, a student of Matisse. He was very old then, in 1956, and we learned some things that cannot be forgotten.

The glassmaking artist never touches her/his creation. The artist works in tandem with a hands-on craftsmen. The artist "talks" the design, but the hot glass is molded by other hands. If a mistake is made in shaping hot molten glass, the artist quickly corrects this, verbally, to incorporate it into a new design. We only saw female artists but the day was short and we were lucky to see the heart of glassmaking. This would instruct Ken in sculpting and me, in writing, for this rest of our lives. A lesson that could not be read about was our guideline for life: Failure was just the opportunity to make something different.

A plane returned us to Stockholm and the Royal Swedish Hotel. The honeymoon suite. (My mother from Heaven, I'm sure, tried to make up for our two-day original honeymoon.) We dined in a restaurant where the owner had known Ken's parents and served an entire roast pig to our table.

Sitting with our Swedish Embassy hosts, they spoke their language and didn't know Ken could understand them. Ken smiled when they said of us, "What shall we do with them now?"

I didn't digest food well for ten days and worried constantly that my baby would now be Harriette's baby.

I feel the grand adventure right now. What it foretold. That the impossible can happen and will. That wishes are thought-forms that manifest. That balance is always there with great prosperous gifts. However, there's a shadow with this memory: I wish Ken would remind me in my meditations the names of the restaurants… the one in a cave… The Golden Fleece? No, Ken cannot tell me right now. He's gone. I think of what Jean Emerson wrote about a Stanley Kunitz comment. The great poet said poetry and memoir are 'the past meeting the present.'

That same year, before we had thoughts of leaving Levittown for good, I had written a poem to enter a poetry contest. It's one of the indelible moments which showed Ken's devotion to my fledgling art. He drove me to Philadelphia to accept the prize and sat in the car all day, in the snow, waiting for me. That was our life together. And I would do the same for his art.

≈

WHAT I WON

The sack dress was in style then
      with a single strand of pearls.
The sack dress was designed to see
      the body move lightly beneath.
That's why I wore it to my first poetry
      contest in Philly,
leaving my four-month-old at home.
      Of course my husband had to
drive, as nervous as I was
so he waited in the car all
day while I sat in the big room, first time out
      since I found my mother
dead and then had a baby two weeks later.
My husband stayed all day in that
car in the snow. I won first prize about
      wanting my mother but
It was said much better than this,
      as you can imagine, to win first.
It even began with *notes upon a phantom*
lute, although The Poet
said what do we know of lutes now?
      But what did he know of
walking into her bedroom and finding
      her a pale shade of lilac.
That just goes to prove I guess I was talking
      about the wrong thing in the poem,
and The Poet was surely on to something.
      I have to say I looked wonderful,
gaunt with grief and colitis, 1956,
      hurrying across the street
where my husband was waiting to take me home,
the first wrong victory in my hand.

      —*Sounds Like Something I Would Say,* Casa Menendez, 2010

27 ~
Pensacola, Florida & Beyond

WE DIDN'T KNOW UNTIL TWO WEEKS BEFORE SHELLEY AND COLLEEN WERE BORN THAT THERE WERE TWO BABIES, NOT ONE. All I knew was, while pregnant, I couldn't sit down from five months on, and could not stand up after eight months into the pregnancy. Ken had to come home for lunch to carry me to the bathroom after that. Fortunately he was water survival officer in the Pensacola training pool for Naval Cadets, five minutes away. I was only 105 pounds when I got pregnant and would lose 35 additional pounds on "the table."

There were no sonograms in the 1950s and since I had constant discomfort, an x-ray revealed two babies due in a month who would come two weeks early.

It was a wonderful delivery with an epidural. Born 15 minutes apart, Colleen Patricia and Shelley Anne, July 22, 1959. Shelley was put in an incubator for one week until she reached five pounds; I called every hour until staff said, in exasperation, 'LET HER HAVE HER!'

My own mother was dead and Ken's mother would not be a good choice to help us at this time.

The first weeks were pretty rough. In 1959 we had an old fashioned, old-school civilian doc in Pensacola for the twins. He believed in throwing babies out in the snow if they had fevers (we did not). Our twins had constant stomach problems and he ordered lactose in some form and it did cure them. I needed to hire some help so he recommended an old lady used as a former wet nurse, about 80 years old who was a Seventh Day Adventist and never left the house but to go to church.

The nursemaid's name was Tommy and she had huge billowing breasts that the twins loved to sleep on. The only thing was, she liked to stay in bed and have her meals served to her, and she was incontinent. More diapers than I counted on, but what we needed was another pair of arms, and she stayed for the first three weeks. We loved her and visited her later in a tiny house the Adventists had built her. They never could afford to finish the steps in front so she couldn't get out easily, and we couldn't get in.

Since our perfect cottage with two small bedrooms was not prepared for the increased population, the bassinettes were put in the small living room and we had to, in three months' time, search for a place that could accommodate cribs.

To leave the backyard on the water was to leave a Heaven that would have to go on without us. But we managed to find, on Bayou Drive, water with an alligator across the street. The house had a tiny palm tree outside and whenever we visited, in future years, I'd make the children see where they lived. It became a family joke, but I haven't the heart to ever visit the street again.

≈

I BECAME A NAVY WIFE AND TOOK BRIDGE LESSONS. I was terrible at that. I participated in fashion shows, had luncheons and poured tea. Wonderful at that. I thought this was the Navy and it was just fine with me. Then it was my turn to entertain the Commanding Officer and Executive Officer's wives plus squadron women. I cooked for three days and they sat cramped elbow to elbow in my small living room while Ken in the kitchen was sous chef handing the items to me, crepes filled with shrimp, crab, pork, and celery, onions and crème sauce.

We visited other Navy couples at 5 pm for drinks and, if we visited senior officers, we left calling cards in silver trays at the designated front door table.

We did nothing but cook and entertain, 50 at a time sometimes, in the backyard of a tiny house. In food preparation, I always had a baby on a hip. Sweet Colleen has a scar on her elbow where once I leaned down too far across some cutlery.

Once I was dishing out individual pizzas made from English muffins hand over fist. All I can remember is bending over a small kitchen oven, making them on cookie tins, while my visiting mother-in-law executed the deliveries for a party to say goodbye to Sally and Shan Trebbe. Sal is gone now, five years dead, and this poem tells all we did.

≈

SALLY DIES

For Sally Trebbe, d:.June, 2008

There goes my past again   the mind worn as thin   as this summer dress

There goes Sally   like the rain against the wall   slighter now   leaving

So we'd have something   to celebrate   together   days so sweet   like

Sunny cupcakes   being young   I mean   I will make a mistake saying this

But I was talking about   pressing 5 children   into a car   to go to the bad

Section   to buy fabrics   under   a lemony sky   before it turned grey

This is   so ordinary   forgive me   the Japanese   dinners   we cooked

And   babies vomited   forgive me   I cannot seem   to   do better

Being with her   the whole of it   I realize   in poetry   we cannot

Say we were young   but the arms   our arms   held so much   that moved

(The tail   of the bird just went by)   outside   now   (a tangle of trees)

I was talking about these hands   our hands   that made so much of color

And food   these hands   the same ones   mine   reach into a temple of
Words to pull out some breath   of someone   once condensed   now
The breath of words   well that makes it harder   telling how we became
Women   in soft wool suits   and high heels   and umbrellas   rushing in
Restaurants in Washington   a lawyer   and a producer extravagantly
Available shamelessly   big   with love   for each other   when it could
Have been otherwise   I will make a mistake saying this   but there goes
Sally   with her laugh   and that   makes it all the harder to remind you
When the day sheds itself of Sally   and her box of paints   and flowers
Let it not be forgotten   there is   someone left   one of us is always left.

—*Sounds Like Something I Would Say,* Casa Menendez, 2010

28 ~

EastCoast, WestCoast

PENSACOLA, FLORIDA + SANFORD, FLORIDA + DEL
MAR, CALIFORNIA + WHIDBEY ISLAND, WASHINGTON

JEAN EMERSON, EXPERT MEMOIRIST, SAYS WE ONLY
CAN TELL THE TIP OF THE ICEBERG NO MATTER HOW MUCH WE SAY. There's
no ability to field the rush of all those feelings, the sensory smell
of the bayou nearby, the children playing outside, the company of
women. Pensacola, Florida.

Every day at 11 am the twins would take a nap, like little clocks,
and from 11:30 to 1 pm I would entertain friends for lunch. Women
were my stability and my ground. Their stories, dissatisfactions,
dreams, denials, all between 11:30 and 1 pm. My pattern is the
same today. I usually cook dinner for some woman friend at least
once a week and enter their stories, dissatisfactions, dreams, denials, memories.

But this was shore duty, and no one lived in fear of that knock
on the door from the designated officer of death. All I cared about
was how many fresh-caught crabs I could pick in one hour to
freeze, jar after jar, for party time.

The back yard was filled with our beer parties and the neighbors were family. Paul Murphy from Trenton, Ken's and my oldest
friend, came through monthly on business, to share beef tenderloin
on the grill. He became a staple with the neighbors and remained
fast friends with them long after we moved.

The twins, at 18 months of age, and Cindy were to find a new
home with us in Sanford, Florida, inland near Orlando. Ken went
ahead to buy a house and I trusted his taste 100 percent, as we were

identical in values and esthetics. And he didn't disappoint me, finding a rambling stone front house with marble floors, sun room (still no air conditioner in those days but we had one window unit installed in a bedroom to escape the heat), 106 East Coleman Circle. A cul de sac of Navy families. The girls rode trikes through the house. Ken built a beautiful brick floor in the Florida room where the twins would slide our precious long playing records across like skateboards. We made beer and wine in vats. Grocery stores in Florida would only sell ten pounds of sugar to customers at a time because of this rampant hobby.

Two-year-old Colleen and Shelley would put socks and small items in the beer vats, discovered, to our surprise, when the huge jars were finally emptied. We rationalized that they may have improved the flavor. An object to register bubbles was not yet invented, so I'd have to count the bubbles for the correct rise, and when it hit the maximum, I'd call Ken home from work to bottle the beer.

This was not to be a new profession. At night, while sleeping, one by one, the bottles exploded. This was a huge loss for we'd spent weeks collecting, washing, sterilizing, the glass bottles. The beer that remained was amazingly good though. Sweet light champagne like wine (could be the socks) and a delightful light beer (punctuated with small plastic toys).

Ken was at sea on short cruises, one and two months at a time, and I enrolled in graduate school, with the help of a good babysitter after bedtime. Cindy was first-born and the head of the household from age six. She herded her twin sisters into magical games; and delivered newborn kittens when I was too squeamish. I think she gave me strength or I'd never have had the stamina to go to "college" after hours.

Teachers at Rollins were pretty rural. My main professor at Rollins used to say I "might could," before his sentences. My Princeton bred college professors were different but this guy was sweet, he let us do research in the library for our A grades, and had an afternoon party at his home for the class. I was always nervous driving although it was only 20 minutes away. And I remember writing a paper on the robotic mechanized future—which has indeed come true—but mostly I remember running outside to see the girls on their tricycles after every sentence. My Remington-before-electric-typewriters stuttered out ideas. And so that I wouldn't miss Ken too much, I plowed on. But there's no one playing outside today, as I write this now, just the snow and an empty winter street.

Ken was always saying goodbye in Sanford. But when he was home, the picnics with the children at cold Sanford Springs, and the imagination we shared with the children and our own romance was beautiful. We were too housebound to do nightclubbing. Ken would say, "Let's go out for dinner tonight." And we'd set up the card table in the sunroom with candles, while the children whizzed by on their stomachs ruining the LP records on a brick floor.

Some people sift through memory; I'm faced with a sand storm. Down the street in Sanford was a Navy doctor's wife who became my buddy. Helen Morosini from Boston; she was a reader like me and a great smoker and drinker. She and Chuck were like the Great Gatsbys of the neighborhood. They ate steak with martinis at midnight. Chuck would come home noontimes for sex, and she was so full of life and brains and humor. I adored being with her while her little Debbie and younger daughter played with my girls.

How could we know our future? Chuck and Helen would get out of the Navy. Helen would have a third baby girl, Dana, when I had my fourth, Angel. All the Morosini girls had glamorous lives as Chuck became a renowned cardiologist near Manhattan. Helen would have a limo take her to work at Lloyds of London in New York City. Dana Morosini, after a dazzling courtship, married movie star Chris Reeves (the original Superman). Chris would become paraplegic from a horseback fall; Dana left show business to become a spokesperson for spine research. Chris died a hero of valor. And soon after, Dana died of lung cancer. She never smoked in her life, but she had sung in clubs where people did smoke.

That year Helen died of lung cancer. And Dana and Chris Reeves' son, Will, would be turned over to Chuck, the grandfather, to be raised.

Two years ago to my heartbreak, I read an interview with Chuck in a book called *Serial Marriages*, about Chuck's new love/wife. He disclosed the fact that he never loved Helen at all but married her because she was pregnant. I wonder why this disclosure was necessary. I thought about Helen's girls, two daughters, who would read this.

How could we have guessed all of this when we were happy, living on a sunny street in Sanford in 1962, when Helen and I talked of Jane Austen and books during the day, while our girls played together. Many times we four would go to dinner in Winter Park, in cutting-edge restaurants. I can remember one place and exactly where we sat. I remember the taste of tomato aspic. I'd never be able to make one like it.

This was the year of the Bay of Pigs and the Cuban Missile Crisis. Both times, Ken was flying over the Mediterranean Sea from a carrier. Once he was told he had to wear a white flash suit. To their horror, the pilots learned why. They were carrying atomic bombs in the bay of the plane. Ken said we were twenty minutes from a full atomic war and President Kennedy went to brinkmanship. Later I would learn Ken had a bailout plan, in an emergency to land near Turkey; and I can't remember the details. It was unthinkable. He became a pacifist that very day.

I too had small wars erupting. At night I would receive strange phone calls in the middle of the pitch black night, with my three children sleeping in the next room. The voice had scary music playing, not the blues, but some combination of pop music I could not identify, and the voice would say, "I know you are alone. Your husband is at sea. I'm watching you." This was during the Bay of Pigs debacle and Ken was gone of course.

I was never a risk taker, or athlete, or courageous person, but I knew that the man who came near that house would never match my strength. Yet it was frightening and all I could do was go to the Commanding Officer's wife and report it. And squadron wives were then told to take the decals off our car windows, for these showed our squadrons—so it was too easy to know by insignias, which men were dispatched to sea.

This stalking eventually subsided and I'm convinced my fury was a thought-form that scared the creep away. My protective instincts were stronger than his predatory ones and I know I could have broken him in half for the sake of my children. The strength flooded through me. I was afraid but angry as Hell.

During the Cuban Missile Crisis, while Ken was gone, all the wives in the neighborhood went home to their families. My father had remarried a sweet woman but one not capable of housing me and three little ones: twin three-year-olds and Cindy, age six. Chuck Morosini, Navy doctor, stayed on the base and I remember going to him constantly for stomach medications. Helen and her two girls went home to Chuck's mother. I could not entertain the thought of travel alone even to drive to an airport then. Harriett, Ken's mother, was having marital problems. I could not go there.

We had bought the house in Sanford because we were told we'd be in Sanford for a four-year tour of shore duty. Suddenly Ken got orders to the West Coast because another Landing Signal Officer was on deck when a landing plane snapped the tailhook wire, cutting off his legs and killing him.

This was the real Navy. No more fashion shows and tea parties. No more bridge clubs with peppermint sticks crushed into ice cream, before such flavors were imagined and sold commercially.

Before we left town, I visited the woman down the street whose husband never made it home. There were always plane crashes. Her two boys were so wild, I trembled to think how petite Donna, with no parenting skills, could ever survive now.

We left our house to have it foreclosed as no one would buy it. And five years later Disney World, Orlando, was built nearby. Our house then would have made a small fortune, by proximity. Ken and I always laughed about our bad business karma. We were Hansel and Gretel in the forest, not knowing where we'd turn next, lost, but together.

It was an eventful trip across country to beautiful Del Mar, California. We'd rented/pulled a large pop-up tent that slept six. One night in the mountains, Ken got violently ill. There was a lamp next to him in the back of the tent and he got carbon monoxide sickness and I pulled him out; we rethought our survival skills. He was a survival expert and taught it in the Navy. I guess they forgot the chapter on the kerosene lamp.

I fell in love with California—its palm trees and ocean. When we arrived in San Diego we stayed at a marina for four days, putting the girls in school there before moving north to find a rental. I never wanted to leave those boats, that sky, the cool wind and the hot sun. I would live there still but life did not hold that luxury.

The real estate man took us up the hills to Del Mar, where Jimmy Durante and Ricky Ricardo lived within a mile, down the hill on the beach. They were seen from time to time, especially Ricardo, walking drunk on the sand.

This house! Amphitheater Drive. On top of the highest hill, this house, all glass windows, a swimming pool, a view of the ocean where we could watch dolphins and whales migrating, a screened in porch (which Cindy chose as her bedroom). If life was a balance, our good fortune had come.

Ken was one of the pilots who, while stationed there at Miramar, initiated the Top Gun school which would later be the subject of a movie by that name with Tom Cruise. Ken was the first "adversary pilot." It was fine duty and the other Navy couples were the best company, and fun. If in Sanford "The Twist" with Chubby Checkers ruled our parties, here in California it was a Trini in the trunk (Trini Lopez). We'd always have records, ready for dancing wherever we went, in the trunk of our car. 1964. Party time again.

We entertained constantly. One time Ken and I planned and prepared an authentic Swedish Smorgasbord. We spent days hunting down the imported ingredients. A huge Gloog, all kinds of delicacies, and we flamed individual Swedish crepes for about 50 guests in our small, gorgeous, all-wood living room with full-length windows, inviting the sea. Crepes were Ken's specialty and the month before he died, 2013, he had just ordered a new crepe pan which cooked crepes on the bottom of the pan, as in French restaurants. He never got to use it.

Ken's mother had sent me a gold brocade outfit for a Japanese buffet we created. Tempura all over the kitchen but served with all the accoutrements. It was an elegant evening in my silk slacks and long Asian tunic. Over the years I was showered with designer clothes from this woman whose aesthetics were a high Art. Clothes were her vehicle of love; and I was so grateful, many days, to come exhausted to the door with a baby on a hip, and find a white cashmere coat delivered or a wardrobe of the newest fashions.

Every time we entertained, Harriett would express an outfit for me that I could never have afforded in a 100 years of Navy pay.

A significant event, among many others in Del Mar, was when we heard from Tony Nolte's widow that she was moving her six children to Hawaii where she was to teach swimming. Tony was the most adored man in the squadron in Sanford. He was our Executive Officer, whose plane went down in a routine mission. The Boeing inspector had dropped a ruler into the engine from his shirt pocket and this was revealed during inquiries. Incredible. One would not believe that this ruler was not located and seen on a quality check. There it was. And several men dead. Our beloved Tony was so funny. When he heard Ken made "fluffy ruffy eggs" on Sundays, he bullied us until we gave such a breakfast for him and other friends, featuring Ken's specialty.

Now Maggie Nolte, a confirmed alcoholic, was coming through Del Mar to God knows where. She certainly didn't.

The tent we'd driven across country came in handy. We erected it in the driveway for her and three of her children. The others would bunk with ours. That was the week that was. All I can remember is Ken coming in every day with bags and bags of groceries and my cooking and cooking. After dinner, Maggie would drink and cry until her head hit the table and she was out, cigarette still burning. We didn't know what to do.

One morning Maggie's boys pushed their sister in the pool. She couldn't swim. Cindy had just learned how to swim but jumped in and pushed her to the side of the pool. It was an eventful ten days.

During the day hours Maggie was thinking more clearly and decided they had to move on. We sold her the tent for a negligible amount, and she somehow got the brood to Hawaii. I heard she had that job teaching swimming.

≈

AFTERTHOUGHT: Two tours on Whidbey Island

Somehow I've managed to skip two tours of duty in beautiful Whidbey Island, Washington, near Seattle. I know the first tour was about 1963 for one year and when we drove in and I saw no outdoor swimming pools I was scared to be left with tiny children with Ken gone. More rain. The wood fire smell was everywhere and houses blended in with the gorgeous rocks and trees.

I see one temporary housing address in my files from letters Sally Trebbe left me when she died: 3181 300E Apt 6, Oak Harbor, Washington. Oh yes, I remember Ken driving the twins around all night in the back of the van when they had ear aches so they'd sleep. This would be before he'd move me into a house and leave for sea the next day.

Also, I see 1025 Mountain Drive, Washington. This must have been two years later. I thought the apple trees were ugly shapes which didn't portend well. I know this was the house where the children saw J.F.K.'s assassination interrupting their cartoons. This must be the place the girls made tents over the clothesline and Colleen got clunked on the head by a rock from their architecture.

When we returned another time we lived on-base at the Naval Air Station: 8163 875E, Oak Harbor. Ken was home more then. We went out our back door to the sandy flats pulling oysters, cold with sand, to wash and steam for dinner. I remember listening to Dinah Washington a lot there.

One night before Ken was to leave for a long cruise he and I went to the Base movie *Bye Bye Birdie*. Never has a musical been filled with so much pain. When I hear the songs today, I get vertigo.

But the drives across the country were fun, until Cindy fed a bear a banana out the window in Yosemite and the bear almost pulled the car window out. I guess the sign meant what it said. Then Cindy sat on a bee hive. And somewhere in the Great Plains a stampede of wild horses sent us under the picnic table til they passed by. As Lucille Clifton said in her poem, "oh children/ remember the good times."

29 ~

Extraterrestrials in Pensacola, Florida

FLASHBACK: I'D NEEDED SOME THERAPY HELP, 1955, IN JACKSONVILLE WHEN I WAS PREGNANT FOR THE FIRST TIME. I'd had huge fears about returning to civilian life and great distress about leaving the conviviality and friendship of being part of squadron life, and about leaving my teaching in a school where I could unleash all creative powers.

Ken and I had met two women friends who lived at Jacksonville Beach. We used to spend weekends there—eating chili, reading, talking, playing board games. Many times Ken sat with the two women playing scrabble all night. I remember sitting up reading Thomas Wolfe's *You Can't Go Home Again*, till dawn.

They were psychologists and suggested I talk to someone in their firm about my apprehensions—there were problems that I thought were waiting for me at home in civilian life. What I learned is that energy shifts and the problems would have attached to new circumstances, changed form, or dissolved. Nothing stayed the same. Good information.

The connections we made with these therapists were priceless. When we returned to the Navy two years later, back from civilian life, we reconnected with some of our psychologist friends, among them the great Haim Ginott, who'd later become an authority on teenage guidance. He was from Israel and the most provocative and stunning individual. We were at dinner one night at a friend's home, a Navy widow, and she asked Haim what to do as her young preschool daughter was touching herself. Haim said, "It's fine, just don't let her use any sharp objects. Wood blocks are ok." I, a product of a Victorian society, could not believe people were saying this at the dinner table. Haim became an international celebrity in New York by the next decade, and his various books on *Between Parent and Child* are still on the shelves.

Haim used to play a dissonant harmonica. The mournful sounds of his country. He died very young, at fifty-one.

When we moved to Pensacola, we were sent by our Jacksonville psychology friends to meet psychologist Dan Overlade and his wife, Renee, our favorites. We felt at home bringing our three little girls to their home for Sunday mornings to play with their two little boys, eating peanut butter on toast. Dan fascinated us the most. His PhD was on laughter and that summed up our times together.

However, Dan's professional specialty was not on laughter, but on extra-terrestrial abductees. Pensacola had sand made not from ground dirt but quartz. Space ships had been sighted there for years causing a clan of the faithful—some nut jobs, some military intelligence, and many serious scientists.

Since Dan was an expert in hypnosis, he soon became the official person in charge of interviewing those who claimed to have been abducted. After extensive interviews, he'd send the candidates to New York without prior information to allow fresh interviews, to receive the same results, doubly assuring accuracy.

Of his findings, Dan had one consistent observation—each abductee had a blackout for three days with no conscious knowledge of where he/she'd been. Each person had come to him with a triangular piece of skin missing from a shin bone. One could only conjecture what the reason for that might be. Another consistent report was that there were painful experiments, usually in the abdomen and stomach areas, probing not in cruelty but investigation.

I later wrote a play, now lost and unproduced, about the idea that the ETs were so highly evolved they had intellectualized away from humanistic qualities and were searching for what human beings still held. In short, they were seeking the element of Love.

Ken was a fan! He'd followed the idea of extraterrestrial travel since childhood from science fiction, turning then to evidential information as a Navy pilot, and actual sightings from other pilots. He also was privy to Navy intelligence and its documentation.

Ever since Ken was a boy of 14 he told me the Space People were arriving and that he would go with them in 2013. Dan cautioned him not to. That it wasn't as glamorous as it appeared in print and film. Ken was unafraid, a risk taker, and felt it was his calling. Of more than casual mention is the fact that Ken died in 2013. I told my grief counselor this story and he said, "Maybe he did go with them."

But long before that time, to our great shock, we learned Dan had died. This was scarcely ten years after we'd met him and we were well into a new Navy life in Washington, DC.

Renee, Dan's wife, told us he'd gone alone to a wedding in New Orleans and drank some vodka and passed out. Three days later he found himself in his hotel room with a triangular mark on his shin. Soon after, in the Pensacola hospitals, 13 doctors could not diagnose the virus inhabiting Dan, until it won over western medicine and Dan succumbed to the mysterious disease.

And of our psychologist friends, then there were none.

But the Pensacola sightings continued.

30 ~

Mary Ellen Long

AFTER DUTIES IN PENSACOLA AND SANFORD, FLORI-
DA, AND ORDERS TO WHIDBEY ISLAND WHERE ANGEL WAS BORN, we had
that memorable one-year-stint in Delmar, California.

Immediately upon moving in we found we were in the center of a thriving arts community, where an artist named Beverly
made hand-woven textures, Wally threw pots, and Mary Ellen,
a neighbor, one hill/street away, was a silk screen artist. Marlene was a ballet dancer; her husband an architect. Ken went to
work daily to Miramar, his Navy duty station, but when home,
the Navy felt very far away to him.

Ken promised himself if he ever made it home from Viet Nam
alive, he'd buy welding equipment and turn to his first love, making art. Ken converted the California basement to a studio and
he began work. His first bronze sculpture, Prisoner of War, was
of Chuck Klusmann whom he'd tried to rescue from capture in
Laos, 1964.

Ken was too modest to declare himself an artist, but Mary
Ellen entered his finished piece in the California Arts Exposition
where it was accepted and honored. Ken's first bronze sculpture.
Chuck is on his knees on a rock but his back is straight and un-
bending. He's surrounded by barbed wire. Chuck was the first
man to escape the POW camp in Laos where he was shot down,
and he walked through the jungle to safety.

Mary Ellen's husband, Wendell, was a teacher and Mary Ellen

was a stay-at-home artist like me—she had two small boys who played with Shelley, Colleen, and six-week-old Angel.

I started writing every day, and I could watch the girls playing in the pool from the window while I was jiggling Angel's crib. I was able to read all of Pierre Teilhard de Chardin while rocking. Multi-tasking didn't have a name then but I could do it. I remember finishing Kazantzakis' *Odyssey* while walking twins in their stroller in Pensacola. Ambulatory reading was my skill, and philosophy my salvation. I was becoming amazed with Jesus, and filled with gratitude for something I could not name. I think I was a Jesus freak then. I found a reasonable logic in Teihard de Chardin.

Mary Ellen was inspired by the bold colors of the 1960s and by the California art movement, the swaths of brilliance produced by Sister Mary Corita, a war activist who eventually left the order and became a renowned artist, Corita Kent, muralist.

MEL and I teamed up; she made large silk screens featuring my poetry, which were eventually sold in galleries throughout the country. My house is still filled with her colors. And we wrote a book together. I produced the book, *Little Line*, and each page was designed with an original Mary Ellen silk screen illustration.

For 40 years we sent that book to publishers and in 2000 we published it ourselves—because it's beautiful. I realized that at some point if you don't love your work enough to publish it, why ask anyone else to. The publishing industry has lock-step rules. One, is that they choose from their own stables of artists and rarely will accept the writer's choice of art, much less a finished illustrated product.

Making something that did not exist before is to be in collaboration with God and so is sacred work. To make a book is a splendid thing. Another collaborative joint effort was *Migrations*, with Mary Ellen's heart-stopping photos of broken dolls completing my text about the loss of children.

If the previous year had been hell for me, alone without Ken, and a frightening birthing experience with Angel, this year balanced it with art and beauty.

Down the hill, two blocks away, was the ocean and beach where Marlene (a dancer), Mary Ellen and I would practice dance on the sand while the children played. There was a restaurant on the water. I can still see Ken and the children there at the window watching the mist form on the glass, and the water roar. That window seat, that window, these moments at sunset are branded in my soul.

Mary Ellen and Wendell, native Californians, introduced us to nearby La Jolla with its art galleries and foreign film house, where we parted a curtain to walk into a black box theater. We four saw *Woman of the Dunes* there one night and Ken and I were transported. After moving to DC much later Ken and I would see every Warhol film. Even the one where the subject sleeps for eight hours. We stayed for three of the eight. How large the world had become.

Ken and I and our four children together in Del Mar, California in a gorgeous house on a cliff near the ocean. No sea duty. The arts. This is where we belonged.

Mary Ellen and I sent our book, *Little Line*, to Dr. Seuss who lived in La Jolla and he sent us an encouraging note. I don't know what I expected, but the response from him was reason to go on together. Mary Ellen and I were an art team.

In Washington, DC, Mary Ellen visited us from the west coast, staying in our condo. I was working at the National Endowment for the Humanities in 1987. After that, we didn't see one another until 2007 when we visited their new home in Durango, Colorado. Now Mary Ellen is a site sculptor. For 40 years, she has adorned forests with paper trees, water with paper lilies, etc., and is respected and recognized nationally in the field.

Fort Lewis College in Durango staged my play reading on Mary Wollstonecraft, "Hyena in Petticoats," in an outdoor amphitheater. An indelible experience under the stars and Colorado sky.

And it was powerful to walk through Mary Ellen's new studio to see her inimitable works.

Colleen came across country with us to Colorado, and she helped Mary Ellen set up a retrospective exhibit where visitors would walk through strings dangling with her objets d'art. My poem "MAP" was read while we watched dancers reenact it. It is about our friendship.

≈

For the poem "Map" see the APPENDIX TO CHAPTER THIRTY, *page 267.*

31 ~
My First Poetry Grant

WHAT BOTHERED ME MOST WAS SPENDING KEN'S EARNINGS ON MY ART. After settling into Annandale, Virginia from the west coast, 1966, I was writing every day and sending poems out to magazines, and also focusing on small stages for my first plays. Money was limited but our life was prosperous, our house brimming with color and colorful people, and the energy was resounding. I wanted our daughters to have what they wanted and needed, as modest as that was.

Yet I worried about my piece taken from the pie. Was it too large? I contributed nothing materially to our income. I was mailing every day to literary journals and theaters—perhaps a few hundred dollars a year allotted to furthering myself. We could add an extra zero to that these days.

The DC Commission on the Arts and Humanities professed to support artists; and so I wrote them a letter requesting support. The Commission at that time had no mechanism for funding individual artists and I had but a few publications and a host of dreams. A thin resume.

Oddly enough, I received a call asking me to meet with the Council to submit my case in person.

The room at the DC Commission was filled with many stern and august persons seated around a long oval table. I was asked why the urgency and intensity of my letter demanded that the Commission develop a resource for individual artists.

I said I had four children; I spoke of my endeavors; I admitted I was at the beginning of my career and needed assistance.

This was the height of the Cultural Revolution where women were burning their bras, and here I had to be driven into DC from Annandale by my husband.

The room was disdainful. One member actually said, "So what are you, some kind of suburban housewife artist?"

I shouted, *I AM AN ARTIST!*

A black guy, a sculptor, stood up in the back and raised his arms in a fisted salute and said *YES!*

I received $200. The Council began a plan to fund individual artists and to this day has a full blown system that does important work which has benefited me many times with projects over the years.

Forget the postage. With that $200 I bought a maxi coat. A beautiful long black coat with a huge collar. Just like Janis Joplin wore. If they wanted "an artist," not a housewife, they'd get one.

≈

For the poem "The Red Porsche and the Model"
see APPENDIX TO CHAPTER THIRTY-ONE, *page 273.*

32 ~
Teaching Poetry: Glen Echo Park

WHILE TEACHING AT ANTIOCH COLLEGE, 1969-1974, I WAS IN MY ELEMENT. All those students wanted poetry. I felt I had to match the creativity and urgency and passion of those who came to Antioch. They were mavericks and many as close to genius as I have met. It was a magnet for the kind of student society had no use for—the inventive—the truly original—the risk-takers.

Although much of my day was spent in hour-long poetry tutorials, group lessons called upon other efforts. I was determined to introduce poetry differently because Antioch students came to us disenchanted by other academia. Introducing poetry as other than an intellectual pursuit called for some thinking. Among other creative exercises, I found Viola Spolin had a book on theater workshops and I was able to convert those into poetry exercises.

There was a period of time, 1975-76, when I'd left Antioch in exhaustion. Brilliant experiences burn brightly, but burn they do. And I had more I wanted to do. I wanted to continue my MA at the University of Maryland and wanted to relax into my own poetry more. Commuting to and from Baltimore daily the final three years at Antioch was debilitating

Glen Echo Amusement Park had a checkered history. It was a magnificent arena of 1940s carousels and arcades and buildings of period structure. In 1973-74 the now-defunct park was being converted to artists' residencies, where every area was taken over by some artistic endeavor, all under the auspices of the Park commission. The Park had a shadow over its history because in the early and mid-20th century no blacks were allowed. Like every other facility, it was not integrated for the general public. Now, lying defunct and abandoned, artists entered to breathe new life into the sleeping amusement park.

The Writers' Center (now 40 years strong) started out in the shooting gallery. I was at the initial meeting with Al Lefcowitz where a group of us, with excitement, heard of plans for this great mecca for writers starting right there behind the ducks.

The Spanish Ballroom was set into operation as a great dance studio and big band stage; the potters worked in yurts. When life at Glen Echo was restored, and lights were on again, the public wandered through marveling at what could be created before their eyes.

Ken and another metal sculptor cleaned out the empty swimming pool and created studios behind its huge façade. They had to first remove the items left from the 1930s and 40s. Woolen bathing suits! Boxes of Kotex! The world had abandoned the park but left its detritus.

The sculptors were allowed to charge $5 per student and, although they loved to help people, they had to pay most of that fee for insurance by rule of park authorities. Although Ken had strict rules, a young hippie got her long hair caught in a machine, and no harm was done, but there were health risks and vigilance was always required.

Ken taught welding and, like all artists who teach their art, finally found more energy was going out than was coming in. But until that time of teaching exhaustion, from 1974-77, it was a heyday.

This is where I set up the Glen Echo Writing Workshop in the main building, and tutorials were given in the lifeguard's room, above the swimming pool where the broken glass windows allowed birds to fly through, punctuating our poetry.

At the main house I met David Bristol, lawyer and poet, and also Charles Hart, a now-retired lawyer living in Alabama. Sauci Churchill was there. We had a vibrant group. My tutorials were mostly with Jane Flanders who had twins as I did; she was just beginning to write. After a while, she moved to New York State and became a well-established writer and, after a fine career, she died, too young, in her sixties. My press published three of her books posthumously, edited by Steven Flanders, her husband, and designed by Cindy: *Sudden Plenty, Dandelion Greens, Manifesto d'Amore'* and *Uncollected Poems (1940-2001)*.

Charles Hart has communicated with me and this month (March 2014) I'll see him again in DC at a Library of Congress event. He's flying up from Alabama—40 plus years between visits, not too often for friends to meet. Charlie has kept entries in his journal that are historical treasures of 1974, Glen Echo Park. I wish I'd done the same. I was too busy living it.

After I met the psychic Bryan Christopher, I received many ideas that developed into poetry exercises in later years.

Bryan said to imagine our lives as a building with every floor a year and to get into the elevator and go to the roof. At the end of our lives a helicopter will come in and swoop us away and the building will crumble. And that is death. But until that time we have a building and if you are five years old, there are five floors, and even if you are 80 years old, there is a building with 80 levels. It occurred to me that on every floor there's a story and if we get into the elevator, we can stop at a floor and look around and tell that story, and if we don't see anything we can get back on the elevator and find the next story.

My good friend Robert Sargent at 90 was still finding poems to write about his childhood. He didn't realize he was going into the elevator of his life, getting off at floors, but he was, and he had all those floors to choose from.

This exercise has unleashed at least 1000 minds I know of; and it continues in schools and workshops across the country. It's now worldwide and has spread like a good virus through creative writers everywhere.

33 ~
Goddard College

GODDARD IS NOW A UNIVERSITY AND IS A VANGUARD OF INDEPENDENT THOUGHT AND STUDY. I ventured in after teaching at Antioch to finish my Master's Degree. I'd been simultaneously at the graduate school of English at University of Maryland, College Park. The solid foundation I had from Maryland is still a platform for confidence in my work. Goddard was the tribal fire where one is burned into submission and excellence, depending on who your mentors are.

This was the time (1974-76) for cultural upheaval and defiance of all authority, systems and bureaucracy, and although Goddard was not an Ivy League institution, the demands were eclectic and anarchistic enough to have me running back to therapy.

My immediate supervisor was compassionate and fair-minded, radically chic and very smart. Her superior mentor seemed out to get me.

Here I was, again seen as a suburban housewife playing at the arts, and a Navy wife at that, with Viet Nam souring the air. What could be more a betrayal to the Revolution. And my heart squeezes when I think of Ken's suffering on a carrier in Laos, how he never dropped a bomb, how he believed in Concerned Officers for Peace, yet he was branded by the ignorant and the self-righteous as a war hawk.

Ken finished his B.S. degree at Antioch College in 1974 while I was there. And paid a great price due to some professors who treated him badly for his Navy profession. But he endured because he knew who he was and what integrity meant.

My Goddard off-campus mentor held seminars and meetings which were bullshit, but the other students I met were top notch. I was allowed to research on my own. My field was Creative Writing and Education. I had the Education credits from Rollins, in Florida, when Ken was on a cruise, and University of Maryland as cherry on top; also, five years teaching writing at Antioch had some heft. My thesis would combine all these experiences into a book on teaching; and my final product in addition was to write a full-length play.

For this task I was grateful. Writing always seemed to take time from my family and, it being an MA project, somehow made writing more legitimate. I didn't have to feel guilty writing while waiting to prepare dinner. For some reason, when we plow the earth or scrub a floor we know we're doing the right thing. But reading a book and sitting at a desk staring at paper feels wrong—surely we should be contributing to the family, society and humankind. At least that's where I was, yet unformed, 40 years ago.

On a Remington Rand typewriter that was a foot high and weighed easily 20 pounds, I worked on "Best of Friends," the story of my childhood with my dear surrogate sister "Little Grace." She will always be my little sister instead of cousin, and will be here Saturday for lunch with another cousin, Carol Hurtt. Threads that never break.

I wrote because I had a legitimate and official reason to write, after ten one-acts and ten-minute plays, I finally had time assigned to myself to write a full-length play.

To allow a shift in atmosphere, Ken and I decided to rent a cottage in a shore resort in Delaware. Cindy and Shelley were excited as they were planning to pitch a full scale tent erected by tent master Ken Flynn in a nearby recreation area to have an excursion. Colleen was spending the week with a friend in Maryland. I would be in an empty space with Ken and Angel to get this MA done, and my loving play, long remembered, was waiting to be shaped into form. Ken would cook. Angel was used to having the typewriter take up some of her space, and had accommodated beautifully. Ken was my savior and dedicated his life to supporting my art and I dedicated my life to his. This is why we stayed together, besides the reason that he was the most interesting person I knew and I was the most interesting person he knew. That is an aside but worth saying. And as for Angel? She always forgave me for being a writer.

As the gods would have it, a gigantic storm swept the eastern seaboard and our drenched daughters came knocking at the door—adventure ended, tent collapsed, writing aborted. But a good time and a single day to write—working from dawn to dusk—something I would have the chance to do many times again, even now, and in the future.

But I would do anything to hear rain-sodden children knock at my door interrupting this thought right now, anything; and thankfully they are not very far away although 40 years have passed. The play written served me well and saw many stages after that.

But my MA thesis was to be delivered verbally to the Buddha of Goddard's alternative education in May that year.

I was scared because his method of overseeing my work was ridicule and derision. I shored myself up and memorized my oral report so many times that it took one month to get it out of my head. When I complained to my psychiatrist, Dr. Evans, about this obsession, he said, "Well it was very important to you." I think of that after any event where the words still linger in my mind, obsessive thoughts that are slow to go.

But what of the presentation? My "Orals." I had eye shadow on, I remember that. An attempt to be dressed up. This was a time when women didn't shave their legs or underarms, and I had blue eye shadow on.

My mentor looked at me as I rose to speak and said, "Well, I see we have on our war paint." My heart deflated, but showmanship kicked in, my brilliant defenses I tried so hard to dissolve through psychiatry came to rescue me, vindicated by bad habit—a fake demeanor—fake confidence. He brought out the worst in me. But I got through as bright as metal.

Ten years later when I was a senior program officer at the National Endowment for the Humanities, this same churlish gentleman from Goddard was now heading one of our state humanities councils. He needed to consult with me for what his council needed. I was working on the national level, in the organization from which he got his funding and support.

I was always professional in dealing with him; I never mentioned the war paint, although the war with him would never see a truce. I don't know why the following poem about childhood has the same feelings of unfairness, but it does.

≈

TO THE OLD WINE OF MEMORY

You have no place here
for your intoxication is
different from mine ...Amir

What is your place here
the more I give you
the more I keep

the trees were closer than
next to the steps
close as the moment
I will walk through

It is Christmas
at my Grandmother's house

when the family says
Let's Pretend
She's Not Getting A Doll
And See What She Does

Four years old,
but wise, I stood near
my sister's doll.
blue velvet
with yellow curls,
the most beautiful
I'd ever seen
as if I were happy for her

so happy
I didn't need one of my own

The joke didn't work
my father said
So Here's Yours
That was the box
I never opened
and never will

The house is imagining me again
It whispers Come Close
Forgive The Past
It warns
If You Lose Love
Where Will It Go

Winding up the clock with
its language of meaning,
I sit in the sun
steam rising to my face,
If its heat suffocates
I'll leave
taking my memory with me

I say to the past
"You were never a well made thing.

Now what will your world be without me."

— *Trenton*, Belle Mead Press, 1990

34 ~
WPFW-FM

WPFW WAS FILLED WITH JOY AND TURMOIL AND, AL-
THOUGH I LEFT IN 1997, AFTER 20 YEARS ON AIR, I STILL DREAM OF IT. I
dream recurrently they are waiting for me in the studio and I can't
get there…they cannot find my tapes…my microphone is not on.

WPFW was the culmination of a life's dream. Yet, WPFW was
that mix of positive and negative, a cauldron for all the happiness
and conflict bubbling together.

My love for radio exists because it was the mirror of my fulsome young imagination in the 1940s at WBUD in Morrisville,
PA. I was part of a children's show on Saturday mornings fashioned after the national success "Let's Pretend." We acted out stories and used sound effects made by hand (under the guidance of
professionals). Footsteps in the leaves were people, on-mic made
by crackling newspaper, etc. It was the perfect expression of a parallel universe. Magic was everywhere.

When I think of the education in Trenton throughout the school
system, I see it as the source of freedom and guidance to creativity.
And WTTM in Trenton permitted us drama club members to have a
show on air. We worked next to the great Ernie Kovacs, who would
go on to become famous as one of the first personalities on "live"
TV, a technology just catching some steam in the early 1950s. And
Ernie would die in an auto accident much too young, circa 1956.

In 1970, I bought a reel-to-reel portable professional tape recorder. It was the first toy I ever bought for myself. And it's true,

I never before had anything I wanted like this. I recorded a talk with my cousin Marilyn Gaston, a ballet dancer with the Stuttgart Ballet, and sent other small art segments to NPR, which went discreetly unnoticed.

Radio was me and I was radio. WBUD, Morrisville, PA, had an all night slot open when I was in college and I wanted to talk and play music and share my thoughts with invisible masses. My father said *NO* and how could he have done otherwise? I had no car, I was pretty unraveled in college, and I would be in danger alone in a studio all night. He was, of course, right. And the yearning went on.

While at Antioch, 1974, winding up my teaching days, the prize student and my friend Paz Cohen, from Chile, translator, writer, mentor, found out that Pacifica was getting the last available FM band on the dial in DC. It had been in litigation for nine years because Pacifica was a lefty organization and Congress was not. WPFW would be the newest station after four other Pacifica stations in Berkeley, LA, Houston, and NYC. And Washington's WPFW needed a Drama and Literature Director. What kind of place would think of such a thing? It had my name all over it, and I spent hours lying on the couch in a state of anxiety, plotting and planning. I had survived a hippie college and could certainly face alternative systems. Nothing could beat Antioch, I thought in my mind's struggle. But WPFW did that and more.

In 1975 I was teaching writing at Glen Echo Park, finishing up my MA, and scheming how to get the next brass ring on the carousel. Somehow, I think through Paz Cohen, Antioch student, I found the General Manager's name and sought a meeting. Dear Ken waited outside in the car for me, as he did my whole life, letting me pursue my ambitions.

Fortunately the new manager, Greg Millard, was interested in me for my poetry, so I brought five poets along: Ethelbert Miller, a prominent DC writer, gathered some friends, among them Adesanya Alakoye, Essex Hemphill, and other African-American poets who had, up to this time, no real poetry platform on public air. Howard University had a radio and TV station but WPFW was to be *the first black-managed public radio station in the country.* Greg was black and saw that poetry was missing in the DC environment. No radio station was committed to poetry, whatsoever, and I was proposing poetry from, by, and for the people of DC.

Sigidi Brodie, genius musician and engineer, recorded our session, and promptly lost the tape, my introduction to how it would always be at WPFW. Triumph was always followed closely by a tragedy. Greg named me "Drama and Literature Director" and now all we needed to do was raise money to get the station on the air. This was something I was glad to do. I spent the rest of 1975 and all 1976 working with core staff: Paz Cohen and Tim Frasca (News), Lorne Cress (Public Affairs), Sigidi (Music Director), Denise Oliver (Program Director) and Bob Frasier (Chief Engineer).

I still had my Porsche from Antioch days, and drove from Maryland to Southeast Washington to squeeze Sigidi and Denise into a single seat where they ate cupcakes for breakfast and talked about things philosophical, to go into DC. How I miss their advanced minds. We drove to our first radio station, a ready-made studio on top of a drugstore, corner of 15th and L Streets, NW, across from the Washington Post building.

I managed to get an appointment with Leonard Randolf, then head of the National Endowment for the Arts literature program, and Greg Millard came with me. We laid out our story of poetry forestalled by poverty. We were able to secure $40,000 in the name of literature to get us partly on the air. That would serve to be salaries for me, Denise and Sigidi for three years. I was on fire.

This was a sandbox I'd always wanted. And my family was patient, well taken care of but always bemused, watching a mother who flew like a hummingbird to some nectar away from our home.

February 1977—We went on-air with Sterling Brown's poetry and Duke Ellington's "A-Train," not the "Star Spangled Banner," the first black-managed, jazz *public* radio station in the country was making its purpose known.

Throughout 1978 I was able to create and produce eight art shows a week: Writing Workshops on the Air which gave three credits (from Prince Georges Community College) to audience members who sent in manuscripts for discussion and critiques. I produced children's radio, live radio drama, film criticism, poetry recorded at venues around town, Expressions (an art talk show), and my beloved THE POET AND THE POEM, the only show of its kind giving poets prime time (Sunday nights, 8 pm) for one hour. Now at the Library of Congress, 37 years later (as of 2014) and still going strong, I have presented and celebrated approximately 3000 poets in 37 years.

There was one significant problem with Writing Workshops on the Air. I had the best poets and novelists and teachers rotating weekly, discussing on-air the work sent in by writers. But we found that sensitive creators did not want their shortcomings discussed on 50,000 watts so we dismantled that brilliant (I thought) but ill conceived project.

The station was primarily run by African-American volunteers. The news staff was white and off in its own world, Chief Engineer Bob Frasier as well. I was working it out with Lorne Cress, Black Nationalist, and Denise and Sigidi, non-militant. If Lorne overstayed her time in the studio while my guests waited, I confronted it. And it became racial and we talked it out, because we each knew we loved the other but had some problems that needed declaring. I was being tested. And I would not fail the test. Antioch had honed me to the task of race problems, but I was not guilty when charged.

From L Street we went to the heart of what was then a drug inflicted inner city ghetto at 18th and U. Now, 40 years later, it's the chic part of DC with its new shops and restaurants. Not then. Our offices were donated by RAP Inc. and we operated in front of that drug rehab facility. Good spirit, bad section. I was not worried. Daytime, nighttime, my radio love would call me. I now had an all-day Thursday on-air shift, engineering, where I ran the board and operated the station as well as being live on-air. I had to study for a third class radio engineer's license then, now no longer required. It was challenging but I studied and took the test with Angel waiting in the back of the room while my car was on a meter. I passed. I had no time to fail.

On Thursdays we featured Dial-A-Poem, an addition Sigidi Brodie invented, where people called in their poems and I work-shopped them on-air. Let me say that I thought I knew what was out there but everyone in DC had a poem: drunks, taxi drivers, grandmothers, prizefighters, and we didn't have a "bleep" system, so I stood in fear of the FCC. Some great poets also called in—the jazz poet Fareedah Allah, for one, Ambrosia Shepherd, another. The poetry community in Washington, DC was coalescing and a certain circle of black writers would rise to prominence. Surely these good poets would find their audience: yes, a regional listener-ship of 200,000 helped.

One Thursday summer morning, I came for my usual morning shift, after David Selvin, who was to be on-air also. David was an artist/painter and producer who came to us from NYC's WBAI. But David was not there. The station was locked up, which was un-usual, but anything could happen at WPFW. I had to get someone to help me climb into the second floor window.

I was technically untrained to turn on the station's transponder and knew some things but not enough beyond running the board and being on mic and rolling out records that were played, at that time, on turntables. I think David showed up finally and helped get the station on the air as I was so shaken, with Bob Frazier on the phone talking us through it.

David, brilliant artist/painter, would die 30 years later of drug use, having lost both his legs to the disease, and being homeless in Martinsburg, West Virginia. As they said of pianist/musician Bill Evans: "He was just too sensitive to stay alive."

The station, after five years, moved to 7th and H Streets in Chinatown, before Chinatown became a destination spot and tourist haven. We were on the fifth floor of a place that was nice but for the rat infested basement, which Denise Oliver finally had exter-minated; and forever more we would smell that poison, whatever it was. When I came home I would have to rip my clothes off, toss them into the washer and scrub my body.

At that time, 1980, I would run my own board, engineering, while interviewing poets on The Poet and the Poem. That was hard but I liked the assurance of knowing I was the engineer who would show up on time and my tapes wouldn't get erased. Finally a young man showed up who would be with me for the next ten years. And I loved this engineer dearly, and always will. Dwane Goodman.

One night I was invited to a dinner at novelist Susan Shreve's house to honor Margaret Atwood, the Canadian novelist. Poet Linda Pastan was there with her scientist husband, Ira, and their daughter Rachel, who would become a fine novelist in her own right. In fact, I recently reviewed her second novel, some 30 years later.

Margaret Atwood sat on the couch and never said one word the whole evening. Then I packed her up in my car, drove to the station, and we had a good hour on air; she talked about her son beginning school. Before leaving to drive her back to her hotel I ran back into the station to make sure I'd turned off the transmitter. We laughed, seeing how much it was like running back into the kitchen to check on the stove. We sat in my car for one hour and I told her my heartaches and she spoke of hers. Her child was then five years old. She talked like a woman friend—so different from the evening at Susan's.

WPFW was my life force and I spent too much time wining and dining poets, chasing them, transporting them. I have guilt about this but the girls were well. Ken was prospering as a realtor and, although he went to southern Maryland and I went north to DC, we'd meet in the middle, and the girls always had one of us. He supported us, and I was allowed to follow my dream because of this.

I feel bad about all the women/artists in the world who do not have a Ken to plug them into their purpose in life. My girls saw me as independent and a great role model, they tell me now; but that was only allowed because I had a roof over my head and the bills were paid, for after the first three years I was a volunteer at WPFW for 20 years. At the same time, during the WPFW interim, I did have other jobs that actually paid salaries. Although I wanted the careers, I cared less about earning money than following my passions. However, with the thought of colleges, even on a modest scale, money was needed for the girls.

When I left the WPFW station full time in 1978 to go to PBS, I still kept my weekly show, "The Poet and the Poem," appearing weekly on-air live, no matter where else I worked. It was a shadow life, a parallel universe, I was at WPFW every week. The wacky station where, in the beginning, we had to keep people from sleeping on the floor at night, where we forbade marijuana in the bathrooms, where tapes were erased if someone needed a blank one, where editing was done with scotch tape and scissors for years; and, where I met the great jazz and blue singers: Big Mama Thornton, Little Esther, Anthony Braxton, and Betty Carter, among others. They all came through the station in the early days. Life was a jazz paradise.

There's always trouble in paradise, life balancing out the way it does. I naturally went to the music clubs where our artists were appearing, and came home late, also becoming acculturated with the scene. So different from Oxon Hill where four girls were sleeping and Ken was brushing against flirtations never to blossom, but designed to make me take notice.

I wonder if it could have been otherwise. This kind of growth. Years of pain between Ken and me. I would say there were five years of what therapists call "a rough patch" (1977-82). Ken was handsome, dashing, seductively charming and he loved to entertain women in his business attire. I was living the life of Southside Chicago, and I knew more bluesmen than neighbors. It would not be until 1982 when I met the psychic Bryan Christopher, and he said, "You will never leave your husband. This is your commitment in life." At that point we said *ENOUGH! It is only the other each of us wants.* The escaping was over. And the real party began. We called it Marriage No. 8.

Of the multiple times that dramatic events happened on-air, I must recount my hour presenting Henry Taylor, Pulitzer Prize poet. The telephone lines were switched in the control room and everyone who buzzed outside to come into the station came in *over the air in the midst of our program.* Some people outdoors wanted cigarettes, some wanted in to work on production, some needed the restroom.

Henry, after being interrupted a few times, braided the calls *into his poetry* and it was spectacular. Instant art. A true creator.

The haphazard affairs of WPFW can only be explained in some incidents which exemplify 100 others. When the station was to move again from 7th and H Streets, NW, to Adams Morgan, the fashionable, multiethnic Tribeca of DC, I was called by a frantic program manager. My shelves of tapes were in the dumpster, and if I wanted them I'd better hurry to DC. We were living in West Virginia full time in 1988. Ken and I grabbed our coats, piled into the station wagon and drove down Route 70/270 into DC to back the car up to the loading dock and pull my programs out of the dumpster: poets laureate, the famous and near famous, the cherished, the blessed, the poets I had paid in flesh and blood to gather. We filled the station wagon and headed home.

I spent that summer in an unairconditioned garage, sitting on the floor to label and box about 500 tapes. These would be carried in that same car to the loading dock of George Washington University Library to unload what would be the beginning of the DC Literary Special Collections. "The Grace Cavalieri Papers" in the GWU Gelman Library now houses at least 1000 of my first shows, plus poetry books that I've reviewed and donated from my reviewing, all my writings, manuscripts and publications, etc.

We never would have initiated such a fine collection if we'd left those tapes on the radio station shelf to be discarded.

Yet more mishaps: A typical day in heartbreak hotel. I secured an interview with Hazrat Pier, the great Sufi mystic leader who was coming to DC, via Avideh Shashaani who was my precious friend and still is. She many times contributes to support my radio series. The Islam community in DC was listening and we promised—as this was a fund drive Special—that a donation to the station would provide a tape of the program with the great Mystic. I had the poor judgment to go home that night and leave the master tape. The next day someone haplessly erased it because he needed a blank tape for his own show.

I was sick with grief. Avideh, the spiritual person that she is, had me send the cassette Ken had made on the radio at home, and she personally duplicated it to satisfy the subscribers who'd ordered it.

From 1977-1997 I was an on-air volunteer at WPFW, even while working at PBS and NEH full time. From the year 1975 (before we went on-air) until 1978, I worked 12 hours a day for the station and ran all the arts shows. WPFW was the happiest time of my life. And it was the hardest time of my life.

In 1997 the series moved to the Library of Congress where, for the last 17 years, it's been engineered by Mike Turpin and sent out to public radio via NPR distribution and Pacifica Radio with the greatest skill.

≈

BIG MAMA THORNTON

Last time I saw her
she wasn't so big. Actually
she was downright skinny,
singing the final time
in Washington, D.C.

Backstage she drank a
quart of milk
mixed equal parts with
gin—
Seagrams, she told me.

Then she got the idea.
Could I contact the Seagrams
people and then she could
advertise for them and
they'd like her for
drinking a full quart a day—their gin.

I said no, I didn't
think so, and I didn't
think the milk people
would like the commercial so much
either. She still felt bad
about Elvis stealing "Hound Dog,"
The way he did, even though
she was much too much of a lady to say so.
Once she talked about it, long ago,
before she started milk with gin.

I guess the drink left a
sweet taste in her mouth.

— *Cuffed Frays,* Argonne House Press, 2001

35 ~

PBS 1978-1982

WORKING FOR A YEARLY HONORARIUM AT ANTIOCH, and then for three years at WPFW as a full-time volunteer began to bother me. It was all about my own self-fulfillment; but we had four daughters looking at colleges and even I had to look life straight in the eye. I believe I was a responsible person, but I had to follow the star trails first. I began to fill in my day from poetry and playwriting gigs with substitute teaching at John Hanson Junior High in Oxon Hill. It was suddenly polyester to my satin life. And I came home from that job gasping for breath and lying across the bed in shock. No creativity could balance the forces of unruly teens vs. a substitute teacher.

An engineer at WPFW, Ken DeWire, told me of an opening at corporate PBS for someone in Education. This was the office of national PBS scheduling and I was no longer in control of my senses. I was a dog with a bone. Forget the fact that I knew nothing about Television, I knew I was destined to use my educational fervor to the good.

I was interviewed by the Director of Children's Programming (Education) who coordinated all the PBS member stations with the instructional aspects of PBS' daily schedule. Linda was young, vivacious, and spiritually hip. She was the one who would eventually introduce me to psychic Bryan Christopher—a lifelong spiritual guide and friend. I did everything to hypnotize Linda, convincing her that my radio experience was essential to simulcast TV (an idea just beginning at that time). Although I didn't know how true it was, I knew I was being guided in that direction; and Ken DeWire had given me courage because anyone named "Ken" would be a caretaker, I figured. I didn't know that Linda was hiring an assistant as indentured servant, buddy, and loyal jack of all trades, who would wind up helping to cook for 100 guests at her home more than once.

I had walked out of a radio station with rats in the basement in northwest DC, into a palatial reception area in the L'Enfant Plaza Offices, southwest DC, with the luxurious L'Enfant Hotel restaurant across the street, where PBS employees were hurrying out to dine with producers and artists and fellow broadcasters.

Linda had come from Instructional TV (ITV) in California at a local PBS station and knew the field. I knew only what I saw on "Sesame Street." The PBS management saw Linda as an enemy who wanted to take over PBS for education while they had plans for it to be a fourth network—which indeed it is today. I was Assistant Director to the enemy; but with a secretary, office, expense account, and private parking. I could do this. I just needed a few designer suits.

The first day I sat in the board room with the other management staff and was introduced, and I don't know why I wore that plaid long sleeve blouse I used to wear while substitute teaching. I had tried to make my hair go up in a barrette, and some was falling down. When Chloe Aaron (VP) welcomed me (like the bubonic plague was let into the offices), I said, "I hope I can be of help." She sneered, "Oh I'm sure you will be *of help*." She had no use for instructional television and especially no use for one more staff to champion this. That was Day One.

Day Two: Linda was vivacious and smart but she was not a manager. I had no training at all. She came in and said, "Write a policy for PBS Education to send to all the Instructional TV program managers in all the stations and get me in touch with Jon Cecil."

I had no idea who or where he was, nor what the policy should be. She had handed me four huge three-ring notebooks of overall TV policies. I was a good enough writer who, when desperate, could turn verbiage via alchemy.

I used to teach my poetry students at Antioch to choose ten words and from that develop a story or poem. I leafed through the documents and extrapolated words and let language lead me to thought—whose thought it was I'll never know. It was good. I knew enough about education to make up for what I didn't know about broadcasting. The directors in stations should know the rest. And then I leafed through all the rolodexes until I found Jon Cecil. He would later be hired by Linda in some capacity that had to do with PBS videos.

That was the time of my menopause and I recall rashing up at every important meeting with PBS upper management. I would have to leave the room, the stress was so great, but I would not want to be anywhere else. I was able to develop programming with producers, and fly to NYC on Fridays. I helped develop and inaugurate the series "Reading Rainbow" and a host of other memorable children's series. I was in charge of the daytime schedule, which meant organizing series into timeslots and notifying stations, and I worked on the first closed captioning application in television history, because PBS, in education, was a pioneer. My education background was essential but my creativity was the catalyst.

PBS was high minded. No commercials. No mention of any product that may have perceived interest in the content. Example: no mention of cereal on children's shows, etc. Today it is the fourth network with all the accoutrements that make it so, commercials are paramount, however more tasteful they are than other networks.

I left my hippie life behind, a new wardrobe, with the help of Shelley who was managing the Limited Stores then—suits and high heels, and everything fine. Jewelry too. No more shorts and halters a la WPFW.

This was also the time when I snapped the ligament in my right leg playing tennis with Ken in a ferocious doubles match. That was painful, but I couldn't leave my precious job to have surgery so I stayed on crutches for six weeks. Linda was not deterred by the crutches, thankfully, and we steamed ahead.

Something happened in the dark recesses of executive thought at PBS and Linda was fired. She left her Georgetown home, her past lover, and went back to California to start over. She was always a fabulous cook. (Oxtail soup. We went all over town looking for an oxtail for her party, once, while I was on crutches.) She began making candy, designer chocolates, in her home in San Francisco and now has a huge cottage industry supplying hotels and gourmet shops.

I was thrilled to be Director by default, and naive to think they'd want me. In my new state of excitement I moved Mary Ellen Long's silkscreen art work, featuring children, into my new Director's office, hanging the walls, and rearranged the furniture to a more welcoming appearance. In a few months Linda popped in to visit, and was not happy. Also, PBS Management must have smiled at my new décor, knowing it was temporary.

A new Education Director was brought in from Texas and she was truly qualified, with a new assistant, also competent, working with the Instructional PBS ITV feed to schools. They were PhDs with years of TV instruction. I had the creative savvy to help put on new shows for broadcast. This was additional to the regular daytime programming, so I was still managing children's programming and the general broadcast schedule during the daytime feed to stations.

My work in poetry was well known by then and I was called into consultation with someone who had an idea for a prime time poetry program, "Voices and Visions." Bill Reed, a vice president of PBS, and overseer for Educational Television, called me in and thought it was a wonderful idea. PBS was committed to something new. All the producer had to do was find the funding. The forces of the universe are strange and unknown, but after PBS I went to the National Endowment for the Humanities (1982) where I would be able to shepherd funding for this 13-part series within the course of three years.

Due to protocol, the position of Director for Children's Programming, Linda's position, had to be posted. I could not inherit my dream position I now occupied. So I was my sparkling best. Wayne Godwin was Bill Reed's assistant, and everyday he sat with me while I taught him all I knew and all we'd accomplished during the preceding years. He loved sitting with me and seemed so encouraging and eager to hear about education that I thought I was auditioning for the part. I didn't know I was rehearsing Wayne for the part. He took over and I moved to a smaller office. I was still indispensable as I had the corporate knowledge by then, and they needed me. But Wayne was to be promoted again in six months and then, would "my position" be mine again?

PBS hired a man from commercial television for they wanted that expertise as PBS was moving toward Network status. Frank Allen Philpott was hired—nice enough person to bring in while I concealed a broken heart. I had to then teach him Public Television and we started all over again, training a man to do my job, which I was doing very well alone. But Frank Allen and I became friends. PBS Management still did not like any of us in Education but we had our own world and occupied it nicely. When Frank Allen got married for the second time some 20 years later, I wrote and read the poem for his wedding. So we were good friends and I can't blame him for taking the job he was offered.

Before Frank Allen had been offered the position, I attended a workshop on assertiveness training to attempt to win this job back and keep it. I needed to confront Bill Reed who was 6'4, many pounds of muscle, an ex-football player, and a glare-er.

The workshop taught that we needed a bottom line in negotiations; that we needed to have a line that could not be crossed. And in my mind, my line was that I would leave if I didn't get to be the Director of Children's Programming. So I sought a meeting with Bill, I wore a handsome grey pinstripe suit. Nothing could be more authoritative. And we talked and talked and talked and I finally came to "Well, then I guess I'll have to leave." I did not expect Bill to say, "Well, we're certainly going to miss you Grace." I shouted *WAIT WAIT I CHANGED MY MIND.* All my training went out the window.

Also, let me get rid of guilt by one final confession. I never touched "substances" at Antioch, and was eventually introduced to marijuana in WPFW's foray to the underworld of jazz. I knew cocaine was rampant at Mount Vernon College. Coexisting with PBS, I was teaching a course on radio at Mount Vernon College in DC and I knew the students were giving drugs to each other for graduation presents. I was shocked. My own daughters didn't smoke or drink and disdained "altered states." They were comfortable with the traditional and conventional, it is true. And I loved them for it.

Our secretary Patricia, through my affiliations with musicians coming through town, was living the life, and offered to have me and the PBS accountant, Ellen, come to the jazz club, Blues Alley, and try some cocaine. I only had $7 in my purse so I only got a little sniff on the inside of her long fingernail. We all three were crammed into a stall in the ladies' room. I didn't see why people went to jail for this. It just numbed my upper gums and made my heart race. I would never try it again! I rushed home, and lay in bed all night in fright of having a heart attack. I kept envisioning the newspaper: "Navy Captain's wife. Mother of four children dies of an overdose in her Oxon Hill home after partying at Blues Alley."

There, I feel better now.

The final scaffold for me would fall when PBS was to be restructured. This was the media industry. Personnel were replaced every six months. I never saw an industry like it. Vice President Chloe Aaron would go to California's station KPFA. Bill Reed and Wayne Godwin were to go manage regional TV stations. And children's programming would be incorporated into Arts and Humanities. The A&H, then run by Suzanne Weill, would be taken over by new Head, Catherine Wyler, the daughter of famed Hollywood director William Wyler. I was to be her consultant and teach her children's programming. Suzanne would go west to be Robert Redford's associate at Sundance.

Cathy Wyler was lovely and beautiful. She flew in from California and, next to her, I felt as if I had on the original plaid blouse I wore to substitute-teach. But I didn't. I had a grey silk gabardine and I was to lunch with Cathy to ease the transition. She told me that when her father died her left side was paralyzed and that it was an emotional response. I liked her very much, and admired her ambitions as a filmmaker. But I was to be her consultant and teach her my job. This I did with cheerful aplomb for several months.

Note: In 2012 Catherine Wyler appeared at a poetry reading I was giving in DC at the Italian Ambassador's residence, hosted by Mrs. Laura Denise Bosigniero. We want to renew our friendship now. She's just completed a documentary film about her famous filmmaker father.

Back to my waning star at PBS. One day I faced my disappointment. This had been my dream job for five years—creative, lucrative, highly stimulating, and of service. Communication with ideals, and a contribution to television. But it was over. I was now merely a Consultant, rather than a Director. I went home one afternoon. The girls were still in school, Ken was at work running a brokerage for Long and Foster.

The house was quiet and still, and I threw myself on the bed to fall into a long deep sleep. My mother appeared to me so perfectly I could see every pore on her body. This would be 26 years after her untimely death. Psychics have told me that it took her that time to gather the gravity to come to me completely formed. And she was a complete version of herself. The odd thing was she was so beautiful but I saw no concern in her face, no empathy. She was just there. Total. Serene. Complete.

Later I learned that the dead have no feelings as we do. Feelings are human crystals we carry within us when in human form. The dead have care, but no concern. I was so used to seeing worry for me in my mother's face, and now there was just placid beauty. The most incredible part of all, she—who had no education beyond high school—was wearing on her head a mortar board with a professor's tassel. Nothing could be more ridiculous than for her to arrive, after all these years, wearing that head piece. She wore clothing, a dress, perfectly normal clothing as I remember. But with that mortar board set slant on her head!? It was off-putting.

She stayed long enough for me to absorb every facet of her as she stood quite close to me. She was not a bubble or a vision that burst. She stayed there, standing. But then she left and I sat upright. What did it mean? What could it possible mean?

The next day I was to find out. I was in my office when I received a call from Marion Blakey, a Director from the National Endowment for the Humanities, a government organization that funded scholarly projects. I had worked alongside that agency various times seeking funding for children's programming and we had great rapport. Blakey said the Endowment was setting up an initiative for funding children's programming in media and she would like me to be the Director to develop that mechanism.

Thanks, Mother, for the message. Or for doing this for me, for, from the depths of my despair and broken heart, a golden apple was handed to me—via the other world perhaps—or messaged through from behind "the veil," but I turned from forlorn to ecstatic in ten seconds. I could continue this work I loved. Now, instead of broadcasting, I could make it possible for other producers to develop programming of value for children in the humanities, for radio and television. I was on the right path. Thank you dear Nettie. My faithful mother.

I would miss PBS. I worked with many celebrities and had the fun of being hand-in-hand with the creators of Nickelodeon. That channel would compete with us but we were friendly advocates of children's programming. In my view, all good material was welcome to drown out the cartoons staining children's minds. At PBS we lobbied Congress for an Endowment for Children's Television; as the Annenberg studies showed cartoon violence, bigotry, ageism and sexism were making an indentation on all minds, not only children's. We had worked with the Annenberg Foundation and universities to move our cause forward.

Among the good luck I had with this creative, productive, spectacular workplace was to become personal friends with "Mr. Rogers." We met at a PBS conference and spent much time together. At dinner one night, we were eating and talking about poetry when suddenly there was a line of children forming at our table. Fred Rogers stopped eating and spoke to every one of them, never finishing his meal at all.

I sent him a poetry book of mine with some bold poems—excellent for the poetry community, not for sainted Mr. Rogers or my bosses, also unwelcoming recipients. Where was my radar? Fred Rogers wrote sweet notes for all subsequent books.

Here's the contribution Fred Rogers made to our culture and civilization. Before his appearance on local Pittsburgh TV, the nation was watching the program "Captain Kangaroo," with Mr. Green Jeans and an arsenal of people in costumes. My children grew up on these and they were wholesome entertainment. But Fred Rogers was the first person in the history of broadcasting that appeared before children as a person, unadorned, talking about feelings. A genuine person. He *demonstrated* authenticity instead of talking about it.

I had long thought because of him we could turn children's TV into a more socially proactive tool, even speaking to abused children to let them know someone was aware of their plight. I never got to do that. It was probably unrealistic in that PBS was headed toward commercials with all those corporation-pleasing limitations.

Instructional TV (ITV) comes close to changing conditions for children, but those programs are focused directly for classroom content, and little emotional healing for children has yet been addressed in media.

I learned while at PBS that "the hardware drives the software" and since the future is going to provide the equipment, perhaps we can someday provide higher levels of consciousness for children.

36 ~
National Endowment for the Humanities

I HAD LEFT FIVE YEARS OF THE MOST PERFECT JOB AT PBS. I'd gone from being a hippie at WPFW to become an executive in public television, with designer suits, trips to New York, exciting producers and their creative ideas, a good salary, a secretary and YET the realization that nothing mattered more than being with Ken and the girls. This shift in jobs was also turning a corner in my personal life to the better, back to what I had been brought to earth to do—a marriage of commitment to Ken.

The building NEH occupied was an old established gray building at 15th and L Streets, Northwest. There are two 15th Streets in DC. I started WPFW with a group of raggedy, brilliant entrepreneurs on one 15th Street; and now on another 15th Street I would walk in to be among the most scholarly, erudite, serious individuals, perhaps in the entire city of high-toned people. It was the Shoreham Building and, fortunately, downstairs was a coffee and doughnut shop to give me courage as I walked into the sober halls of learning. Gone were the plush carpets, the fancy reception room, and the glitter of media. Here people were silent and thoughtful. All action was inward. All progress, mental.

I have always said: I've never entered a group that wanted me to come in nor one that wanted me to leave. Whether it was group therapy, or a classroom, or the board room of National Broadcasting. The workplace is nothing but a laboratory—the place where we work out our differences. We were all brought here with a career that was to serve our life's journey, but so many people with clashing journeys will always create conflict.

Some people thought I was an outlander, others thought I was a star coming from the world of popular culture. Some people were jealous that an outsider was brought in to be a Director of a program, to newly establish a children's funding mechanism when surely there could be others as qualified within the existing organization. Don Gibson was the first one to see how alone I was and he offered friendly hellos, and they were valued; his wife, Dai Sil Kim Gibson, at first thought I was a flaky poet, but later became my best friend. I was a flaky poet. I was also enormously competent, hard-working, knowledgeable and caring. Also, no one knew the field of children's media better than I did. I had that under my belt now, whereas when I entered PBS, I certainly had started on shaky ground.

Today Don is gone. He had become the Chair of the National Endowment for the Humanities. I composed a poem for his memorial in 2011, I saw Dai Sil almost 30 years after our first meeting— love and sisterhood, now, instead of work colleagues. My small press (Forest Woods Media Productions) has published Don's Memoirs and one of Dai Sil's books, which I edited.

In NEH, as we struggled in the rooms of intellectual debate, I was the only one without a PhD and some days I felt that was used against me, but no one else knew broadcasting or children's media or programming for children, and I also had the entire public television network in those fields at my reach. I had made no enemies in the world of broadcasting.

My first job at NEH was to write a strategy for how government funds could be used to better children's television and radio. Surely this was the next step in a road laid out for me that I couldn't have imagined. All that I loved about creativity for children could be applied in this difficult workplace.

My boss, Marion Blakey, was an iron maiden and I admired her. I think because my own mother was positive, loving, and non-judgmental, it allowed me to work with the most difficult and impossible women. I was drawn to magnetic, forceful, demanding women bosses, and to fellow artists who were impossible to get along with. They interested me. I could get along with them without fear of criticism.

At NEH, I operated somewhere in the vicinity of other people's rejection, disdain, competition, and admiration. It was a weird place to be. My first "panel" would be comprised of the biggest and best from the field of children's television and radio producers. They were called together to judge the first competition to find new projects for children's media. It was a stellar group. I brought in the producing "stars" of public television whose programs were being watched by the people I was working for and with. Of course many producers who worked at PBS with me to develop their children's shows were now lining up at the door to get funding for those very shows.

Along the way someone would be hired in my domain and would remain a friend to this day. Candace Katz has a PhD from Harvard in literature, a law degree from George Washington University and 30 years later our press would publish her two books on "Schaeffer Brown," detective stories. By that time she would also have gotten a detective license and a license to carry a gun. She was five feet tall, blonde, adorable and modest. She's recently retired in 2013 as the Deputy Director of the President's Commission on Arts and Humanities. This very week, March 2014, she's a member of a new committee I'm chairing—a new National Book award—the Marfield Award (under the aegis of the DC Arts Club). The threads have not broken from those old relationships although struggle was at the original core.

The National Endowment for the Humanities moved offices to the beautiful old vintage post office at 11th and Pennsylvania Avenue. It was called the "The Pavilion" and was converted to restaurants and tourist treats below, while on the fifth floor we worked in silence. Since that time the building has changed hands to a "Trump building" with a different purpose.

One of my humiliations was that someone, out of jealousy, said that I could not write well for the National Council books. We had to formulate written decisions for funding programs in a Council Book, for the annual meetings of the National Council of the

Endowment. Because I was a known poet and still broadcasting my show, someone who didn't like my jurisdiction spread the rumor that poets could not write linear thought. Let me say, a group psychosis formed where everything I wrote was slashed, analyzed, torn apart, and disparaged. This was bull shit. But it was also not helpful to someone vulnerable, without a PhD. It has brought me great pleasure that, 30 years later, the same people now read, and praise, my columns and articles on literature.

I repeat: The workplace is a laboratory for the human spirit that allows us to overcome the obstacles we need to overcome in order to find out what we really want. The "wall" people put up for us is a perfect way to find what we truly want on the other side. It focuses. Desire is made better by the wall. I never said it was easy.

≈

UPON DREAMING A PROPOSITION
THAT ALL TRUTH IS A CONVERSION
FROM NEGATIVE TO POSITIVE

This may not sound like
Much to you
Who know Coleridge's waking
To write the secret of the
Universe only to find
In the morning that his scribbles
Said the world smelled like oil
But my theorem is different and
as if touched by God, I,
At night
Saw that all
Which exists comes through a
Transmutation
From dark and can you name one
 Principle to which this does not
Somehow apply? Say, for instance
"All people are good," a
Result from the contrast
With "bad," so I take that back
Scratch it
We're stuck with dualistic thought
And logic here which is not
At all what I meant to dream
I saw, I tell you, for one
Moment what all truth
Was about, as if suddenly I knew the
Specific weight of water and
Hot with it rushed to work

To ask if anyone had thought
Of it first
It reminded me of a piece of silk
I used to love as a child
And naturally they all
Said YES
"Streams of people had,"
One damn thing after another
I thought, but I am not talking of
Hegel and others studying
Something as ordinary as
Good and evil
Dark and light
Please listen, I am telling
You that something touched
Me while I slept at night
Beyond "A or not A" kind of
Thinking. Beyond that. It was
Told to me
Like a kiss
In my sleep
And I am right at this moment
Crying
With the thought of it and how
Happy I was
Burning with it waking up on that most
Ordinary Summer morning of my life.

—*Bliss*, Hillmunn Roberts Publishing Co., 1986.

≈

I was soon to find out about the politics of money. Money at PBS was sparkly fairy dust that created Roman candles of programming and Joy. Money at NEH was filled with the dust of academia, yet the currency of NEH funding made brilliant television and radio. The Endowment funded many scholarly programs and our job was to make radio and television that held the NEH government money answerable to the mission of "the humanities."

I worked under two ideologues as Directors: Bill Bennett, a rampant Republican who used philosophy to suit his purposes, and Lynn Cheney whose husband would become Vice President of the United States and who was quite unfair in judging the media as too progressive. I'll always believe Bennett and Cheney answered to high-powered Republicans.

My single run-in with Bennett was not to be about politics. My first major project as Director of NEH Children's Media Department was a one-hour PBS Special, "Big Bird at the Metropolitan Museum." Sesame Street, of course, was well known, via PBS, and so the idea of having Big Bird locked in the museum to explore the treasures was a magnificent idea. The producers were top-notch and the content was undeniably good.

Children's shows had not been aired prime time before on PBS and it got good numbers. Bennett upbraided us because he thought the content wasn't "measurable" for preschoolers and early-age children. One of the criteria for judging humanities content was not to be "intuitive." We know children absorb information but we were being scored because it was seen as too soft as information. This would be an awakening for me, and a test to my resistance.

After that, the first few years were more fulfilling. Children's Media was folded into a larger program department and I was absorbed as one of the many media program officers. I was a GS13, a fairly good government rate, so designated because of my former senior position at PBS. It was my great pleasure that "Voices and Visions," the first primetime series on poetry, was hatched at PBS, where I had helped birth it. This would once again come across my desk. Everyone at NEH was in favor of it and, since its inception, the series has made broadcast history.

To obtain an NEH award, a project director submitted many applications before several panels of judges. For producers to gain planning funds, there's first a "planning" application. If funded, the applicant had to accomplish planning tasks for a year, in order to return to apply for "scripts" for the next phase of the program. If the scripts passed panel, project directors could embark upon production. This could take several years and indeed it took my entire five years at the Endowment to see "Voices and Visions" created.

What a pleasure to work with the material from our greatest poets—the luminaries who created the canon of literature that we depend on today. This series made broadcast history, is now on videos, has been shown in classrooms, is in libraries, and will live forever as scholarly and entertaining programming.

Now that Ken and I were back on the same path and had felt the isolation of separate worlds, we wanted each other more than we wanted our careers. The fulfillment of a partnership is only as good as the success of each partner. Ken now knew that real estate, cutthroat, was not in his nature; and some of the seductions of the commercial world were not to his liking. He wanted his art and he needed a studio.

This was the time that our West Virginia home would be completed, every weekend, and Ken would eventually build a separate sculpture studio which was bigger than the house. Our five acres were to become his place of work three days out of the week, and my place of rest and writing every weekend.

At the time I joined NEH, we sold our home in Oxon Hill, Maryland, where we had raised our daughters through elementary, junior high school, and high school. Shelley and Colleen had gone to college in Florida; Colleen then finished her degree at American University. Cindy, after attending St. Mary's College of Maryland, was raising a two-year-old. Angel was at the University of Maryland becoming an architect. Ken and I moved to a condo on 16th Street with a view of the White House, where I could walk to the old post office, "the Pavilion," to work at NEH every day.

I used to take the S3 bus down 16th street on days I didn't run to NEH at 11th and Pennsylvania. I would always look out the window at people having breakfast in the swank hotels, I envied the silver teapots on the table. So naturally Ken said "Let's go."

We sat in the window so the people on the S3 bus could watch ME and my silver teapot, but when they charged $25 for an egg, Ken had to talk me down. Oh we were truly two people out of O. Henry's "Gift of the Magi," stuffing each other's pockets with dreams fulfilled.

During my five-year tenure at NEH, my daughters would evolve—Angel would come home weekends to the DC condo; Colleen was now at IBM working; Shelley would figure as a major regional manager at The Limited store chain. Cindy was working and living in Virginia and transitioning with her baby Rachel.

Weekends found me holding up ceiling beams in the living room while Ken hammered out our West Virginia "healing place." I still ache with the thought of carrying in that fireplace with Ken, and managing its massive structure up the steps. I've never forgotten the terror of being on a step ladder holding glass windows that were slipping from my grip. I do not like physical work. But Ken created a dream house that gleamed with his mastery of wood and glass and brick. Later we would build a loft upstairs where I would work in the trees with the birds, that would be in 1988 when I left NEH to write full time.

However, throughout my NEH years, three days a week Ken was away in West Virginia. I reviewed plays and when Angel came home from college we would go to theaters together, and art would sweep away any sadness from that day. I treasure those times and the restaurants where we would go. I'd see each of the girls every week somewhere, thankfully, although they had a mother who was cursed with the gift of work.

Friday nights Ken would pick me up and take me to West Virginia, and there I would write and write and write. Sunday nights we returned to DC to WPFW, and I would be on the radio Sunday nights with "The Poet and The Poem." Ken went back to West Virginia on Mondays and he did good work there.

In fact Ken, along with sculpting, built an airplane from scratch, and flew it. That took him three years. I never wanted to move to West Virginia, but it was Ken's turn now. He deserved it after holding my poetry life in his bare hands for so long.

I left NEH in 1988 almost at the end of five years—a few months short of the term which would allow a pension (a whopping $2,600 a year). A mistake. If I'd opted for social security my pension would have been doubled. Another wow.

The first day I was in West Virginia with the knowledge that I could be with Ken every moment, I remember walking up the hill to the mailbox and feeling the sun on my shoulders and loving the forest and birds and everything West Virginian.

To complete my five year tenure at NEH, I commuted by MARC train to DC three days a week. Ken drove me to downtown Martinsburg (a town that needs a fresh coat of paint), a 30-minute drive, and I got the dawn train. That was almost a two-hour ride before I got to Washington. Then a cab from Union Station in DC to The Pavilion at 11th and Pennsylvania. At night, reverse the process and I was commuting 5 hours a day.

I loved to read on the train and looked forward to that reading time, so one day I was alarmed when someone sat next to me who couldn't read. She was blind, and would doubtless want to chat to fill time. I squirmed inside but it turned out to be the most wonderful surprising hour of the decade. In the time span of one and a half hours, my traveling partner told me something she'd never told anyone, and I told her a secret no one else knew. Then she got off the train and left, never to be seen again, and both of us were changed forever.

≈

HELPMATES

I remember the train ride with the blind lady
where we each found out something about ourselves,
She asked me what beautiful means and if she
                              looked that way.
I told her about the child who died in my arms
with an article stuck in her throat.
                    It was the word "I"
I told her about the baby who disappeared from the back
seat of the car where she has been playing –
When I picked her up I couldn't wipe the dirt from the face.
I told about the twins who were borrowed and how I feared
the new owners would take them and keep them in playpens
without their favorite snacks.

Where do the babies go when they grow?
Like trains out of the tracks they come
but where do they go?
She replied that at my age why did it matter.
She asked how people know what *beautiful* means.
            I told her that because of pain
in losing my children
my eyebrows grew together forming a beard.
She said if she didn't see it, it didn't happen
and to consider it a passing fancy.

— *Migrations*, Vision Library Publications, 1995

37 ~

West Virginia

I REPEAT, I NEVER WANTED TO MOVE TO WEST VIRGIN-IA. I'd been in therapy talking about it, dreading, fearing isolation, afraid of leaving my energy center of Washington, DC. I liked our beautiful little cabin to visit weekends where our marriage occurred while the children were in college, leaving our Maryland house empty. In West Virginia at first we would cook on a Coleman stove, building the house on weekends, living under the rafters.

We bought just a wooden frame structure without insulation. One square room. No bathroom. No kitchen. And this was in 1975, when my father drove with us to see this place. It would be five years before he would die at age 80. He had loved the Poconos and when he saw the laurels growing around the house and the greenery on five acres he said, "If you don't buy this, I will."

My father knew a bargain. He never made a mistake when it came to money. We knew this was a good investment—only one and a half hours from Washington, surrounded with forest, graced by a brook and surprised by every species of bird including pileated woodpeckers.

I would move there full time in 1988 and stay until 2002. But I never left Washington in my heart and sometimes we would commute to DC three times in one week for poetry and family events. As Ken said, we burned out route 70. By the time we left in 2002 and moved to Annapolis to be near our daughter, Angel, and her newborn twins, our West Virginia house had become a mansion of beauty. Angel, our architect, had designed a tower to connect the lower level with my writing loft. In this tower Ken's sculpture would shine. The house in West Virginia was turned from a one-roomer to a multilevel creation—the house that Ken built. It was called "the healing place" by all who visited.

I can't believe this, but the first year we lived there we had weekend guests from Washington *every weekend of the year.* Each of our children would come with their families, and every artist and poet in DC loved a weekend away in the country. After the beginning deluge, we surely had visitors at least one weekend of every month for the 14 years we were there full time.

An unforgettable, near tragic experience occurred when the poet Barbara Goldberg visited for dinner with her soon-to-be-husband, Israel's poet, Moshe Dor. He didn't know there was tuna in the lasagna and I never thought to say so. Thank God he happened to ask the recipe because it looked good to him. When he heard he became alarmed because of his fish allergy. He was verging on the first bite. I quickly grabbed a steak from the freezer and silently thanked God I didn't kill Israel's top poet before dessert.

For the first year I remained quiet in the countryside and did my writing. I liked being anonymous. I liked walking up the gravel road every day back and forth, a mile. I liked running the country roads and Ken would follow me in the car very slowly to keep my safety. I did not like the surroundings once we got away from our enclave, because there were Confederate flags and cars with guns on the racks. A depressed economy makes for depressed people and the consciousness was very low.

However, after I was there awhile my cover was blown as someone wrote about my poetry for the local newspaper. From then on it was all fun because I met Jeanne Mozier, astrologer, writer, entrepreneur who had come to Berkeley Springs 30 years ago and changed it from a mud puddle to a Mecca of artists, musicians, actors and festivals.

Jeanne also managed to get funding for a defunct building that had once housed bulk ice within cork walls. Over the years she transformed this to theater, workshops, teaching centers for the arts, and a hub of galleries and resources in the arts. She remains today one of my dearest friends and a guiding light for the arts in West Virginia where she was once an arts commissioner, travel writer, and still is the light of the state.

I embarked upon a West Virginia career identity and had my play "Pinecrest Rest Haven" produced at the Ice House, from which it then went to New York. J.W. Rowe would direct this and I still find him unsurpassed as a director all these years later. I had many wonderful poetry readings there and Ken enjoyed beautiful recognition for his sculpture, including many showings. He was heralded throughout the state for his innovation and genius. This was a good time for our arts.

I received grants from the WV Arts and Humanities Council, which allowed me to produce good radio and arts commentaries on their public station. The funding also supported my playwriting, and a book of poems which was "New and Selected." When our home was still a shack in 1979 I wrote *Body Fluids* in a broken arm chair with a wooden board as a desk. That place was transformed into a magnificent dwelling by 1998, when I wrote the *Pinecrest Rest Haven* poems, and *Heart on a Leash,* plus dozens and dozens of published poems and a lot of theater writing.

My writer's loft at the top of the house, surrounded by birds and trees, was where I had a gigantic Atari reel-to-reel tape machine I'd bought from NPR. Here I would take my twelve-inch tapes from my Sunday shows on WPFW and edit them to send nationally or to keep in-house at the station for emergency days, if I couldn't make the station for my Sunday night show. Snow and ice were prevalent in West Virginia, although we valiantly sloshed to DC every chance we could. We started watching the weather with apprehension on Thursdays, calculating the danger through the winter mountains for my "live" program on Sundays.

The most wonderful part of my time there was working with the literacy program. West Virginia had 20 percent illiteracy which is one fifth of the population. I was on the state board and Ken and I traveled the state to hear people's stories and to record their triumphs when they learned to read. Even if one achieved a third grade reading level, this allowed a person to escape a house of violence or sexual abuse, find a job, get a driver's license, and pick out groceries at the store by reading a label. Nothing touched me more deeply than to speak to these people who struggled with the greatest disadvantage anyone could bear: disenfranchisement, scorn, shame.

I produced a documentary for radio, weaving all their stories together and it's heart moving and heart lifting at the same time. Parts of the state of WV where we stayed were not pretty. One motel Ken and I stayed in actually had brown water and leaves coming out of the spigots. I don't deride the state. It's economically a poor state but there is a dignity and intellectual fervor and activity; and certainly a place of natural beauty.

We dined with Governor Gasper Caperton and his wife, Rachel Worby, at the Governor's mansion. I had performed in Charleston a piece called "Migrations" from my book of poems of that title. The work had been illustrated with photographs by Mary Ellen Long. I talked about how I worked 'in consciousness' with my illustrator, Mary Ellen, although she lived in Colorado and I was on the East Coast. After dinner at the Mansion the governor took me aside and put his arm around me and said, "One day, would you talk to me about how a person can maintain a relationship across the miles?" I knew he spoke of his wife, Rachel, living and working as an orchestra conductor in Pittsburgh. They had trouble and she even made a scene at the dinner table that night, decrying life in West Virginia. I was touched by Gasper Caperton's sincerity and vulnerability and I'll never forget the concern on his face. If we think art doesn't make a difference, I think of this moment where a high-ranking official was moved by poetry, and my story of artists who could reach each other where a married couple could not.

My happiest times were when Cindy and her younger daughter Elizabeth, and Shelley and Colleen would visit Hedgesville. Angel, Danny, and their twin boys enjoyed the sun deck, the outdoor shower and a world not imagined in their urban life.

When twin grandsons Sean and Joe were two years of age, we could no longer stand life without them and we put the house up for sale to go to Annapolis to be close to Angel, Dan and the boys. Cindy, Colleen and Shelley were but 45 minutes away in each direction. We'd been commuting to Annapolis twice a week, to be close at hand and help Angel, and it was a two hour trip each way so it made sense to give in to a world by the water, to the beautiful people, to the boats, and to be close to our Navy community.

Ken was not mercenary. In fact, when it came to money he sold low and bought high. I always teased him about this. He was wise and practical, not parsimonious, and always thought of the other person before himself. So when we put the house on the market and the realtor said that according to the zip code we should go for $92,000, I stepped in. This was a three-level, gorgeous house with solid oak inside, made by artists, encased in glass inviting the outdoors into the indoors. I said, "Advertise in the *Washington Post* and if we don't get a buyer I'll agree with the realtor's paltry assessment."

At this time, as if a warning by Edgar Allen Poe, a northern rat took residence inside the wall of the kitchen. We had the exterminators use poison gas shot into the wall, and every new method of extinction. We hope we got him, but if not, we were leaving someone a pet.

The person who answered the ad was a retired artist from the *Washington Post* with motorcycles that would occupy the studio where Ken's art was made. We got $120,000 for this mansion and would go to Annapolis searching, to find only twelve houses on the market and all of them over $300,000. Year 2002.

On August 31 our buyer would move into our house in West Virginia and we had no place to go.

Many readers don't believe in the divine. Many readers do not believe in providence. Most people do not believe in prayer. They give it up after church service. And we certainly don't believe in magic upon demand. But that very week something happened that can only be called other-worldly.

Ken's mother's fifth husband, Hank, was someone we loved very much and someone who had made her very happy—beyond her previous wealthy husbands. Hank showed her a life of substance and true authenticity in a relationship. He had oil land in New York State. When Hank died he left the property to Harriette; when she died she left it to Ken. It had been in litigation because of a property manager dispute. This very week when we had no place to go, and not enough money to get there, $100,000 came our way from this land that would finally be sold.

We moved to a house we found on Glade Court in old Eastport, one mile from the water in every direction, between the post office and the library, and a walk away from the most beautiful parkland, Quiet Waters Park. The Eastport bridge we traveled into "downtown" overlooked a line of yachts summering in Annapolis, the sailing boat capital of the nation and, as bumper stickers claimed, 'a drinking town with a boating problem.' Whereas West Virginia was solitude and beauty, this was party time, with its quaint Amsterdam-like streets filled with young midshipmen from the Academy, and there was a fabulous swimming pool at the Academy where we could swim daily.

I still have tremendous bonds with West Virginia artists: Hilda Eiber, the great potter and sculptor; my dear poet friends, Ethan Fisher (recently gone) and his wife Uschi; Sonia James, my former poetry student, now a world-class poet. Ken and I would return every July so we could attend the Contemporary American Theater Festival that we saw born there in 1987. I attended /reviewed theater there this year, 2014, with my friend Ann Bracken. It was CATF's 24th year, and its second season without Ken. Everywhere we visited, in every restaurant, Ken was there. West Virginia was his place. Ken and I only moved there because of the land which gave him space to create his great art. I do not regret it.

≈

A POSTSCRIPT OF NOTE: Ken's time in West Virginia allowed him time to make sculptures for clients all over the country. We traveled to Texas, Florida, New York, among other places;

but during the last three years of our life in Hedgesville, Ken turned his time to designing, creating, and building an airplane. This had always been his wish and now the sculptor's studio was draped in white cloth, illuminated with special flood lighting. Ken bought a single engine kit plane but imagined and invented everything else, including the electrical system.

Ken had a rocket attached to the plane so that if any mishap occurred the parachute would lower the entire plane gently to the ground. My daughter called one day, and I said, "I have to run. UPS is delivering a rocket. She said, "You're having a rocket delivered by UPS? No one has parents like mine!"

Ken flew his creation. Imagine building a work of art you trust enough to place your life in it. Sadly, when we decided to move, we had to sell the plane. A dentist from Connecticut bought it, and promptly ran it out of fuel, crashing the magnificent aircraft. The doctor never pushed the button to parachute the plane. He walked away. But Ken's finest work of art was broken.

≈

Poem celebrating West Virginia Governor
Gasper Caperton's Inauguration:

LETTER

If you ask what brings us here,
staring out of our lives

like animals in high grass,
I'd say it was what we had in common

with the other—the hum of a song we
believe in which can't be heard,

the sound of our own
luminous bodies rising just behind the hill,

the dream of a light which won't go out,
and a story we're never finished with.

We talk of things we cannot comprehend
so that you'll know about

the inner and the outer world which are the same.
Someone has to be with us in this,

and if you are, then,
you know us best. And I mean all of us,

the deer who leaves his marks behind him
in the snow, the red fox moving through the woods.

The same stream in them is in us too
although we are the chosen ones who speak.

Please tell me what you think cannot be sold
and I will say that's all there is:

the pain in our lives
…the thoughts we have…

We bring these small seeds.
Do what you can with them.

What is found in this beleaguered
and beautiful land is what we write of.

38 ~
Judy's Murder

MY SISTER JUDY AND I HAD NEVER BEEN CLOSE EVEN IN CHILDHOOD. Two years older than me, she was a curly haired, blue-eyed, protégé to become tops in her class and the nation. I truly believe she had something of genius and could learn a language in three weeks, and learn to play the piano instantly. She was remote, she was icy, and if she had needs one didn't see them except in her excessive weight as a young person. She was the kind of person who had one friend to my many. I went to the senior prom; she did not. I was told that the difference between an introvert and extrovert is how they transmit information. I was gregarious, Judy turned inward.

But she had something I wanted. My father. I truly believe Judy is the only woman he ever loved. And they bonded in a circle of personal reverence from which my mother and I were excluded but were chosen to serve.

I regret that I didn't know more when I was young so that I could cross that bridge to her to ease the anger and resentment inside me; instead, I turned away to the crowds of people—seeking a sister in every woman, and to this day I'm gratified with so many good ones.

Judy went away to college at New Jersey College for women—the female equivalent of Rutgers, then an all-male college. I visited her once there for the weekend and it was extremely awkward. We tried to be sisters; and now I know that we came through the same mother but were not of the same mother. Surely we both wanted each other and had no tools whatsoever to communicate this.

Judy met a man at college and married him. Frank Volk came from a wealthy family and was to go to Harvard architecture school and live a life of aesthetics. He was not a centered person, he was not kind, and in fact saw me as Judy's nemesis and, at the end of all, was my father's Executor and stole my estate.

That is the background. But why was Judy murdered? This still seems impossible. This is the person who was an exemplary teacher of English, who had been offered, while in high school, a scholarship to the Sorbonne, which my father elected she not accept. She was number one in the country's national Coca-Cola science exam. She bent the bell curve at Trenton High so far that people felt like leaving the first day of class when they saw her enter the room. She had three sweet children and lived in a mansion on the water; and she lived a quiet life, and an intellectual one.

Frank was a philanderer, not a well person emotionally, and had many affairs to which Judy turned a blind eye. I think she was very sheltered her whole life and truly lived in an ivory tower. But one day Frank said he'd like a divorce unless she would live with him and his lover in a ménage a trois. I remember her housekeeper telling me Judy threw a jar of olives across the floor, and that was her answer.

Remember, Judy had no experience in dating. She had one boy in high school who liked her very much. He was valedictorian; as she would have been, except she was a girl—tops in the class of 1000 graduates. Her beau was Jewish and his parents called our parents and said it was best if he married a Jewish girl, so there would be no sense in their dating.

To my knowledge that was her total dating experience before Frank. She was devoted to Frank. And he made her feel like a woman. And I think she felt the same love from my father, that she was an adored child, and sacrosanct.

When I think about the murder, I feel things that could have gone differently. It was about an attitude Judy could not help—an imperious bearing which was rejecting. It could've been a defense and now I do believe it was, but for the person at the other end, it was infuriating.

Frank and his lover moved to North Dakota. Judy dated a few men in the Michigan area and for the first time had a social life. She lost a lot of weight and was very pretty with beautiful sparkling blue eyes and a dignity that looked like royalty. But she was really a babe in the woods about life.

A man came to Michigan who owned a cement company and was also a part-time resident in Florida. He was Italian and reminded Judy of my father in his gait and speech. She fell in love. She thought he was divorced. Remember she had no known knowledge of the world, no abrasion to rub against to find the sharpness of clarity. If a man loved her, like my father or like Frank, then that was her divine right. She apparently didn't question or analyze the attention.

I'll never recover from the fact that Judy didn't see warning signs. She knew this man's wife was dogging him—and she believed he was divorced, not separated, from a woman who was clinically insane—but why wasn't Judy afraid? So protected by her father's emotional umbrella of safety, she did not know fear. Our father had died four years prior to this event or he would have certainly protected her. Judy sold her house in Michigan and moved to Florida.

I find it very touching that Judy had previously done so little alone that she took several days driving to Florida, and kept a notebook of each thing she spent, each sandwich she bought, and each tank of gas. It was as if it were a Girl Scout trip and she would be accountable. Well, she certainly would be.

Once in Florida, this man moved her into one of his townhouses in a large community he owned. The "ex-wife" appeared. Judy thought she was crazy and ignored her. She stalked Judy. I would have called the police and I advised Judy to do this. Judy felt inviolate. Why? Because Judy was "superior" to this woman? Once on the golf course Judy and her lover were affronted by his ex-wife and had her removed by security. Once on his yacht the ex-wife showed up and threw Judy's clothes overboard and they had the trespasser removed by security. Here is where I would have felt terrified. Here is where Judy felt nothing but disdain, and that would be fatal. Had she insight or humility, or reality, she would have seen red flags, but Judy was above this and felt *This Man Was Hers*, through entitlement and privilege and history.

This sounds harsh, but this is the only way I can understand what would drive this predator to murder when she could have been assuaged. Yes she was crazy. Yes she was desperate; but why not kill her husband? Why Judy?

The Wednesday before her death Judy called me and apologized for the way her husband Frank had treated me and illegally absconded with my inheritance from my father. Ken and I never wanted to go to court. This was still family. We didn't have the stomach for it and it's not a good thing emotionally or any other way. I loved Judy's children and still do, and the money was not worth maiming them.

In this phone call, Judy said Frank was a crook and 'we should have punished him.' She said of herself, "I was weak and dependent and should have stopped him." In her 53 years she'd never opened up to me, reached out to me, shown love to me, although I know it must have been there. I was so grateful for this call. The past was wiped away in an instant.

That week she would be dead.

She finally had the life she always wanted, so she thought, resting, reading, playing tennis during the day. Playing tennis *at the same time every day.* And so it was at 11 o'clock in the morning that she came home in her tennis outfit and someone was waiting for her, someone who had keys to the townhouse because the intruder had access to its owner. The police say Judy put her hand up in front of her face; and one only does that if she knows the intruder, because the gesture instinctively is made to stop the person. The gunshot went through the hand into the jugular vein in Judy's neck. So, to look as if it were robbery, the murderer pulled some jewelry into a brown paper bag and left. The murderer had her grown son with her.

The neighbor's child next door was outside riding a bicycle and saw "a grandmother" coming out of Judy's house holding a brown bag and said "the grandmother was crying."

Ken and I were in West Virginia when my Uncle Freddie's call came, saying Judy was dead. It is easier to have someone lost from a rich life's union than to have someone die who lived side-by-side with you, but never heart-to-heart.

I wish so much it had been different. Somehow my father kept the rivalry going as if it were some game that would have a good ending. My sweet mother never knew how to settle discord and so she went to church Novenas instead. As a consequence I only had my sister's true heart in that one phone call days before she left forever.

Judy was living in Sarasota, Florida, and I did what I always did under duress. I called Bryan Christopher, the psychic. I then called the Sarasota police and asked if they were interested in speaking with the psychic, and they were. Bryan had never been to Florida and yet he told police precisely about a bridge over water, and the foot of that bridge, where they would find a brown bag filled with jewelry and a gun. It was certainly there and the wife was arrested.

To my horror, the Sarasota police—or the newspaper—termed Judy his mistress. This was the most painful part to me because if she were, she certainly didn't know it. And her innocence was her downfall. I wrote an extensive letter to the editor citing her accomplishments, her standing in the community in Michigan, her background, her fine career as a teacher. It was never published.

Would you believe that this woman with intent to kill and who committed first-degree murder received only three years in prison? She is out now, released. Bryan Christopher said not to fret about that. She has the darkest karma of any human being he'd ever seen and her own background was one of abuse and torture as a child in Italy. I often wonder what her teenage son suffered psychologically from watching his mother murder his father's love. Judy's lover called us and I was sympathetic with him. Maybe I had the same blind spots as Judy did, but I felt his grief.

Ken and I drove to Michigan with my daughter Colleen for the funeral services. Frank, Judy's ex-husband, was there and her children. I realized my estate financed the banquet. Well spent, I thought.

Today Judy's daughter Claire is like my own daughter. Judy's granddaughter that she never saw, Grace Anne, is, by lucky default, my treasured granddaughter.

This was 1984. This was the year of three significant deaths for me. Of course the major one was Judy; there was also Devy who committed suicide, and Greg Millard, my dear friend who started WP FW and who died of AIDS.

My sister died at age 53. My mother had died at age 53. When I reached 54 I said, "Thank you."

≈

JUDY AND ME

From time to time
someone would ask
how many children were
in our family.
It was always the same,
I'd snap (ready) "just
one – me – and a broken
umbrella handle."
My father always laughed
at that entangled wit,
hardly funny now
it seems, my sister as
an object.
Did description amuse him?
Or the use of skewed language?
What did it mean?
What did it say?
Why such a thought?
How is it
my father smiled at
the idea of a handle
so crippled?
What if the umbrella
could have opened?

39 ~
Ken's Swimming Career

W<small>HEN</small> K<small>EN WAS</small> <small>SWIMMING FOR</small> L<small>EHIGH</small> U<small>NIVERSITY</small>, <small>AND</small> I <small>WAS STILL IN HIGH SCHOOL</small>, <small>WE USED TO FOLLOW HIM TO ALL THE</small> <small>REGIONAL EVENTS</small> and humiliate him by yelling, *"Come on Kenny-baby."* In the next 60 years how many pools would I sit by, how many grassy slopes would I sit on, waiting for his next event, how many swimming meets did I time with a stop watch in a funky college in West Virginia or in a grand set of multiple pools in the Hall of Fame, Fort Lauderdale?

From 1982 to 2008, from April through summer, we were on the road while Ken competed in local, regional and national events. I didn't want to write about this because it's so hard for me to relive those sunny times, the excitement it brought him, the discipline he showed, the passion for excellence. These things still live in my heart. We have plastic boxes filled with hundreds and hundreds of medals. I once wanted to find a room to mount them from floor to ceiling, but the room would not be large enough.

The framed picture of Ken I have now on the kitchen table is him winning the national breaststroke gold medal 2008. I look at his extended arms, I remember snapping the picture as his red swim cap emerged from the water, every muscle rippling like a young man. He was toned; he was fit. He was an athlete.

I never understood how swimmers could talk about one swimming pool as compared to another, hour after hour, but then I finally understood the detail of performance—how the side of the pool could affect your time, how the lane lines mattered. Ken bought every new kind of racing suit; he shaved his body; he wanted to win. And since desire is what drove Ken, and desire is what keeps us living, when Ken no longer felt fit to win he slowly lost interest. His rotator cuff needed surgery. His neck had painful arthritis. Yet he swam every day for recreation until his death in 2013.

Ken had a rich interior life, and every sculptor loves to live in the bunker of his soul—lost in time—looking for a miniscule change by which he can transform some object. The energy Ken had was so magnificent there was nothing to do but pull it through his body physically, and swimming was something that only those people who can be alone can master. I can only swim 30 minutes without getting bored. Ken would amuse himself longer than that by turning his finger a certain way to get better traction, or holding his arm closer to his head in the back stroke. He was always improving his stroke. These tiny cogs in the wheels of the body, that don't interest me, interested a man who could spend hours dripping molten bronze on the heads of steel nails to create his sculptured works.

We only knew Ken had a heart problem when he had to stop a race once in Fort Lauderdale. Shelley and I were there and we were alarmed, but he was not. However, stress tests did show a problem. After triple bypass surgery, and what he called "a modified engine," in six months' time he swam better than ever.

Just as poetry events became the rubric for our partying, Ken's swimming meets all over the country were reason for our travel. I can recall every hotel, motel, timeshare, restaurant, blue Martini and meal.

The DC Masters Swim Team was his mainstay, and he was a loyal participant over the years. That team came to his funeral at Arlington. He wanted that. I had his pictures displayed at the funeral luncheon at the Officers' Club, when he made "Masters All American" with that special group.

It's very hard for to write about Ken's swim career. I watched a scrawny boy of 128 pounds at Lehigh, eating bananas and drinking beer because the coach instructed him to gain weight. I watched as Ken raced against the clock his whole life, and up until the end, he won.

His time at age 70 along with his team mates:

1. Steve Hogan 3:32.26
2. Art Smith 3:37.35
3. Ken Flynn 3:39.38
4. Dick Cheadle 3:48.80
5. Jill Hoover 3:53.46
6. Dale McGinley 4:05.95
7. Stephen Hogan .... DNF
8. Carlyle Carpenter .... DQ (illegal swimsuit)

Thanksgiving Weekend, 2014, I was searching for an old swim bag to pack for an Ocean City weekend with my family, and I found a crumpled red paper from a swim meet:

D.C MASTERS. National Short Course Championships. Fort Lauderdale.

Age 75. Kenneth Flynn	Seed Times
Men 50 Breast	40:40
Men 100 Fly	1:39:30
Men 50 Freestyle	33:90
Men 200 Breast	3:34:80
Men 50 Fly	43:10
Men 100 Breast	1:35:30

In 2008 Ken became National Champion Gold Medal Winner for 200 Breast Stroke. Age 78.

FIXATION

Every day I go to the Naval Academy pool where Ken and I swam
    together

And I plunge under the water and pretend Ken's in the lane next
    to me

And I know he moves two laps for every one of mine

And I pretend we're in the Key West pool and he's in the next lane

Where it is shining ribbons off the bottom

And I'll get out first and go along the white stone path

Through the hibiscus past palms by the water

Into the shower room where I always slip on the floor

Then I'll be waiting for him outside at the picnic table watching
    the scuba divers

And he'll come out and we'll wonder where to eat lunch maybe go
    into town

For conch soup but I have writing to do and he needs to rest after
    such a workout

But whatever happens we need to be up at 6:12 because tonight

That's sunset time and everyone claps on the pier and we're never
    late

With a martini for him and a tequila for me in plastic cups

Then a sound breaks my trance and I realize that it's coming from
    my own throat

Like the clacking the cat makes when watching the birds outside

It's caught like a squeal under water a squeezed sob and I climb
    out

And I rush past midshipmen who're laughing and telling their
    jokes and complaints

And I take a fast shower with the sound still coming from the back
    of my throat

Hoping no one has heard me as I dress and move out fast already
    planning when I can

Return.

—*The Man Who Got Away,* New Academia/Scarith, 2014

40 ~
My Poetry Books

IN 1975 WHEN I LEFT TEACHING AT ANTIOCH, JOHN McNALLY AND I STARTED THE WASHINGTON WRITERS' PUBLISHING HOUSE, and we published three inaugural chapbooks. Mine was called *Why I Cannot Take a Lover*. It still holds up today—about love, domesticity and, like everything else I write, about *relationships*, and their many guises.

There is a poem there called "The Abortion" and I've always wondered about my children seeing that, even though in 1975 I was a liberated Catholic; I completely believed in abortion for women. In my case, it was a medical necessity, life threatening perhaps in those days when RH negative blood formed toxemia, there was no reversal. Still, it always bothered me that the poem was out in the uneven world without context. It was repeatedly published in progressive journals.

As I seem to be saying, there is this divide between respectability and inner freedom, and I did pretty well with that balance throughout my marriage and motherhood but I learned one thing since then: You cannot send poems out into the world and expect anyone to love them more than you love them. I'm much happier today because I don't print or publish anything unless I can take some pride in a gift to the world. There's nothing but this anyway.

However, I still like that little Washington Writers' Publishing House chapbook. John had a wonderful graphics artist, Jim True, who did beautiful covers and so was launched the Washington Writers' Publishing House, from an old building near Dupont Circle, Washington, DC.

One year later Ken and I were going to West Virginia weekends to build a house and I would sit in an old lounge chair that previous owners had left. Ken made me a writing board to go across my lap—just a plank of wood—and I would write on that while he hammered away. It was terrific because I could just write without interruption—we didn't have a stove or a bathroom those first years so we would always go around the corner to the little diner, and the little mom-and-pop store, so I didn't even have to worry about cooking. In this haven I wrote *Body Fluids* almost in one stretch.

My practice is to collect imagery so, since I always have scraps of paper and notebooks, writing a book of poetry is sitting down and knitting it all together; and that's the fun of it. This is playful because it's like stringing beads together—I already had the thoughts and images and, of course, since I was the source of it (or at least the one who brought it all through) all the particles belonged to me, were of me, and somehow it was, and still is, great fun to shift phrases around to get a poem.

Body Fluids was a groundbreaking book. Each poem was about the circus and all the characters in the circus, the hurtful things they did to each other and about gender oppression and subjugation.

When I think that I really gave this book to the vice president of PBS, my boss! Why did I think that poetry that was cutting edge— so that you could hurt your fingers on the paper—would really suit people who would never read a poem in the first place? The book, however, stands up, strong and capable. The subject reflects the time of turmoil, cultural revolution and discord.

I was in a lot of emotional pain around the time of *Body Fluids*. The 1970s. Feminism was strident. A lot of injustices were coming to the surface about women. I myself was transitioning from teaching at Antioch College, to what I did not know. There was a lot of cultural argumentation, and also I think much of the emotion I felt was left from childhood disappointments.

When I read these poems I'm really surprised all over again, because they are extremely strong, and extremely painful. They are also said to be very funny. If ever we want to know where humor comes from, it's just failed tragedy. The readers who appreciated my work in 1976 were other poets who had a tremendous license and latitude, and commonality.

In 1979, *Swan Research* came out. The Word Works produced this. Deirdra Baldwin had birthed Word Works at that time, and for the last 40 years Karren Alenier and Jim Beall have navigated this elegant small press. In the poetry community, this book was admired and still is.

Bliss was published by John Roberts with his Hillman Roberts Publishing Company. John was an interesting guy, loved literature and was a bouncer in Baltimore in the stripper section. He'd printed a couple of my plays after they won playwriting contests. John had a small printing venture but he was in constant demand in Baltimore (carried a gun) and the physical book that was produced is not great. The production had faulty covers and I remembered finding out John was in his garage, night after night, trying to rectify things, personally gluing on the perfect binding, fixing the printer's problems. It's a very good book because it's unafraid. The long poem "Bliss" occupies one half of the book; and is an exegesis on the profound deaths I'd experienced in 1984: Greg Millard, my WPFW station manager; Devy Bendit, my anorexic friend who suicided; and my sister Judy who was murdered.

All in one, *Bliss* was one long lyric. I remember sitting on a chaise lounge in in our condo Pensacola—the girls were at the beach—and from then on Ken always joked about the fact that any time I saw a chaise lounge I could write a book. I wrote nonstop for a week, with interruptions for meals and walks, but pretty much this is the way I spent my vacations, now that I look back on it. I'm completely unashamed about being such an obsessor.

In 1986, I was working full time at the National Endowment for the Humanities and was a busy program officer with a lot of "drudge" writing to do, I certainly couldn't find much poetry time other than these vacations we took with the family. The girls of high school and college-age were self-sufficient. Ken loved solitude. So in Pensacola, until cocktail time, and family dinners, I wrote *Bliss*. The title poem is a weird connection of disparate images, but altogether it tells a powerful story of incongruity, disjunction, and loss.

In 1990, I wrote a book I was very happy with: *Trenton*, is now in its third printing and people like it very much. *Trenton* is autobiographical and talks about growing up as an Italian-American child. I believe I was finally learning to say what I wanted to say, but it took this fifth book to get there.

Herman Ward had been my professor at New Jersey College in Trenton 40 years prior, but we'd always kept in touch and he was certainly the flame that kept burning in the temple of poetry for all who studied with him.

Ward started a small press in the village where he lived near Princeton, New Jersey, thus the name Belle Mead Press. He liked the manuscript and made a few recommendations. He suggested two poetry title changes, but he was generally enthusiastic. My artist daughter, Cindy, had designed a cover for *Body Fluids* which was an imaginative drawing of a clown. I'd done the photograph for the cover of *Bliss* (trees from our back deck in West Virginia), now, Cindy would design the cover for *Trenton*. It is wonderful. We obtained a photograph from the New Jersey historical archives of the Roebling Steel Mill which was the biggest manufacturing entity in the city when I was growing up. There are silver stars coming out of the smoke stacks on a white cover, a lovely book. No matter what press published me, for 20 years, it was agreed that Cindy would be the cover artist.

In 1995, I was hungry to work with Mary Ellen Long again because we made fabulous works of art. We just jived—with her colors and my words. We produced silk screens for galleries all over the country. Mary Ellen's photography was heart-fracturingly beautiful. For some reason, I was going through a throwback of feeling about mothering because I had been such a career seeker, so ambitious, always working, always having very high level jobs of national stature, or else spending my time in the armpits of hippiedom teaching poetry. I was feeling all that.

The book we made was *Migrations*. Its introduction states: "Migrations is about the journey we all share. /Although the metaphor is motherhood, the subject/ is loss. The poems speak of mother and child. We/are each the mother, each the child."

Migrations came from anguish, and is poetry of grief in that the only way the children go is away—the only road there is. So, as usual, I never keep anything inside and I assembled poems which are said to be really wonderful poems, all spelunking. Going to the deepest part. Not your usual Mother's Day gift. Mary Ellen's photography with antique dolls, broken and lost, was the perfect component to change this book on a richter scale of beautiful to a visual masterwork. I'm not surprised that the book wasn't a best seller, but I still maintain that it is one-of-a-kind and I am very proud of that combination of words and photographs.

An aside on this, my composer Vickie Rudow created the music to bring in the light that was very badly needed to the words. Her music transformed a lot of joy from the darkness of loss.

In 1998 came my favorite book of all. *Pinecrest Rest Haven.* Ken and I, above all else, were playful together. We joked about our relationship. In a way we'd play "dress ups" metaphorically. Most of the subjects in all my plays and poems are about Ken and me. He'd been with me for 200 lifetimes and I imagined us going to an old folks' home where Mr. and Mrs. P would not remember who the other person was, but would fall in love and hate again and again every day. It was a winner. These are prose poems and I love every one of them, even the clunky ones. I can't say they're lyrical, I can't say they're immortal, I just know they're terrific. They are, as one critic said, champagne and rum, because it is all of our relationships in marriage; how we changed some of the dangers into hilarity as part of our day. This became a play that I wrote of that same title, and was wonderfully done in New York although it wasn't premiered until after 9/11—the date it was scheduled to open.

I had back surgery the year that the Pinecrest poems came out, 1998, and I was recuperating while writing. Once again I can remember sitting up in bed with the board across my lap. By this time Ken had converted the plank to a tiny desk that was portable. A breakfast-tray writing table. This year I had two books come out at once. A lovely girl, Laura Qa, had Red Dragon Press in Alexandria, Virginia. I don't know whether it was the Percocet or being able to stay in bed, but I managed to put together a bunch of sharp poems that are half sparkling and that chapbook pleases me. *Heart On A Leash.*

In 1999, Ron Baker's Argonne Hotel Press put out *Sit Down Says Love*, a chapbook I like. The same press, in 2001, produced *Cuffed Frays*. Originally "Cuffed Frays" was a play that had won an award in West Virginia. The play reading was in a Charleston library, and I'm fond of it as the piece has a rich history. I produced it first as a radio play. A very good Baltimore director, Michael Makarovich, helped me get top-of-the-line actors. But I have a bad memory associated with the recording, because the only studio that he could find at this time was on the top floor of an autistic children's hospital.

The radio play was premiered in my living room in Oxon Hill, Maryland, after a five-course dinner. I laugh when I remember Baltimore critics and classicists and theater elite, probably armored by alcohol, huddled about a small audio recorder. After that, I converted "Cuffed Frays" from radio to a stage play and then to a book-length poem. There's nothing like plundering your own work to keep it going.

In 2002, I put a few poems together and Pudding House Press produced a chapbook called *Greatest Hits*—a handful of favorite poems written from 1975 to 2000, poems I liked.

41 ~
My Poetry Books, Continued

In 2004 I fulfilled a life's dream that had been burning since 1974–1975.

When I was in graduate school at the University of Maryland in the English department studying 18th century literature, I discovered Mary Wollstonecraft. At that time there were only about four or five books written about her—today she's the toast of literature. I couldn't believe how this woman had gone unnoticed since the 18th century except by a small percentage of scholars. Her daughter was Mary Shelley, who wrote *Frankenstein* and was the only person every reader knew, Mary Wollstonecraft Shelley; few knew her mother. Mary Wollstonecraft was the first woman to write a book in English that was serious. I fell in love with her.

For 25 years I carried Mary inside of me while she incubated and while she simmered, and finally she would stay inside no longer. I did some more research at home and found the first draft of a play which I'd written in 1975; and I found some audiotapes about the people who surrounded her, Edmund Burke, conservative philosopher (her nemesis) plus the Revolutionary War notables, the French Revolutionary writers as well. She was writing politics and she was the only woman to stand shoulder-to-shoulder with male writers.

It interested me that Mary Wollstonecraft was also a person who was quite a flirt and quite an active sexual being and so she had this terrific conflict about whether or not she wanted to be opposed to a man or whether she wanted to seduce him. I wrote the poems in her voice. That means that all the facts are true but I imagined all the words that she would have said.

Jean Emerson, who'd gone to Antioch College in the early 70s, and who I mentored for her Masters Degree, was enthusiastic about premiering this historical woman. She and husband Bill had a small press, Jacaranda Press, in San Jose, California. The finished book has a beautiful cover, produced by a California photographer, and from this book came my play, "Hyena in Petticoats." This is truly a play I value, I think the only play extant on Mary Wollstonecraft.

The book *What I Would Do For Love* has just been reprinted now in 2014. In 2013, my Italian translator and best friend Sabina Pascarelli translated the work to Italian. *Cosa farei per amore.* This is now a gorgeous rendition of Mary Wollstonecraft in Italian and it will live longer than I do. Sabine is a noted poet and therefore every vowel has been attended to in both languages. The premiere reading was held at the Italian Ambassador's residence in 2013. Laura Denise Bosigniero, the Ambassador's wife, hosted to a full auditorium, with translucent chairs from Milan, lighted from above by Murano chandeliers.

Flash back: In 2006 I assembled many new poems that needed a home and submitted them to Bordighera Press, winning their national book award. The award allowed $1000 to pay for a translator. Maria Enrico was a friend from the early 1970s and was now a professor of Italian in New York, so I enlisted her services to translate the poems and we had a great reading at the City University of New York. Ken, along with my granddaughter Rachel, went with me. Cindy painted the image for the cover of *Water on the Sun* and it's quite beautiful. It's a watercolor, and the yellows and blues are exactly what I wanted.

My next five books were all from one publishing house, Casa Menendez, and I had a great relationship with this cutting edge publisher. Dan Murano was the cover photographer for all these books.

I'd seen a lot of activity online from the creative and imaginative DiDi Menendez, who at that time was living in Miami. She was an innovative magazine editor, curator, and producer. Her taste was beyond Andy Warhol and Mary Cassatt. Didi's sense of style and grit and sparkle attracted me very much. I don't remember when I first submitted poetry to her but she took a liking to some of my poems and she was producing several things at that time. One was *Ocho*, which means 'eight' in Spanish, a literary magazine, a compendium of poems. I edited one edition inviting Poets Laureate for my edition. Still in publication is DiDi's fine *MiPOesias*, which is a magazine with radio-on-line, as well. *MiPOesias*, in Spanish, means 'my poetry' and it's still is in existence, a stunning magazine. I was a columnist for the radio series and Didi Menendez allowed my programs and commentaries on poets "streaming" online in a series called On Location. Another Menendez magazine, print and digital, is *Poets&Artists*—the major showcase for American painters and poets. I contribute poems to these editions regularly. DiDi is the empress of 21st century poetry and art; she is a great benefactor.

Along with all of her other projects, she produced my books: In 2008, *Anna Nicole: Poems*; in 2010, two books: *Navy Wife* and *Sounds Like Something I Would Say*; in 2011, *Millie's Sunshine Tiki Villas*; in 2012 it was *Gotta Go Now*, a beautiful little chapbook with elegies for my lost friends. Not sad, actually upbeat.

After writing about Mary Wollstonecraft, there was nowhere to go with women's history but Anna Nicole Smith. Everyone thought Anna Nicole was a train wreck because she was a showgirl without any talent. She was beautiful but untamable; she was a public clown made to take drugs and then behave mindlessly on a reality show.

Anna was a gorgeous woman and had been a model for Guess Jeans. I was struck with her vulnerability when I saw her in the hospital with her new baby, Dannielyn, and I had to write about her. I saw her sweet side and I wrote a book of poems—not in her voice, but about her—and most people say the book has changed their opinions of her entirely.

I found, within Anna, the child that was killing the mother, and I was passionately connected to her. In fact, Bryan Christopher was in my sunroom one day and he said he heard her talking to me when I was writing. I had dreams where she held me against her with energy that was radiant. I believe she was grateful to me for showing another dimension to her life and revealing the broken and beautiful cut glass person that was inside of her. I still love all of those poems.

Navy Wife was another important book to me. In 1950, I'd been given a blue book called the *Navy Wife's Handbook*, the way officers' wives were supposed to behave. It was successful because it included how one was supposed to hang a chandelier, what kind of cocktail shakers should be brought on travel and how you should wear your skirt (not above your knee). My favorite tip is to pack a candlelabra because temporary quarters may not have one. It was very 1950. I was telling my friend Laura Orem this, and she promptly found the old book on eBay and bought the book for me; I had a wonderful time rereading it, and Ken and I would laugh so hard about the way a wife must address an enlisted person. You were supposed to say, "I say there, Blue Jacket," if you wished to address one at all, because it was a class system back then.

Upon reading this vintage book with its absurd behavior standards, I realized how different my real life experiences were as a Navy wife; so I took portions of the old-fashioned book and juxtaposed them with the real story. All the pieces arc not pure poetry because they are anecdotes in response to arch directives. It was lots of fun and filled with truth I'd never told before.

Navy life was so difficult. I'd been left with children alone, and there were frightening times where I had to never be sick or falter; never show my fear; and I always lived in the concern that my husband would not return. I wrote some of these life sketches and held them up against the superficiality of the ancient principles that we were supposed to live by as 'officers wives'—how to give a cocktail party, how to treat the servants—not reality. *Navy Wife* is a large chapbook. It should be circulated. It should be marketed. It should be read; but right now remains a hostess gift that I give to my friends. (Navy Wives were told to give hostess gifts, remember.)

That same year, 2008, Casa Menendez published *Sounds Like Something I Would Say* and the most wonderful thing about this is the cover with Dan Murano's photograph. He captured Ken in his triumphant sculpture "Sister Mary Corita." This book is very important to me because I have Ken's sculpture with me on the book; and because the title poem is about my first date with Ken at age 15.

In the 1980s when I was living in West Virginia I wrote a novel called *Millie's Sunshine Tiki Villas* about old people in Florida in an 'old-age resort' where the women were chasing the men, and writing memoirs, and having craft shows. It was satire but as a novel it just never got anywhere—I'm just not as comfortable with prose as I am with poetry. So it seemed natural, in 2011, to transform Millie to a poetry novella, a more energetic short form. I was able to take each episode and make it a prose poem so that it became a series that tells the same story as the novel, but more succinctly and with much more compression. It's one of my favorite books. Dan Murano did a photo cover of palms in brilliant greens and yellows.

In 2012, a chapbook *Gotta Go Now*. Once again, my genius Dan Murano did a memorable cover of my swirling around in a gypsy skirt that he had photographed at the launching of (Sabine's and) my cookbook.

In 2013, *Cosa farei per amore* came out, an Italian translation by poet Sabine Pascarelli of my *What I Would Do for Love,* Mary Wollstonecraft's book. Mary is now international.

Two new poetry books came out in 2014: one from Bordighera Press, *The Mandate of Heaven*, about my Italian childhood; and the other from NewAcademia/Scarith, *The Man Who Got Away*, a year's worth of poetry about the death of Ken.

I've never submitted a manuscript to a major publishing house; I think because I'm basically a poetry guerrilla, and anarchist, or believe the Big Houses are conglomerates. Many of my poems are published in major anthologies by dominant presses, yet my poetry 'small press' publications rise like cream; and I'm content in that respectful community.

≈

For a list of Grace Cavalieri poetry publications see the APPENDIX TO CHAPTER FORTY-ONE, page 277.

42 ~
St. Mary's College of Maryland

St. Mary's College might as well be back water Mississippi or that's what it felt like on my first visit, 1977. Cindy was a sophomore there, an art major, and the professor who reached in and calmed her life was a poetry professor, Michael Glaser. When I visited, I fell in love with the college. Here's a place that's an oasis of greenery surrounded by history. It's where our first settlers arrived, and unfortunately an area where black slavery was prominent. It was history with a liberal college at its center and at the heart of it was Michael Glaser who, despite whatever academic politics came and went, kept the human spirit alive. And so he did with my daughter.

Michael and I hit it off right away. He knew my radio program. He listened to my poets on WPFW. We sat until three o'clock in the morning talking about poetry and I felt validated. I had left Antioch's faculty just two years before and was still animated with the thrill of reaching young people. Michael was, and always will be, about the same thing. He had an annual Poetry Festival where he invited poets, at first from Washington and then from all over the nation, to come for a weekend every May, which was nothing less than a bacchanal of life and language. The workshops offered four credits, undergraduate or graduate; and for two consecutive weeks, 12 hours a day, potential poets realized their greatest dreams by immersing themselves into reading, writing, discussing, and creating, in an informal, safe world.

I was Associate Director for this, taking leave from whatever 'real' job I had for the month of May, every May, for 28 years. I don't think there's a poetry experience in the country that can equal what Michael Glaser imagined and created.

The students that I met are friends still. It was freedom with and within structure. And every ripple of imagination saw reason to emerge and manifest. That was during the weekdays. On the weekends came professional poets from Washington and further.

In 1998, my embarrassing moment happened when I was readying myself to go to the first class of the first week of the first session of the first poetry festival of the year. I had driven down from West Virginia and carried a box of books to WPFW on my way down, and I remember having a pain in my back because of the weight of the books. The next morning I was dressed, and ready to enter the great realm of meeting new students, when I fell to the ground and couldn't move. The campus phone was within crawling distance but my purse was upstairs with the necessary information to get dialing help.

I was crawling along the floor when Maggie, a beautiful student, happened to come by to walk me to class—instead she called the ambulance. This would be the first year I'd miss teaching at St. Mary's. I had a herniated disc and lay in excruciating pain in St. Mary's Hospital. My husband made the two-and-a-half-hour trip immediately. They tied me to a board of some sort so I couldn't move, and put me in the back of his car. A friend had to come down with him later and pick up my car. That was the only year I missed the ebullient entry to the secret garden, the party of the soul.

Other than that, every May was St. Mary's College. Lucille Clifton, the celebrated African-American poet who would win the National Book Award, came to the campus—enriching, broadening, deepening everyone's experience.

She stayed until retirement and I believe the college was put on the map because of her presence—although I'm not sure what to say about celebrity, because the college should have been on the map just because of Michael Glaser and the great work he was producing. However, brilliance never hurts. Intelligence never fails.

Humanity always wins. So working with Lucille was enlightening and fun.

I had some hard life lessons there. Antioch College had been my playground and there I could develop whatever courses I wanted. But there wasn't as much freedom at St. Mary's because many people there were jockeying for a personal 'purchase' in the college; it was not a world insulated from competition. Although poetry was its own haven, it was really not valued by everyone in the academic world, and within the poetry world there are always people who wish for some aggrandizement, also.

The poets who came for the weekend were all poets I knew because Michael allowed me to help him invite the poets; and so it was family time. Dear Michael, on top of everything, would go out and personally purchase all the food for the weekend parties; the poetry readings were embellished with his gourmet touch.

I find it difficult to talk about the past in writing all of this, I guess simply because it is the past.

Michael Glaser went on to become a Poet Laureate of Maryland and took his gifts into the classrooms of the state. Lucille Clifton had been Poet Laureate of Maryland early on.

The fiction workshops were presented by Wayne Karlin, marvelous novelist, who'd been an 18-year-old helicopter machine gunner in Vietnam. He's spent the last 40 years rectifying this by visiting Vietnam, building playgrounds and schools and publishing Vietnamese writers, especially North Vietnamese who were his enemies. He has personally dedicated his life to building bridges, and repairing the ones Americans had bombed.

I don't think this type of poetry education exists anymore, because the 70s, 80s, and 90s had not yet succumbed to technology when I was there. That human interaction without interference from the outside world was a precious cocoon of creativity.

≈

TAROT CARDS X: WHEEL OF FORTUNE

for Michael Glaser

Alone in my backyard –
my daughters were gone and
even the rain
kept the flowers
from needing me.

The cats
could not be comforted
so they were put outside.

This is why
I sidestepped my own life
putting on a large scarf
the color of pink and yellow
streaming across the sky.

And I came here to see you

To share the puzzle
of how love comes to us
unevenly, inescapably.

How it births… but does
not sustain us,
found in small places
when you reached up
from a dream holding

what is floating in the night
above your head...
coming down from the heavens –
that love. Well my breath stops
with the wonder of it.

This gave me a map
 of my own time and
brought me here –
my heart strapped
to my back
like a peddler,
a refugee from Poland or Russia
a peasant singing in the road
a merchant with something to sell
clanking and calling out
with spoons and cups rattling –

Calling: Here I Am
I Am Here
to tell you what I love
by what I write. Here
I am again
stumbling down the road
like an old Jew
complaining of my happiness.

—*Poems: New & Selected,* Vision Library, 1994

43 ~
Vivian Adelberg Rudow

WE CALL HER VICKIE. When Alice Houstle headed the theater department at the College of Notre Dame in Baltimore, Alice accepted my play "Best of Friends" for its premiere. She suggested that I link up with a composer she knew who would be wonderful for the soundtrack.

Vickie and I were both very much suburban mothers and progressive passionate artists at the same time. We each made dinner at six o'clock, took care of the children, and gave dinner parties. Her husband David was, and is still, a well-known tax lawyer in Baltimore; and my husband was, at that time, a Navy Captain. We had a similar rubric for our lives in that we maintained the armature of middle-class predictability but yet we were both avant-garde. We were artists.

It was thrilling to be with Vickie because she thought like no one else. I say composers have round brains because in communicating with them I keep feeling I'm falling off. She would visit my home in Oxon Hill, Maryland, and I would drive to her home in Baltimore.

In 1975 we premiered the play "Best of Friends" with a wonderful production that's not been equaled since. Alice Houstle used lithe undergraduate students to play the two young girls who spin the play around them.

When Vickie did the sound for this, we sat in her home and she played mournful train whistles. There were screams, there were cries, there were beautiful, ominous, haunting sounds, all created by Vickie's technology. She'd gotten her MA from the prestigious Peabody School of Music and was a 21st century composer in the 20th century. I remember hearing an imaginative piece where she played a cash register backwards to make the sounds she wanted. My play was about danger and loss. She captured that, and when I asked her how she could do it she told me she heard the music in her head. That would be horrible for my thinking as a writer, if I constantly heard words in my head every minute. But I'm sure it balances the life of a musician.

When she moved to a house in Roland Park, Baltimore, I loved to take a day off from work, whether I was at PBS or NEH, and sit in her big music room with the grand piano, a room alive with clutter: compositions, books, and technical wonderments to make it all come together.

Vickie's little boy, Lenny, was asleep upstairs along with his brothers when we were working on the play. The sounds made him wake up screaming because they were so emotionally penetrating. I regret this. We had no idea how effective we were. Lenny's a man of 48 now who still remembers those nights in his childhood.

When Devy Bendit committed suicide, all Baltimore knew about it, especially the Jewish community where Devy's mother was prominent. Vickie wanted to memorialize Devy in music and had the idea of a one-woman opera telling her tale.

The usual procedure in collaboration is for the writer to write words first and for the musician to accommodate music to the words. There was never that choice for us because Vickie is a very strong personality and I tend to be more dependent when I collaborate. So Vickie wrote the music first and I had to paraphrase the words to the notes. It was a great experience for me because I really didn't read music beyond the fifth-grade level and I just had to listen to each note and phrase the meanings to what I heard. The notes on the page were less important to my imagination than what I heard.

I can remember sitting up in my loft in West Virginia writing words to one of our songs and going over the music 100 times before I felt I could approach it. This was a degree of difficulty I've not equaled since, and I'm glad I did it—just because it really *could not be done.* Just because it's impossible doesn't mean we can't do it. All of our songs were beautifully melodic and lyrical and sometimes a little bit too much so, I think, for the current audience. But in the 80s the songs were well received, and still are. I believe Vickie's work will last.

Each of our songs was played at each of Vickie's sons' weddings; and one was sung at Cindy's wedding. These were sung by mezzo-sopranos and sopranos. I never could hear the words in the music clearly enough for my liking, but then again there's the writer's complaint. I just wish that the singers would have slowed down or something. I willed love to my words so I wanted more of my words. Naturally.

Richard Wilbur, the great poet, once said to me that in writing for opera he had to remember that simple words worked best, and that you had to think about the vowels for the soprano who had to hold her note; and I'm very glad he didn't tell me that before I wrote all these things because I would've never been able to do it at all.

Ken and I socialized with Vickie and David. They came to our house sometimes, but our lives were very productive, and they had whole communities they belonged to, as we did.

Where we came together, Vickie and I, was in the great stream of consciousness where you create something out of nothing. Where you have disparate ideas which come together into a unified vision. Where there is a likeness of spirit and consciousness, where your ideas blend with compassion for the other.

We had sensitive discussions sometimes because Vickie was deeply hurt by anti-Semitism and was offended by images that appear to be Christian. I remember having angels in one piece and it bothered Vickie, but then I showed her that they were in the Old Testament and she agreed. Also I had an Easter egg in another piece she felt was offensive. We combed through these things and Vickie always honored my integrity, as I did hers.

The only difficulty I had with any of the public presentations was about a single piece called "The Healing Place," where I'd imagined Devy Bendit's death. I saw her coming through the wall in a secret garden from this life to the next life and Vickie chose a very tall, well-known black male basso profundo as singer. His deep voice always threw me off. It didn't seem to carry the meaning of this delicate and fragile sprite-like person who was moving from fear to eternity.

The *One-Woman Opera* about Devy was extremely effective. It has one part of screaming music where Vickie really caught her in turmoil and tumult, and it's really quite a magnificent mono opera. I wish I could see it again. Sometimes we plundered our own work and re-phrased it. One group of songs became "Purple Ice," another, "String of Pearls." Now we're working separately, but at one time it was unthinkable for either of us to commit the adultery of working with another composer or writer.

If Vickie needed words I would be there for her even now, but she seems to be doing more symphonic work and I need to return to the wholeness of my expression, rather than being a piece of the pie, however wonderful an experience it was. At this time, Vickie can't drive a car because of a health condition and since Ken died I can't drive to Baltimore; Ken and I used to go all the time together. Last week Katherine Wood, my dear friend and spiritual buddy, my "daughter sister," drove me to meet Vickie at Cross Keys, in Baltimore. The healer/musician Jeffrey Chappelle was there and we had a memorable lunch together, where we investigated and proved that the "other world" could guide us in this world.

Of all the "near death" technological experiences this time in history pummels us with, my most terrifying one involved working with Vickie. I wrote a libretto called "Seven Colors for Victoria Blue" and worked many weeks on it—1988, West Virginia—in the world of floppy disks. For those old enough to remember, I simply clicked one sweet button in a rush of ecstasy, having finished the piece, and it all disappeared as if by magic.

I believe I faced my mortality that day looking at a blank screen, and seeing how quickly reality can vanish. I remember going to bed and staring out the window at the trees and birds. Then called Candace Katz whose husband is a techie genius. She said she'd never heard any person sound so destroyed. Then, I called Vickie. Vickie lectured me on printing hard copy, and then became sanguine. Vickie had a cousin in the Northwest working for Microsoft who could recover material. I forget what was sent to him or how but *BY GOD HE DID. HE DID IT!*

Every word was found. The only trouble was they were not in any particular order. Yes, all words were retrieved but they were dancing all over the pages, each to its own tune not in alignment with literal thought. Pages and pages of sparkling words unconnected. Finally free of me.

I think I rewrote the damn thing. But it was never set to music. I have it, though. It's back.

≈

AN EXCERPT FROM THE POEM

Art Museum

...
Spirits speak fervently
and often before they go

...
I, on the other hand, travel with gold silk in my pocket on
        the dry beach
entering the span of the forgotten line—the Latin rich moon.

—*Sounds Like Something I Would Say,* Goss 183: Casa Menendez, 2010

44 ~
Visitations

IF A PERSON BELIEVES IN THE INVISIBLE, AND SEES A MIRACLE EVERY DAY, it's good training to lift the veil and communicate with the other side, which is never very far away. Eternity is right here in the living room with us and our loved ones are in eternity and they travel their spheres of consciousness; but whenever we think of them, they come to us. And some of us have that extra awareness where we can see people, visibly, actually in human form, those who have gone on. Ken and I were very intuitive and we had both experienced supernatural phenomena and trusted what we experienced.

When psychic Bryan Christopher was here after Ken's death, he saw him and described Ken in a blue shirt. He described the shirt we bought from Travel Smith. That exact shirt, no one could make it up. Bryan saw him sitting in a chair with his legs crossed. Bryan went on to describe Ken in many areas of the house.

In my own case, Ken's appearances were more subtle. One day, a few months after Ken left us I had cleaned the top of his desk and there was nothing on top of his laptop. When I came downstairs a little later there was a gold coin with an angel sitting on top of his laptop, one I'd never seen before, one I had never seen in any store or circus or antique bin. I knew it was from Ken.

I asked Bryan how an object could be physically moved by a spirit. Bryan replied, "The same way you do it." I said, "He has no hands." Bryan went on, "Movement is made of energy, and hands are just the gesture of that energy. He has the same ability that you have, but not the same gesture." This was a lot to take in, but there is, at the heart of it, something I understand, and quantum physics will make it clear to us, someday, when science and knowledge of the spiritual universe come together.

The bathroom towel rail was broken and on the floor the night Ken died. It was plain wood and Ken had been promising to paint and replace it. The week after he died, when I walked into his bathroom I saw it was white and on the rack. NO one had been in the house. I questioned every remote person. Sons-in-law had been nowhere near this place of sadness that week. They worked a distance away. No one had a house key but the girls who were with me, weak with sorrow, and they were never in the house when I was not present.

After Ken left, he communicated through electronics which is common, the known way that the other world reaches us. "They"— "Spirits" are made of electromagnetic energy, I've been told, like the inside of a battery. I'm used to it now—lights will go on and off in the house, the radio will go on at unbelievable times. When I'm feeling especially blue, something will happen. Perhaps the alarm on the clock will sound. He is always here.

When I talked to Beth Young, a medium, she said Ken is always with me whenever I think of him and especially when I meditate. "He is all over the world helping people and traveling where he's always wanted to be, but every time you think of him he'll be with you. And if you ever want to talk to him you just go to the car because that's the place you know he will be; whereas you won't always know where he is in the house." Upon saying this Beth could see him in the kitchen. She described him to me exactly.

I felt his hand on mine in the middle of the night.

When I'm in trouble and call him, the solution appears immediately. I've always been allergic to milk protein. The day he died my youngest daughter Angel brought groceries which included vanilla yogurt. It looked so good that I tasted it. From that moment forward I've had no milk aversion. He left several interesting reminders of him. He used to eat yogurt every night and now I eat all the things he ate—foods I could not tolerate before. These physical shifts are something the medical community could never solve for me.

I know everyone who has lost someone says, poetically, 'I feel him in the trees; I see him in the flowers, etc.' but Ken is very powerful. Bryan Christopher said he was more powerful than many psychics. Ken can reach through the gauze of here and there and make things happen. I feel protected. I used to be afraid in the house alone at night. The minute he died the house became extremely safe and filled with his warm energy and comfort. Ken made a sculpture now owned by Del Rene Goldsmith in New York—a bronze lost-wood carapace with a translucent egg suspended within. It was his symbol of protecting the family. It was called "Family of Man." I know I am always his protectorate.

What I'm trying to say is, things do not feel better since he's gone, but he took fear away so that I'd be left in as much harmony as possible without him. He thought of everything. He gave me material well-being. And the last gift he had to give was my independence, which I had never had, and he apparently thought I needed. For the last leg of my journey, he gave me the gift of being alone. The gift of solitude. He was always generous.

Ken had driven all over the country to literary events with me; he was not dismayed by this; he was enriched by it, enlivened as part of the community. He now sends me off by myself to see how well I'll do.

We used to do Tarot cards in the morning, and angel/spirit cards. We'd just pick one up, almost like a game, and we would follow that card as a guide all day. Recently, I'd just cleaned off the empty kitchen table where we used to have tea, and I returned an hour later and there was an angel spirit card on the table that said Love. Later, I saw on a tray a page that had been torn out of a book. It was titled GRACE. I get messages every day from Ken.

Once I felt his spirit lying down my bed and I was lying within his spirit as if it were a shadow. I was lying on/in this shadow, this was the best part of him, I thought. I always loved his spirit best.

Today (August 23, 2014), I received my new book from the publisher, *The Mandate of Heaven*. I inscribed the first copy to Ken, as I always did, and put it on his desk. Tonight the book is gone from there. Disappeared. Nowhere in this house. It is gone.

$$\approx$$

AN EXCERPT FROM THE POEM

Messages from the Other World

…

… I agree I'd put everyone's mind at ease to call it
coincidence, or parallels to life
from undercurrents of thought, but did I tell you that tonight
I put the last log in the fireplace—although
it's well into Spring—and without a match, I returned and
it was already alive with flames?

—*The Man Who Got Away,* New Academia/Scarith, 2014

45 ~

Between Levels

WHEN KEN RETURNED FROM HIS FIRST CRUISE TO THE MEDITERRANEAN, flying from the Coral Sea aircraft carrier, his mother and I drove down to Norfolk to greet him. 1954. One of the prerequisites for families visiting this homecoming was a tour of the carrier.

Of course I wore very high heels and a blue silk shantung suit with a pencil tight skirt, perfect for climbing. Those days I also wore a chignon in the back of my neck (a hair 'accessory') that threatened to blow across the Atlantic with every gust.

Now was the moment that makes our bad dreams.

There was an announcement that, as a special favor, we could go up to each deck on steel ladders with no backs to the rungs, extending out over the turbulent ocean. At least it wasn't a floating rope. I hadn't seen Ken for nine months (since our honeymoon) and didn't want his commanding officers to think an aviator married a wimp, so Ken went first and nimbly climbed upward AND upward AND upward.

"Don't look down," he cautioned. No need for the warning; I was frozen in mid-stair, frozen solid. Could not go up one more step and an Admiral was behind me.

Somehow I must have achieved this because I am sitting here writing today. That was the moment I knew I could do the impossible because it was not in my paradigm to be over an ocean with spike high heels.

In a way, that is where I am today. Between levels. Not frozen now, and able to do the impossible, as we all are able, making art, creating some things that never existed before; trusting that there's something at the top of the stairs, and a hand to pull me in.

It's what makes me take the next step.

Appendices

APPENDIX TO CHAPTER NINE

BIBLIOGRAPHY OF PLAYS BY GRACE CAVALIERI, 1966-2013
READINGS • PRODUCTIONS • PUBLICATION

Anna Nicole: Blonde Glory
READINGS
2009 Muhlenberg Library, New York City
2009 Writers' Center, Bethesda, MD
2011 full-length reading, Arias Theater, New York City
PRODUCTION — 2013 New Theater of New York
PUBLICATION — 2012 *Scene4 Magazine*

Lena's Quilt
PRODUCTION — 2011* Harlem Renaissance, New York City

Quilting the Sun
READINGS
2001* Columbus Branch Library, NYC
2002* Manhattan Public Library, NYC
2003* Smithsonian Institution, Washington, DC
PRODUCTIONS
2007 World Premiere Centre Stage, Greenville, SC
2011 Art Center, Beaufort, South Carolina

Jennie & The JuJu Man
Part of "Typewriter Dreams," NYC Theater Festival
2003 Common Basis Theatre, CUNY Grad Center

Hyena in Petticoats
READING — 2010 Takoma Park Theater, MD
STAGED PRESENTATION — 2006 NYC Public Library
STAGED READING — 2007 Ft. Lewis College, CO
PUBLICATION — 2010: *Scene4 Magazine*

Passage
Art, Poetry, Dance Installation. Cavalieri text: **THE MAP**
(see Appendix to Chapter Thirty, p. 267)
2007 Artposium, Durango, CO

Millie's Sunshine Tiki Villa
2011 In process

The Late and Blooming Early Branch
   1968 Polemic Theater, Washington, DC
   1969, 1970 The Corner Theater, Baltimore, MD
   1970 Milford High School, MA
   1970 William and Mary College, Williamsburg, VA

Birds That Call Before the Rain
   1968 The Corner Theater, Baltimore, MD
   1969 Theater Lobby, Washington, DC
   1970 William and Mary College

The Death of a Child by Beating or Not
   1968, 1970 The Corner Theater, Baltimore, MD

What Shall We Do Yesterday
   1968, 1970 The Corner Theater, Baltimore, MD
   1969 Polemic Theater, Washington, DC
   1970 Towson State College, MD
   1971 Trinity University, San Antonio, TX
   1970 Notre Dame College, Baltimore, MD
   1975-76 La Pensee, Seattle Washington, DC
   PRODUCED FOR RADIO — 1977 Pacifica network

Heads
   1970 Notre Dame College, Baltimore, MD
   1970 The Corner Theater, Baltimore, MD
   1973 Theater Prospect, San Francisco, CA

The Planned Escape of Bonita and Bright
   1970 William and Mary College, VA

Old Favorites
   1971 The Corner Theater, Baltimore, MD
   1999 Contemporary Arts Theater, Washington, DC

Eleventh Hour Song
   1971 The Corner Theater, Baltimore, MD

Smarts
   READING — 1971 Antioch College, Baltimore, MD

Backyard Fun
   1972 Upstairs Theater, Columbia, MD
   1973 Antioch College, Columbia, MD

* all plays directed by Shela Xoregos

Cuffed Frays
PRODUCED FOR RADIO — 1962 The Pacifica Network
FOR STAGE — 2001 The Charleston Stage Company, Charleston, WV
PUBLISHED IN VERSE FORM, c2001 Argonne House Press

Best of Friends (performed in several other cities)
1975 College of Notre Dame, Baltimore, MD
1976 Theater Project, Baltimore, MD
1975 The Corner Theater, Baltimore, MD
1975, 1976 La Pensee Theater, Seattle, WA
READING — 1977 Moming Theater, Chicago IL
The Sticker Tree (*Renamed*)
1988 (or 1986) Quaigh Theater, NYC *

Stripping
READING — 1993 The John Houseman Theater, NYC

In the Land of Elbows (*CHILDREN'S PLAY*)
1970 Webster Grove Children's Theater, MO

Hush, No One Is Listening
1970 Festival, Religion and Art, Sacramento, CA
PUBLISHED — 1968 *Kauri*
                    c1972 *Dramatics Magazine*

We Regret to Inform You That the Future Is Uncertain Because of the Inability on the Part of All Nightwatchmen
1970 Theater Lobby, Washington, DC
1969 University of Missouri
RADIO PRODUCTION — 1977 Pacifica Network
PUBLISHED — *Per/Se, The Smith Magazine*

Keeper of the Station
1966 University of Washington, Seattle
PUBLISHED — 1968+ *Kauri*
                    1970 Contemporary Drama Service

Pinecrest Rest Haven
STAGED READINGS:
1998 Clemente del Sole, NYC *
1998 The Ice House, Berkeley Springs, WV
1998 The Writer's Center of Washington, DC, Bethesda, MD
PRODUCTION — 2001 The Common Basis Theatre, NYC
AUDIO PRODUCTION — 1988 Taped reading of poems
PUBLISHED — *Pembroke Magazine*, University of NC at Pembroke

Harvest Kitchen
PRODUCED FOR RADIO — 1976 Pacifica network,

Getting Ready
1972 The WPA Theater, NYC

$$\approx$$

LYRICS AND TEXTS FOR SONGS AND OPERA

String of Pearls
Text and Libretto for Mono Opera
1986 The Walters Museum and Gallery, Baltimore, MD

Migrations
Multi-media performace with images by Mary Ellen Long
and music by Vivian Adelberg Rudow
1988 Franz Bader Gallery, Washington, DC
READING — 2000 Loyola College, Baltimore
RADIO PRODUCTION — 1988, 1989 via NPR satellite
1988, 1990 Pacifica Network
PUBLISHED — Vision Library Publications, c1995

Purple Ice
Lyrics for song cycle with composer Vivian Adelberg Rudow
Several stages in Baltimore

Journey of Waters
Lyrics for song with composer Vivian Adelberg Rudow
for the Annapolis Chorale and Chamber Music Orchestra
PERFORMED — 2006 St. Anne's Church, Annapolis
2006 Har Sinai Synagogue, Baltimore

APPENDIX TO CHAPTER TEN

HYENA IN PETTICOATS
Based on the life of MARY WOLLSTONECRAFT (1759-1797)

MARY WOLLSTONECRAFT WAS THE MOTHER OF MODERN FEMINISM. She embodied a new sense of what was possible for women of her era. The conflict in the play is derived from the fact that Mary longed to stand shoulder to shoulder to men and yet she sought their love and approval. Here is where I got my impetus for the drama!

Punch and Judy came into fashion in the 1800s as live performers rather than puppets. Also, the circus came into being in London in the 18th century. The characters Punch and Judy serve as narrators and tricksters, both.

Synopsis

The play follows Mary Wollstonecraft's life as a girl longing to read and write and to teach her sisters. We see, early on, her manipulation and aggression to "get out of the house" as soon as possible. The play follows her to her first employment as Governess to Ireland's Lady Kingsborough, where Mary indoctrinated the Kingsborough girls to think for themselves. She was promptly discharged. But there she met the American writer Gilbert Imlay. Their relationship was a power struggle, and Gilbert was a womanizer. Mary bore his child, Fanny, out of wedlock.

Mary was a journalist and was publishing articles on the American Revolution, the French Revolution, and the events of the day. This was unheard of for women who, if they wrote anything, penned fluffy romanticized "novels." Mary's masterpiece was her 1792 book titled *A Vindication of the Rights of Women.* She asked that women take responsibility for themselves and reform the world by reforming their own lives. The publisher Joseph Johnson is the one who published Mary and to whom we owe her permanence today. He factors into the play with a surprising twist.

She has lovers after Imlay with calamitous results, especially regarding the married painter Henry Fuseli. Mary argues with the leading male conservatives of the day and has verbal battles that are minor victories but do not win her the affection she so longs for. It is as if she is saying, "If men will not love me, at least they will admire me."

The play shows a major crisis in Mary Wollstonecraft's life. She was not prepared for the women to turn against her and to say she made their lot worse. This broke her heart. She attempted suicide by jumping off the Thames bridge and was saved by a fisherman. Her "skirts" floated her to the top. This is a powerful scene in the play.

Mary meets the philosopher William Godwin who is against the strictures of marriage, as Mary herself is. Yet they move toward a union when Mary finds she is pregnant for the second time.

This is the childbirth that would take her life for often physicians were careless, causing blood poisoning during the birth process. The play ends with her death scene and reconciliation with her sisters, Everina and Liza. A subplot is the formation of a school for girls that Mary abandoned into their hands. Mary had found a few months of felicity with William Godwin, fulfilling a wish that had haunted her life.

(Author's note: Although it is not part of this play, this child born would grow up to marry the poet Percy Bysse Shelley, and become famous as Mary Wollstonecraft Shelley, who would write *Frankenstein*. Because Mary Shelley is renown and her mother is not, I was passionate about writing this play.)

APPENDIX TO CHAPTER ELEVEN

ANNA NICOLE AND ME
(published in Best American Poetry Magazine, September 2011)
by Grace Cavalieri

I JUST CAME BACK FROM NYC WHERE I HEARD THE FIRST DRAFT READING OF MY PLAY "Anna Nicole," a reading by professional actors with the Xoregos Performing Company.* This was just for the purpose of rewriting and is the only way I know to see what moves forward, who loses character—all those issues that you never see when you're rereading your own type-font over and over. One hundred fifty people answered the casting call. There are no lack of big blondes in New York.

I'm writing today to answer the question that always comes up: "Why her?" The question surprised me initially. It started coming at me after my book of poems came out, *Anna Nicole: Poems* (Goss 183: Casa Menendez, 2008). My good friend, poet Merrill Leffler, had it on his coffee table. Another literate person, his house guest, picked it up and said "Why her?!" and dismissed it out of hand. I started to see that this had no audience but the closest of my bosom buddies. Although the book won the National Paterson Award for Literary Excellence, the glitterati did not think it seriously worthy. Even my girlfriends from Trenton High who support everything I do, did not want it. Actually that was understandable: 1) they do not read poetry 2) this does not qualify as poetry to them. Forget the Trenton High crowd.

My affection (obsession) started while watching TV. What I saw was that Anna had less of a human support system than any other celebrity of tragic proportions. Marilyn Monroe, Judy Garland, Jayne Mansfield all/each had more dependable people close at hand. Anna, growing up, had no love, no education, no philosophical underpinning, no self knowledge, and no way to order experience. As an adult, she was fed pills and propped up. Her life was epic, certainly as any Greek tragedy or Italian opera. Did you see her in the hospital bed after she had given birth to her baby girl? The cheekbones? Without the makeup?— The beauty, the vulnerability, fragility, all evident. I loved that in her.

Last month she was in the news again, while they indicted the pill merchants. I kept looking at her on TV and feeling that what we saw was fiction and that my imagined stories of her were more emotionally true. Her wonderment, confusion, blandishments, in spite of a bad case of body custody. Sometimes I exhausted myself worrying about her. I keep remembering Sterling Brown in a poem talking about Ma Rainey, "She jes got ahold a me somekindaway." Anna just gets ahold of me somekindaway.

Critic Geoffrey Himes talks about my trying to give consciousness where there is none. That's a pretty interesting observation. Another aspect of writing Anna is to understand that to be manipulated you have to be manipulative as well. It's a shuttlecock, like so many other human tricks, like fame itself that has to be kept up at both ends.

My basic research was to ask people what they remembered about Anna. Overwhelmingly, the answers boiled down to five slags on the heap: she was a model, she married the old rich guy, she had a son, she gave birth to a baby girl, she died of an overdose. But fiction and poetry are not naturalism. (Well I did get one book order from a porn collector so some are still trying.) We can't cast a value and judgment on Anna Nicole's real life and apply it to Anna Nicole's imagined life. A bad algorithm. So if you try to take apart the facts, all you'll get is what you break.

I want to show Anna's vulnerability and trust in others. Yes she was an opportunist, but I want to show what poor opportunities she was offered; and how, at the core, her essential sweetness endured: a faith and hope in something better that even the merchants of the world could not sell away from her.

Who isn't interested in "FAME?" And why are we all so interested? Maybe because the root word for HUNGER is FAMA (Latin). The answer to the vexed question "Why Her?" is a desire to understand aspects and conse-quences of hunger. Some people are unequal to their hunger. It is bigger than they are. Even some smart people. So really, Anna Nicole is alarmingly not all that unique. Here is a poem of Hafiz.

TWO BEARS

Once
After a hard day's forage
Two bears sat together in silence
On a beautiful vista
Watching the sun go down
And feeling deeply grateful
For life.

Though, after a while
A thought-provoking conversation began
Which turned to the topic of
Fame.

The one bear said,
"Did you hear about Rustam?
He has become famous
And travels from city to city
In a golden cage;

He performs to hundreds of people
Who laugh and applaud
His carnival
Stunts."

The other bear thought for
A few seconds

Then started
Weeping.

—Hafiz

The Gift - versions of Hafiz by Daniel Ladinsky

≈

WE ALL KNOW THE TRAGEDIES OF CELEBRITY. Anna Nicole has been characterized by our society as a train wreck and a clown. She never stood a chance in life with an abusive, rejecting family from the hard scrabble of Texas. But what if beneath that makeup there was a vulnerable woman who longed to be seen. Truly seen. This is the story I wanted to tell and the one I wrote for stage.

Synopsis of play

Anna Nicole is a show girl, managed by Horshel, an oppressive domineering 'handler.' Pushkin is a PhD student using Anna as the subject for his study, measuring her capacity for education. Anima is Anna's twin who died at birth, and haunts Anna's life, causing constant degradation. Anna is in love with Pushkin but she is 'owned' by Horshel. Upon attempting suicide, Anna recovers in rehab to realize she once had a child who died. Anima is unable to control Anna, once alcohol and drugs are out of her system. Anna attempts a stage comeback which fails, but she has great hope for her future as she is pregnant. The specter of disaster follows her into the future in the form of Anima.

The play resonates three true details of Anna Nicole's life: She was a show girl, she married a billionaire, she was addicted to drugs. But it is a fictional work of the imagination.

A workshop production of "Anna Nicole: Blond Glory" opened one night at the New Theatre of New York since I wrote this — and was closed the next day by the hurricane in NYC, flooding subways with water. So my showcase production never materialized after the "reading."

APPENDIX TO CHAPTER TWELVE

SEASIA ONE
by Kenneth Flynn, CAPT, USN-Ret.
Saturday, October 28, 1995

I DECIDED TO VISIT THE PENSACOLA NAVAL AIR MUSEUM WHILE GRACE WAS TAK-
ING A MORNING WALK. It was about 10 a.m. I had injured my left foot, so I was
limping and looking for shortcuts to the displays. Having been to the museum
several times before, I was interested in viewing only those artifacts that were
of personal interest to me. I saw a shortcut passageway to another wing of
the museum, and upon entering I noticed a small table, draped with a plastic
display cover and proceeded toward it.

History

In May 1964, aboard the aircraft carrier *USS Kitty Hawk,* CVA-63, steaming in the South China Sea, at a point later to be known as Yankee Station,
Lieutenant Commander Chuck Klusmann was launched in a photographic
configured F8 Crusader for a photographic mission. Later, as a Landing Signal
Officer, I was summoned to the flight deck to direct an emergency landing by
an F8, which happened to be Chuck bringing his aircraft back with a burning
wing. Wherever he had been, we were now aware that someone was shooting at our aircraft. Soon after, on June 6, LCDR Chuck Klusmann was again
launched for another photographic mission. With him, in another photo version
of the Crusader was Lieutenant Jerry Kuechman. This was to be the final day
in a deployment of over nine months in duration. While performing his photographic run, Chuck was shot down by Pathet Loa ground forces.

LT Kuechman returned his aircraft safely to the ship and debriefed those
officers concerned. He was immediately dispatched to my waiting aircraft, an
A3 *Skywarrior.* Upon entering my aircraft, he informed me that Chuck was
"down," and we were to go find him. Very concerned I said, "Where?" Lt.
Kuechman said, "I'll brief you in the air." My aircraft had been given a very
light fuel load because I was originally scheduled to take a courier package to
Manila. The courier package was removed, LT Kuechman strapped into a floor
mounted "passenger" position, and we were immediately catapulted from the
deck. Once airborne, my passenger unstrapped and said we were headed for
Laos. I was shocked because I didn't have enough fuel for the mission and also
to return to the ship for a normal landing. However, I quickly realized that was
of major importance—we were going to Laos—try to find Chuck and, if necessary, I would make a diversion to DaNang, South Vietnam to refuel at an Air
Force base. This prospect didn't thrill any of us because of the reports of recent
armed attacks upon the base from hostile forces, and the short runways.

Using the flight path information from LT Kuechman's knee-pad we entered it into our ancient analog flight computer and headed for Laos.

Laos was considered a neutral country, and its airspace protected. We legally had no business penetrating that airspace. However, orders from the Oval Office and the Secretary of Defense concerned itself with each individual sortie, and thus dictated our mission. This same protocol had been used which got the photographic missions into Laos previously and the result we now faced—LCDR Klusmann on the ground, hopefully evading capture.

Our old mission computer worked. We found ourselves at low altitude over the Laotian jungle, found the location of Chuck's ejection, and briefly saw Chuck on the ground. What to do now? At the same time I saw a T-28 propeller driven aircraft pass under my left wing, strafing the jungle—the smoke from the 50 caliber ammunition clearly visible. I said on our intercom, "What in the devil is that?" and proceeded to describe what I had seen to the crew. My bombardier, LT Bill Woodward, announced he also had visual contact with another T-28. At this instant my third crewman, Samuel "Rusty" Anderson, screamed, without the benefit of the intercom, "It's coming up the tail!!!" My head jerked to the left and I saw antiaircraft explosions precisely at our flight level, and just off our wingtip. Naïvely, not expecting to be shot at—after all we were unarmed and only on a search and rescue mission, we had been flying very slowly at maximum endurance airspeed, because of my concern for our fuel situation—but we were learning fast! I slammed both throttles full on, pulled the nose up steeply, started a right turn away from the suspected location of the antiaircraft fire, and watched the decay in our airspeed—dropping flaps to keep from stalling. My intentions were to change as many of the flight profiles as I could to hopefully throw off the gunners on the ground aiming at us. Now this very large A3 Skywarrior was a lumbering whale and could only maneuver laboriously as compared to fighter aircraft, and we were an easy target. It seemed that the 37 mm aircraft guns had height finding radar but it didn't appear they had flight tracking capability. Perhaps a flawed hypothesis, but that's what I used. What our A3 did have was electronic jamming equipment—but we were forbidden to use it—even in training—because it was reserved for nuclear war! Decision time. I had armed rescue aircraft with me now, though I didn't know who they were, and we were in imminent jeopardy of joining Chuck on the ground, or worse. "Jam it!" I order Rusty. I hoped this would save us and also give those other aircraft some protection.

The jamming of the radar directed guns seemed to solve some of our problems, and we continued jamming each time fire control radar illuminated on our monitor panel. I never reported the active jamming. I felt that there were no foreign entities with the capabilities to realize who or where the jamming was originating from in the jungles of Laos, and I wasn't about to risk censure just because we wanted to get Chuck out and keep my crew and myself alive. I have never regretted the decision.

My UHF radio suddenly came alive with a booming voice saying, "I'll take over as on-site commander. I'm flying a *Caribu* just underneath you. We have two helicopter pilots hit and replacement helos are on the way. I want you (meaning our A3) to return to the ship and get fighters with 20 mike-mike." (Meaning 20 milimeter machine cannons.) Okay, I had just been relieved of command. I acknowledged his directions, went to full power and headed back toward the ship. We were aware, listening to the radio traffic that Chuck was still evading, he was surrounded by Pathet Lao troops, and the T-28's were keeping the troops at bay by strafing in a perimeter around him. The caribou crew was lobbing grenades out the hatches. It didn't take much savvy to realize that these same T-28's didn't have infinite ammunition, and therefore an urgent need for fighter replacements with full ammunition cans. Our mission now was to get those fighter aircraft replacements as fast as possible.

One way a jet aircraft saves fuel and increases its range is by flying high. I aimed the A3 high. The A3 has a service ceiling of about 44,000 feet. We leveled off at 49,000 feet, still climbing slightly though, and because of our automatic fuel controls I could pull the throttles back to idle and we would still have essentially full power. Now my aircraft was at maximum endurance airspeed, and also at maximum cruise airspeed. We were monitoring our fuel situation every 10 minutes—a very short time indeed when every 30 minutes was normal. The extreme altitude we were able to achieve also gave us the maximum possible radio range with our line-of-sight UHF radio. We tried every few minutes to raise the ship to relay the orders about the requirement for fighter aircraft. No answer. We were still too far away. However, one of the strongest channels on the UHF radio is the *Guard* channel—one used for emergency use—and one that will override all other UHF transmissions. We switched to *Guard*. The ship answered us, although their transmission was broken. I knew we were getting through so I started transmitting, repeating the message three times successively. Then wait. I made the redundant transmissions three times and finally got a clear return transmission that we had been received. I acknowledged and announced that I was returning to a tactical radio channel.

Shortly, in the distance we could see condensation trails from jet aircraft, lots of them, headed right at us. The contrails told us the fighters had been launched and the possibility of helping get Chuck out seemed hopeful, but it was a long way back to Laos. And, time was running out. I observed the condensation trails of two of the approaching fighters blossom, and their flightpath depart on an upward sweep from the rest of the grouped aircraft. I knew those two had gone into afterburner. Only one reason for that—they had spotted our own contrail and thought we were a *bandit*—the enemy! My bombardier switched the UHF radio to the fighter squadron's tactical channel and we made contact, informing them we were friendly, and gave our side number. The two approaching afterburner contrails decayed to normal and we could see their flight profiles start down toward their respective positions in the formation. We exchanged Chuck's geographic position to the fighter pilots as they neared and swept to our rear below us.

Our mission had so far been accomplished. We had found Chuck. We knew he was alive and not captured. We had been successful in getting replacement fighter aircraft on the way to help Chuck.

Now us. Our fuel shortage was becoming critical. When closer to the ship, I radioed and requested a landing at the earliest opportunity. The answer we received was, "Negative. Wait." Now what was *that* all about??? We waited... And we were waited. In my desire to gain as much altitude as possible, we had cruise climb to almost 51,000 feet. Amazing in our old A3! Of small humor with our guest fighter pilot passenger, breathing heavily behind pressure oxygen and saying, "Is it safe up here?" My answer was, "Yes, as long as we don't try to turn," grinning behind my own oxygen mask. And turn we must, because we had reached the ship and protocol required we orbit overhead while waiting for the *Charlie* signal, that is, clearance to land. Because of the delay in landing I had some new planning to consider, and my mind remembered the previous cruise with another A3 squadron, flying from the USS Forestall in the Mediterranean Sea.

Christmas Eve, plus three days, nighttime, snow, sleet, 400 foot overcast, pitching carrier deck and two A3's were trying to recover aboard ship. It was later reported to me that the Air Boss said, "In my 17 years of carrier aviation, this is the worst night I have ever seen." Air Boss—you should have been in my cockpit! Neither of the A3's had operable windshield wipers. Because of my Landing Signal Officer training I knew I was in trouble, so I radioed the LSO on the ship and said, "I think I can see line-up, I have about three "balls" in sight through the snow on my windshield, so I'll keep them all centered, *just help me keep my wings level*." Level wings during landing approach was a critical aspect of the A3, because at slow landing speeds the plane wouldn't make, just couldn't make, quick last-minute adjustments. I trapped (made an arrested landing) on the first pass. I don't think I could have survived a second pass at the ship—my heart rate must have been over two hundred! The A3 behind me in the landing pattern made five passes, all resulting in a wave-off from the LSO. I knew that pilot's panic! He was diverted to a land-based airfield for emergency landing. While trying to locate the field at low altitude and with 1800 pounds of fuel in his fuel tank, as reported by the pilot, the aircraft flamed out and all three of the crew were lost.

Overhead *Kitty Hawk,* remembering that previous loss, and why, I started briefing the other three in our cockpit. My direction was that at 1800 pounds of fuel on board, at an altitude of 10,000 feet, we would all bail out. I briefly explained that in the A3, in a landing altitude, with 1500 pounds of fuel remaining in the large unbaffled main tank, with the fuel pumps in the forward portion of the tank, the A3 was essentially "out of fuel." The surge caused by adding full military power, as was required in a "bolter" from the flight deck on a missed landing attempt, might cause a flameout at even greater fuel levels. My fighter pilot passenger was astounded because 1500 pounds of fuel to him, in his *Crusader* aircraft, would seem like forever. It was time. I radioed the Air Boss, stated my intentions about the bailout, that I would delay that event as long as possible, but make no mistake, that was my command to my crew. I radioed the Air Boss and told him if he wanted detailed information about the fuel management in the aircraft, to get LCDR Ted Mead to Pri-Fly and he would give him all the details. (LCDR Mead was a graduate engineer, and had been the officer who had established the reason for the loss of the crew in the Mediterranean.) I further estimated I could stretch the bailout event to 30 minutes, as I had to leave my altitude to arrive at 10,000 feet. My decision clearly established, my partners and I in the cockpit were making all arrangements for the bailout—cleaning up all unnecessary gear, store maps, clean out our pockets of unnecessary material, double check our bailout oxygen bottles, etc.

Upon arriving at 15,000 feet, with about 2200 pounds of fuel, I informed the Air Boss of my position and I was starting my path to the front of the steaming force for our bailout. And, by the way, was the rescue helicopter airborne? No answer. Now what was *this* all about? There was dead silence in our cockpit as we all contemplated the next few minutes. Suddenly the radio broke silence with the code, "*Signal Charlie*," my clearance to land. Now I faced **another** decision. I was about to make that landing attempt with absolute minimal fuel, no second pass possible, and the fuel surge expected on a bolter would surely cause a flameout. I already had the crew and myself hooked up to the automatic bailout lanyards for a low-level bailout, but there wouldn't be enough time to get us all out. Besides my passenger was sitting on the bailout patch and he would have to unstrap and move before we could actuate the bailout sequence of blowing hatches. Did I forget to say that the A3 didn't have ejection seats???

Committed, I started a steep descent to the final landing pattern. I requested, and received, a straight-in approach to save fuel. I kept the landing gear up until ½ mile from the ship while on the glide slope to save fuel. In the landing attitude I couldn't believe how little throttle was required to stay on glide path. Certainly no Landing Signal Officer I knew had observed or heard such low power—a critical observation by an LSO, so I radioed the LSO, when I shouldn't have, and told him I had never flown an A3 so "light" and he hadn't waived one as "light" so don't be miscued by the low power. It felt as if the engines were in idle! We trapped!!! We were safe. That there was a collective sigh of relief from the four of us in the cockpit was an understatement.

I was ordered to immediately brief Admiral Bringel and Captain Epps, the senior officers embarked on the *Kitty Hawk* about the details of our mission. I was never subsequently informed of the results from the fighter aircraft, however it was believed they returned with their ammunition still in the cans. Later that same day I was told that LCDR Chuck Klusmann was captured by ground forces. He was referred to as a Prisoner of War. However, Chuck was, by Laotian laws, a felon who had purposely penetrated their neutral's airspace.

Two days after Chuck's capture, the Kitty Hawk, delaying on station an extra day at the end of our cruise hoping to find out if he could be rescued, headed east toward the United States. I was stunned and in emotional shock. I was the only pilot from the air wing to have seen Chuck on the ground, still fleeing, but still free, and now to be turning my back on him and leaving him to his fate was to leave a scar in me I can't describe. Rationally I could accept the facts. Emotionally accepting the fact was quite another matter.

After returning home to the United States from a carrier cruise lasting nine months, two days, I rejoined my waiting family. Through classified message traffic I was able to monitor Chuck's situation for several months. I was transferred to another squadron after a time, but I had learned that LCDR Chuck Klusmann had indeed escaped from the Pathet Lao imprisonment. I felt some relief from my anguish, but my mind's eye still saw Chuck on the ground, trying to evade capture. This sense of failure at leaving my shipmate on the ground while I was home with my family would persist for over 30 years.

After settling into a life once again with my family I turned to a long aspiration, metal sculpting. I decided to be a professional sculptor, and remain so today. In my early years I made four sculptures concerning my feelings about Chuck Klusmann. It was an emotional release for me, and at the same time a tribute to my friend. That Chuck might ever have the opportunity to see these works of art never occurred to me.

In early 1995 during a sculpture show opening in Berkeley Springs, West Virginia, I was giving the attendees a brief narration of my motivation for some of my sculpture pieces. As it happened, the gallery owner had insisted on one piece from my collection which depicted my feelings about Chuck Klusmann. One of the men who listened came to me afterwards and said, "Ken, those T-28's in Laos **were my air force**. I was the CIA officer in charge, and what you just described was true." I had heard rumors that those T-28 propeller planes I witnessed strafing over the Laotian jungle had been CIA, but this was the first confirmation, and, from the person who was in charge.

Having accepted two sculpture commissions early in 1995, I was soon to leave for Pensacola, Florida, to install one of the pieces.

After the sculpture installation, my wife and I relaxed for an extra day to enjoy our anniversary, and I decided to indulge in one of my favorite pastimes while in that city, a visit to the Naval Air Museum. While in the museum I saw a shortcut passageway to another wing of the museum, and upon entering I noticed a small table covered with a plastic display case, and proceeded toward it. I observed two or three men, and one woman who was taking photographs. "Vintage Navy visitors like me," I mused and proceeded to look into the right side of the display case. I was now looking at artifacts from our Naval Aviators who were imprisoned in Vietnam during that conflict. There were tin cups, spoons, the model of The Zoo, one of the concentration camps, some photographs. I moved to the left side of the display case, next to another male observer and, leaning near, I was looking at a photograph of Chuck Klusmann with a Laotian political prisoner who had escaped with him, along with the shirt and shorts worn by LCDR Chuck Klusmann when he escaped from the Pathet Lao. I said quietly—I guess to the man next to me as much as to myself, "I wonder whatever happened to Chuck. I was the only pilot from the ship to find him on the ground before he was captured." The man next to me said, **"Chuck is right there,"** pointing to my right.

I straightened, as if called to "attention," recognized Chuck, went to him and introduced myself. He looked very quizzical, like, "Who is this guy?" As we shook hands. I gave him a bear hug and told him, "Chuck, you can't possibly know how happy I am to see you." I proceeded to give him a one minute summary so he could understand, and then our dialogue began. He told me he had just recently located LT Kuechman, his wing man, and said he had no idea that anyone from the ship had reached him. I told him he was probably too busy at the time to notice, but I could surely fill in a couple of pages of his saga if he desired.

That an emotional burden of over 31 years had been lifted from my shoulders was almost too much to comprehend. I know that I have never been happier in my life. The man I thought I had to abandoned is alive and well. Yes, I knew rationally Chuck and been free, but in my heart he was still a prisoner. **Now** the present is more real to me than the past.

It turned out that Chuck and I currently live only about 1 ½ hours from each other. We assured each other that our dialogue would develop—soon.

Chuck and I had a reunion at my home in West Virginia on November 26, 1995, where we reviewed our past—our future—our karma that brought us together once again. At my request Chuck signed my vintage Navy flight logbook, beneath the fateful June 6, 1964 log entry, bringing full closure to that eventful mission.

© 1996

APPENDIX TO CHAPTER EIGHTEEN

THE BUNNY AND THE CROCODILE PRESS
(aka Forest Woods Media Productions)
PUBLICATIONS 1976 to 2013

99 Past 80 by Robert Sargent

A Lover's Eye by Michael Glaser

Altered in the Telling by Robert Sargent

Baiting the Hook by Sonja James

Beached in the Hourglass by Ethan Fischer

Being A Father by Michael Glaser

Body Fluids by Grace Cavalieri

Break by Ilona Popper

British GI Warbrides Among The Alien Corn by Joyce Varney Thompson

Confessions of a Skewed Romantic by Ann Darr

Cycles of the Moonvine by Jean Emerson

Dandelion Greens by Jane Flanders, *posthumous* edited by Steven Flanders

Do Unto Others by Robert.C.Varney

Dream Catcher by Lynn Kernan

Epitaph by Yoko Danna

Fiddledeedee by Shelby Stephenson

Fish Galore by Robert Sargent

Flying the Zunl Moutains by Ann Darr

Gift of Jade by Margaret Ward Morland

House of Change by Stacy Tuthill

Looking for Divine Transportation by Karren Alenier

Looking For Don by Dai Sil Kim Gibson

Manifesto d'Amore': Uncollected Poems (1940-2001) (posthumous) by Jane Flanders

My Emerald Green Dress by Alistaire Ramirez-Marquez (in English and Spanish)

Orpheus in the Park by Rose Solari

Paradise and Cash by David Bristol

Pinecrest Rest Haven book-on-tape by Grace Cavalieri

Rap Goes Deutsch, the Poet and the Poem Special, CD (Goethe International)

Remember Me by Avideh Shashaani

Schaeffer Brown's Detective Fundamentals by Candace Katz

Schaeffer Brown's Detective Observations by Candace Katz

Selling Parsley by Devy Bendit

So What! by Kenneth Carroll

Solid Gold by Devy Bendit

Stealthy Days by Robert Sargent

Sudden Plenty (posthumous) by Jane Flanders

Tales from the Springs, an Anthology edited by Jeanne Mozier

Tales Too, an Anthology edited by Jeanne Mozier

The Cartographer by Robert Sargent

The Corner Ain't No Place For Hiding by Jonettta rose Barras

The Maryland Millennium Anthology edited by Michael Glaser

The Monk That Made His Momma Happy by David Bristol

The Other Side of the Hill, Capitol Hill Writers Group Anthology, edited by Jean Nordhaus

The Tao of Mrs. Wei by Hilary Tham

The Thoughts of Giants by Shirley Scott

The Transmutation Notebooks by Anne Becker

Toad and Other Poems by David Bristol

Voice As A Bridge, edited by William Gilcher

Weavings 2000, A Maryland Anthology for Young People edited by Michael Glaser

WPFW 89.3 Anthology edited by Grace Cavalieri

Appendix to Chapter Nineteen

REVIEW OF ROBERT PINSKY'S PLAY

Wallenstein, an adaptation from Friedrich Schiller (1799),
by Robert Pinsky. Directed by Michael Kahn.
The ShakespeareTheatre Company. Harman Center for the Arts.
610 F Street, N.W., Washington, D.C.
Reviewed by Grace Cavalieri

When Lord Wallenstein (the brilliant Steve Pickering) enters center stage he comes bursting through a projection of words flashed on the door, From that moment the play is a triumph of language, propelling Schiller's work into a meaningful script for today's theater. The stage set is the armor grey of austerity and stoicism. The staging is illuminated at times with colorful flags denoting moments of glory. 1618-1648 was the time of the thirty year war where religious conflicts devastated Germany and S.E. Europe. In 1634 Wallenstein was a Protestant—then turned Catholic—operating with his own private army of immigrants and mercenaries, under the rule of Emperor Ferdinand II. Wallenstein negotiates with the Swedes for what he thinks is the greater good; he's a man of principles and ideals, but for these acts of autonomy, he is plotted, stalked and murdered. Wallenstein's revolutionary road begins with an army devoted to him, but ends with betrayal and death. That's the sum of the story but the true psychological action is fueled by the language which has been updated and made colloquial by poet Robert Pinsky, who is a master of language in form (the translator of Dante), but since form is just a way to hold art, Pinsky chooses to make this a living language.

It's not hard to see parallels to the present religious wars and tensions in the Middle East--how there is no totalizer for tribal and religious conflicts. There are other textual similarities to the present day. Wallenstein at one point suggests that nobles pay higher taxes! Pinsky gets great audience response to these incursions, because he's as savvy about popular culture as he is its higher locutions. But above all, the play is about Wallenstein as a humanist and a soldier. We think of our generals today who so earnestly appear on television. As we watch them, we wonder how they struggle with conscience, and how they must be tempted to run the game. Wallenstein is such a man, who recognizes plague, death, sickness equal war, unlike his Emperor who thinks disease and famine a small return for "victory." Pinsky's play implies a standoff between the spirit of war's law and the letter of the law but inevitably "The only splendor is armor," and "History only wants to know who won."

Wallenstein is disappointed in his first meeting with Sweden. The Swede wants Prague as part of the deal. This will not do, and Wallenstein speaks of Dante's ring of hell where all is ice.

There are secondary plots where Wallenstein's sister wants him to be King; and also a young beautifully tragic love connection; but the message and heart of Schiller's play is the bitter nut: how can we expect peace by fighting more battles.

Pinsky compresses Schiller's trilogy into a single drama. He breaks up the linear action with Wallenstein speaking directly to us, magnetizing, with a sense of immediacy, making the audience complicit. The story is between him and us. This is an effective theatrical device, and one of the many reasons this becomes a viable play of psychological action instead of dramatic literature which would remain between pages. Robert Pinky admits being influenced by Aristotle, Bertolt Brecht (and jokingly adds, Garry Shandling).

No wonder Michael Kahn took to Schiller's play obsessing about a way to mount this work. Wallenstein is a Shakespearean figure, played with perfection by Steve Pickering in a full bodied performance depicting a man buoyed by power and idealism whose doom was shaped by others. All the pieces are here for good theater. Robert Pinsky has taken the tectonics of a German writer whose ideas about war remain relevant, and with governable language presents the strengths and depths of this great leader. The actors and direction are superb. STC is famous for its technical perfection. Poet Robert Pinsky is a spokesperson for the living present and has turned a dour time of history into a vibrant and enduring work for stage. It's a winner. The play runs through May 31. For tickets phone 202-547-1122 or visit <ShakespeareTheatre.org>

APPENDIX TO CHAPTER THIRTY

THE MAP
for Mary Ellen Long

PROLOGUE:
The center to the left provides a clear passage
To the green. This was for the long Run
At the edge of the water.
It is where we may not want to go
It is not what we had in mind,

Imagination within hope
So uncertain the terrain

We went together to deepen our silence.
Half a century saved in memory.
First was the uncertainty of snowfall, powders
Of the heart spilled out with gratitude, which another understood.
We heard the brave voice
Inside the frightened
As we passed through the trees
To find a place we'd know best.
Then we drew a picture on the rock near the sand
And set words around the picture.

Nothing belonged to us – even the rain –
Yet we did our work – We gave it all to the wind – who knew us –
Or sounded like it did.
        So we followed its passage.

The weather warmed our soiled flesh into a glow
Taking the edge off winter's sleeve. Blue Sunset
Lighting up tree after tree after tree.

Are we lost? I asked you.
There seems no path here- our children
Are gone – people are burning the earth -
Our grief is a wound-
Night falls like dark water.

You said: *There is a bright light from the moon*
A knife edge across the desert
Making a sharp line we can cross.
UP? Or DOWN? I asked.
TOWARD and AWAY you answered. And the sun

Exploded hot across our backs
        As we moved through the hillsides that live in
Memory in the sky far away.

1.
IN THE BEGINNING
RED CLIFF RISING

Once we were everywhere at once until suddenly born.

No one can save us now,
Not even the parents
Who helped us go where we didn't want to go.
This is all we'd know of the beginning
And there would be nothing we could do to stop it.
There will be someone waiting. Hurry.
Your grey silk suit will get ruined in the
Rain.

You will meet a man to marry.
You will have his children
Your twin spirit lives far away.
She will meet a man to marry.
She will meet you halfway.
All of us and our children will meet, grow older,
The thought of it still keeping us alive.

The long incline is better than the short
On this beautiful hill.

There was a dream of a house
Each could build but I pictured those whose
Hands could do better. I built our house,
She built her house.
What were those visions
Bombarding us. The world saying,
You are not as good as You are not as good as

We said,
WE ARE AS GOOD AS
And publicly excused ourselves into ART,
Or how our we imagined it to be
Up the greening hill.

We were in separate parts of the country now.
Center to left then left to center,
Right out of bounds on the left
Running running running past maps of despair.

Don't look at them.
Old people dying like slivered glass
Don't think like them.
No more secrets from the world.
It's the same for all of us now. Even you and me,
And the earth we tried to describe, tried to save,
Filling its blank pages here together.

Cutting the corners is the back edge of dark.
Be careful of the stream on the right.

2.
Middle Journey

Pure cold abyss is the middle journey.
Out of a deep sleep, who will bring us to
Ourselves but ourselves alone, untangled with light.

I move center to left center out of the frame.
What is this place neither here nor
There but something in between – a strange state of being.

Move right center carefully.
She takes clay seized with nothing but seeds and
Grows forests, makes books, circles the mountain with paths.
We are ignorant of our destiny
Yet we break open the landscape for all to follow.

One child leaves her.

One child leaves me.

One child is sick. One child is well.

Where is the evidence of where we've been?
Where we're going?

What is pulling the soul from the body to live outside itself?

When our mothers were children
They did not play together.
When we were children
We did not play together.
Our children played together,
        Right over there
Within the garden existing only in memory
Which still reaches your house.

This is the apple pie. This is the bluebird of happiness.
        Over here we danced with our husbands all night,

To the wisdom of the keys
To the bluebirds over the brook
Sparkling through the air.
We praised the music that filled our days.

I bought white satin curtains and new
Hardwood floors.
She planted a pear tree of paper
Feeding the forest floor.
We were sweeping and sweeping the clearing until
We became women SPEAKING
Instead of being SPOKEN TO.
The world started turning to water.
It becomes a circle,
A port we set out from in different directions
To describe the essential loneliness
And beauty of our lives and its earth.

Humor kindness compassion illumination
silence true nature

Where is perfect love?
Where is celestial beauty?

My cat lies dreaming. Her cat lies dreaming.
The soul passes through each one, gray turning to white.
YOU ARE HERE
The sidewalk is a ribbon pink with longing,
Black with regret.
The stars fall down
Sadness leads through the aisles
Our opera is put on
MIGRATIONS from WEST TO EAST
I do not see you in the crowd.
Now we don't live anywhere on this map and
You've already left.

The fool in the circus cried all night.

3.
There Is No End To This Map

The maps of our bodies are different now,
The slender hands, the old hands.

Passing through the door of our age is a garden
Where willows grow upward
Where the rivers run blue.

Scarred by what we've left and what left us,
Our car is packed with hope.

You move toward a place in the mountains.
I look for miracles in *The New Yorker.*

We have dreams and visions before giving in
To the vanishing dark
And to the feelings no language can speak,

The open air of the music in the forest,

The sound of the rain on the wall.

Let us go back to where we began,

The crossing of the street on the way to school,
the piano lessons,
Before our recipes,
Before the dining room tables,
Before the children left a wound that will not heal,
Before the sweet earth replenished us with rain.

Nothing will remain but our song
Following us to the first sound ever made
—by rock—by pen. making a melody
From far away. When I hear it
I know the song must be true.

It is the only place there is.

Did we begin in India? Greece? St. Petersburg?

No, before that
in Atlantis where someone gave us
A magic gift of beads saying. *Carry these*
And in the hearthold of our faith,
We found the colors hidden and broken on
Separate stones tucked in among the rocks.
One by one, the hands who touched these
Touched ours, artists fingering each
Bead to its final end,
Security's silver clasp where we would name them, we
Would plant them.

The center of these hands holds the stones of Atlantis,
now resting beneath the Sea.

Once Atlantis was a city of circles
Connected by canals and bridges

Where each
Bead made a path suddenly luminous

These were directions falling off the string
Leading us here today where the sun
Falls on the horizon from the beginning to the end,

Where we spelled out in our broken way
Connections to all we see
How it felt creating
What we knew of the earth
In a language
From another time.

There is memory in these woods.
The trees on the mountain shine red.
That was a day like this once
While losses damaged and raged

Toward hands and throat,
Making things where nothing existed before,
Or we would have been
Just two more who came and went
Without ever
Having recognizing each other. Or where we'd been.

First Poetry Grant

THE RED PORSCHE AND THE MODEL

I went to the DC Commission On
The Arts in 1968
And asked for a
Grant to buy myself a maxi-coat
They were in fashion
Then and so was I
With four children
Behind me and a manuscript to
Tuck in my hem
They asked if I were
Some kind of housewife-artist
Although
Being called an artist
Is like being called
A child
The child doesn't know
She is one
She just
Thinks she is a person
But in the end
They
Gave me enough to buy
Stamps and so my career began

Now I prayed
To the Angels of Funding
Saying *should I bring*
Art and joy to the world?

They said Hell No,
Just Try To Get Through
The Damn Thing

And so I went
Out again this time to the
NEA
Where I was told
All I needed was to get a
Tall beautiful
Model who looked like a
Goddess
To drive a red
Porsche into the reflection pool
And come out the
Other end where
I should hold up
My right hand
And we could call that
Performance and
All went well
But for the thumb
Leaking and bleeding
Stitched from the tendons
Held up in position
Over time
So it would look good
Acceptable and perfect when
Pulling each artful day through
But lucky for me
The oozing added red
Making
Everything brighter and better

I went to the NEH and
Said I was a scholar
And I could *escape the moment*
As well as anyone
But they asked
That I *manage* the moment
Instead
I saw I was still an artist
As I *imaged* the moment

By accident
They said that the door
You do not **want**
To go through
Is the one you **must**
And it will lead you here
Any way you go
And you'll go through
A couple hundred times
STOP
I said
If there is no money
What I will not take from you is comfort
And I buttoned my maxi and left
In circling the sky
Which will get the prey first
The vulture or the hawk
And how do I sing
The song of the soul
I was told at The Library of Congress
I was in The House of Memory
All spirits will be sent back to earth
To work out their vibration
And until then
I should stretch my eyes
They also said words
Represent meanings
And if I stole a book
Not to expect thanks for that

No Funding
Is what I think they meant
But oh
That marble
Well I loved it

If language
Is used to tell people what you think
It is best to say nothing where at

The Poetry Foundation
they said
I must be a woman before I die
And to try being
A prostitute or a writer
I asked how would I know which I am
In Maine they paint barns
But that doesn't make the farmer
A painter
They answered
You may never know
My child

If you love what you hate
You will not have to hate it anymore
I love
The poverty
Of poetry
I have always loved poetry
The poverty
Took practice
Poems are the bones of God
The flesh
We leave to others
Perhaps we should not ask for more.

GRACE CAVALIERI POETRY BOOKS

2014— *The Man Who Got Away* (New Academia/Scarith)
2014— *The Mandate of Heaven* (Bordighera Press)
2013— *Cosa farei per amore: Poesie dalla voce di Mary Wollstonecraft* (Forest Woods)
2012— *Gotta Go Now* (Goss 183: Casa Medendez)
2011— *Millie's Sunshine Tiki Villas: A Novella in Verse* (Goss 183: Casa Menendez)
2010— *Sounds Like Something I Would Say* (Goss 183: Casa Menendez)
2010— *Navy Wife* (Goss 183: Casa Menendez)
2008— *Anna Nicole: Poems* (Goss 183: Casa Menendez)
2006— *Water On The Sun: Acqua Sul Sole* (translated by Maria Enrico)— (Bordighera, Inc.)
2004— *What I Would Do For Love* (Jacaranda Press)
2002— *Greatest Hits, 1975-2000* (Pudding House Press)
2001— *Cuffed Frays and Other Works* (Argonne Press)
1999— *Sit Down, Says Love* (Argonne Hotel Press)
1998— *Heart on a Leash* (Red Dragon Press)
1998— *Pinecrest Rest Haven* (Word Works)
1995— *Migrations: Poems* with *Mary Ellen Long* (Book distribution, In Support)
1990— *Trenton* (Belle Mead Press)
1986— *Bliss* (Hillmunn Roberts Publishing)
1979— *Swan Research* (Word Works)
1976— *Body Fluids* (Bunny and the Crocodile Press)
1975— *Why I Cannot Take a Lover* (Washington Writers' Publishing House)

EDITED VOLUMES

1997— *Cycles of the Moon Vine* by Jean Emerson (Forest Woods Media Productions)
1992— *WPFW 89.5FM Poetry Anthology: The Poet and the Poem* (Bunny and the Crocodile Press)
2009— *The Poet's Cookbook: Recipes from Tuscany with poems from 28 American poets* (translator, Sabine Pascarelli) (Bordighera Press)
2010 – *The Poet's Cookbook: Recipes from Germany with poems from 33 American Poets* (translator, Sabine Pascarelli) (Goethe-Institut & Forest Woods Media Productions)

ABOUT THE AUTHOR

GRACE CAVALIERI is the producer/host of Public Radio's "The Poet and the Poem from the Library of Congress." She celebrates 38 years on-air and is a CPB silver medalist.

Grace received the inaugural 2015 Lifetime Achievement Award from the *Washington Independent Review of Books*, where she's the monthly columnist and poetry reviewer. In 2013 she received the Association Writing Program's "George Garrett Award" for Service to Literature. She's twice the recipient of the Allen Ginsberg Award (1993, 2013); and, she holds the Bordighera Poetry Prize, a Paterson Poetry Award, and The Columbia Award, among other poetry and playwriting awards.

A recent poetry book, *Water on the Sun*, is on the Pen American Center's "Best Books" list. Her latest books (2014) are *The Man Who Got Away* (New Academia/Scarith) and *The Mandate of Heaven* (Bordighera).

PHOTO BY PAUL FEINBERG

CPSIA information can be obtained
at www.ICGtesting.com
Printed in the USA
FFOW04n0135220515
13527FF